The Adobe® Illustrator® CS6

WOW! Book

HUNDREDS OF TIPS, TRICKS, AND TECHNIQUES
FROM TOP ILLUSTRATOR ARTISTS

Sharon Steuer

AND THE ILLUSTRATOR WOW! TEAM

 PEACHPIT PRESS

The Adobe Illustrator CS6 WOW! Book

Sharon Steuer

Peachpit Press

1249 Eighth Street

Berkeley, CA 94710

510/524-2178

Find us on the Web at: www.peachpit.com

To report errors, please send a note to errata@peachpit.com

Peachpit Press is a division of Pearson Education.

Used with permission of Pearson Education, Inc. and Peachpit Press.

Copyright ©2013 by Sharon Steuer

Contributing Writers & Consultants to this edition: *Cristen Gillespie, Steven H. Gordon, Lisa Jackmore, Aaron McGarry, George Coghill, Raymond Larrett, Laurie Wigham*
Technical Editor: *Jean-Claude Tremblay*
Line Editor: *Eric Schumacher-Rasmussen*
Cover Designer: *Mimi Heft*
Cover Illustrator: *Sabine Reinhart*
Indexer: *Jack Lewis*
Proofreader: *Darren Meiss*
First edition *Illustrator WOW! Book* designer: *Barbara Sudick*
***WOW!* Series Editor:** *Linnea Dayton*

Notice of Rights

Notice of Liability

Trademarks

ISBN 13: 978-0-321-84176-6

ISBN 10: 0-321-84176-X

9 8 7 6 5 4 3 2 1

Printed and bound in the United States of America.

The Adobe Illustrator CS6

WOW! Book

WOW!
Contents
at a
Glance...

Contents

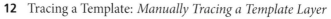

1

Your Creative Workspace

2

Designing Type & Layout

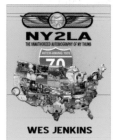

3

8

Creatively Combining Apps

The Adobe Illustrator CS6 WOW! Book
Team of Contributing Writers and Editors

Sharon Steuer has been teaching, exhibiting, and writing in the digital art world since 1983. Sharon is the originator and lead author of **The Illustrator WOW! Book** series, and author of **Creative Thinking in Photoshop: A New Approach to Digital Art**, and the soon to be released **Zen of Illustrator** (info@zenofillustrator.com). In between books, Sharon is a full-time artist working in traditional and digital media (www.ssteuer.com). She lives with her 17-year-old cat and the love of her life, her audio professor husband Jeff Jacoby (jeffjacoby.net). As always, she is extremely grateful to **WOW!** team members (past and present), Peachpit, Adobe, and of course the amazing **WOW!** artists for constant inspiration, and for making this book possible. Keep in touch with her on facebook.com/SharonSteuer and @SharonSteuer (Twitter).

Jean-Claude Tremblay is the owner of Proficiografik, a consulting and training service for the graphic and print community, designed to help clients work efficiently. He is an Adobe Certified Expert Design Master and an Adobe Community Professionals member. He has been deeply involved as chapter representative for the InDesign User Group of Montréal he cofounded in 2010, and also with the launch of the Quebec City group in fall 2012. After serving as a magnificent **WOW!** tester, Jean-Claude returns for his fourth mandate as the **WOW!** technical editor, chief advisor, and resident magician. You can find him hanging on Twitter @jctremblay where he is always directing people to great resources related to design. He lives in the greater Montréal area with his wife Suzanne and his wonderful daughter Judith.

Cristen Gillespie has contributed to other **WOW!** books, including coauthoring **The Photoshop WOW! Book**. She has also coauthored articles for *Photoshop User* magazine. With a decades-long enthusiasm for the digital world of art and multimedia, and an equal interest in digitally preserving and presenting family histories, Cristen tackles step-by-step Techniques, Galleries, and Introductions with avid interest and commitment. She looks forward with every edition of the book to learning from wonderful artists and writers, and hopes she'll be asked to stay with **Illustrator WOW!** for many years to come.

Steven H. Gordon is a returning coauthor for step-by-step Techniques and Galleries. Steven has been an ace member of the team since **The Illustrator 9 WOW! Book.** He has too many boys to stay sane and pays way too much college tuition. Steven runs Cartagram (www.cartagram.com), a custom cartography company located in Madison, Alabama. He thanks Sharon and the rest of the **WOW!** team for their inspiration and professionalism.

Lisa Jackmore is a contributing writer for Galleries, as well as for step-by-step Techniques. She is an artist both on and off the computer, creating miniatures to murals. Lisa continues to share her talent, evident throughout this book, as a writer and a digital fine artist. She would like to thank the sources of distraction—her family and friends—as they are so often the inspiration for her artwork.

Aaron McGarry is a San Diego-based writer and illustrator who spends time in Ireland, where he is from. While writing provides his bread, commercial illustration supplements the bread with butter. He paints and draws to escape and relax, but finds his greatest source of joy with his wife Shannon, a glass artist, and their gorgeous 7-year-old daughter Fiona. Please visit: www.amcgarry.com. or www.aaronmcgarry.com.

Additional contributing writers and editors for this edition:
Eric Schumacher-Rasmussen has been writing and editing copy since long before it was his job. He's currently a freelance writer and editor, as well as editor of *Streaming Media* magazine (www. streamingmedia.com). **George Coghill** is a cartoon-style illustrator who specializes in cartoon logos and cartoon character design. His art can be seen at CoghillCartooning.com. **Raymond Larrett** is a designer, illustrator, cartoonist, and most recently publisher. His Puzzled Squirrel Press (http://puzzledsquirrel.com) specializes in unique volumes on comics, history, and mind control, in exclusive ebook and print editions. **Laurie Wigham** does all kinds of information design, from infographics to user interfaces. When she gets tired of interacting with her computer she goes out on the town with her sketchbook and draws human faces. Find Laurie at www.lauriewigham.com.

Please see **Acknowledgments** and **The Adobe Illustrator Book WOW! Production Notes** pages for thorough listings of the **WOW!** team contributors, past and present.

Important: **Read me first!**

If you're a beginner...

Beginners are of course most welcome to find inspiration in this book. However, be aware that the assumed user level for this book is intermediate through professional. If you're a beginning Illustrator user, please supplement this book with basic, beginning Illustrator instruction and training materials. In addition, don't miss the free Illustrator training videos from the Adobe TV website **http://tv.adobe.com/product/illustrator/**.

Where & what is WOW! ONLINE?

The best way to really learn how to make things in Illustrator is to examine complex artwork created by professional artists using Illustrator. You're in luck! Many of the artists in this book have allowed us to post their works for you to examine and pick apart. Please contact the artists (find their info in the Artists appendix) to request permissions beyond personal exploration. Find these artworks, as well as a free scripts from Premedia Systems, a year's worth of *Design Tools Monthly* newsletters, and other goodies, at **WOW ONLINE**. See the Tip "Look for the **WOW! ONLINE** icon" at the top of the "How to use this book" section, page xvi.

First of all, I am really excited to bring you this twelfth edition of the **Illustrator WOW!** series. This book has been lovingly created for you by an amazing team of people. In order to provide you with the most thoroughly updated information in a timely manner (and as close as possible to the shipping of the new version of Adobe Illustrator), this book has become a truly collaborative project, and is created by a large team of international experts.

The process begins with all of us on the team, testing the newest features of a pre-release version of Illustrator, trying to discover which of the features is worthy of focus for this book by and for, artists and designers. Our astounding technical editor, Jean-Claude Tremblay, marks up the previous edition, identifying areas where we should be expanding and deleting. Steven Gordon and I co-curate the book, finding new artists and artwork that we think deserves inclusion. I work with each co-writer to determine which features they want to concentrate on, based on their expertise in Illustrator, and for the writers who are also artists, we work together to try and figure out which new features they might be able to incorporate into their professional projects. As problems arise, Jean-Claude, Cristen, and I will often pass files and questions amongst ourselves, always attempting to find the most efficient and fool-proof workflow possible.

With my name on the cover of the book, rest assured that as the book evolves, Jean-Claude and I oversee every single page of the book. But it's not just the two of us—the entire team of writers, as well our stellar team of **WOW!** testers, actually test and critique every page as it develops. This amazing group of experts, scattered around the globe, come together by email, iChat, and acrobat.com, all working as a team in order to deliver the best book possible to you, our reader.

With the skyrocketing price of printing in full-color, and the fragile state of the economy, we continue to look for ways to keep the cover price of the book down. We are continuing to emphasize creating art and design with Adobe Illustrator, and will leave the more basic and most technical aspects of the program to other authors and instructors to expand upon. To economize even more, instead of a DVD shipping with the book, we've posted files for you to download from **WOW! ONLINE**.

It's always exciting to assemble gorgeous new examples of art, essential production techniques, and time-saving tips from **Illustrator WOW!** artists worldwide. Nowhere else can you find this combination of gorgeous, professional art, combined with the range of expertise from the contributing writers, and the knowledge that the **WOW!** team has thoroughly tested every lesson and gallery to make sure everything actually works. All lessons are deliberately short to allow you to squeeze in a lesson or two between clients, and to encourage the use of this book within the confines of supervised classrooms.

The user level for this book is "intermediate through professional," so we assume that you have a reasonable level of competence with computer concepts (such as opening and saving files, launching applications, copying objects to the Clipboard, and clicking-and-dragging), and that you have a familiarity with most of Illustrator's tools and functions. Please see the **WOW! GLOSSARY** appendix for a thorough summary of the shortcuts and conventions that we'll refer to regularly in the book, as well as the section "How to use this book…" following, for more details on the user level for this book.

The more experienced you become with Adobe Illustrator, the easier it is to assimilate all the new information and inspiration you'll find in this book. I'm immensely proud of and grateful to everyone who works with me on this project. And I welcome you to the team.
Most Sincerely,

Sharon Steuer

What's new in CS6 (and CS5)?

New features for CS6 include a Pattern Options panel for creating and editing patterns, an enhanced Image Trace panel (replacing Live Trace), gradients applied to Strokes, a quick-access Locate Object icon in the Layers panel, a faster Gaussian Blur, an interface overhaul, and native 64-bit support bringing performance improvements across the board. If you missed CS5, new features included the Shape Builder tool, perspective tools, bristle brushes, variable width strokes with the Width tool, transparency in gradients and gradient mesh, and the Artboards panel.

How to keep in touch with us

We'll post notes on **WOW! ONLINE** when Adobe ships mini-upgrades via the Adobe Creative Cloud, discussing how this might impact your workflow. We'll also post announcements to **WOW! ONLINE** about future ePub versions of the **WOW!** books, **Zen of the Pen™** courses (when they're available), and CreativePro **WOW!** expansions. Communicate directly with Sharon via Twitter (@SharonSteuer), facebook.com/SharonSteuer, or sign up for her occasional eNewsletters (STEUERArtNews)_, or send her links to artwork, via http://ssteuer.com/contact.

How to use this book...

Look for the WOW! ONLINE icon

When you see this icon, it means that you can access related artwork or files for that project or artwork. To access a separate zip file for each chapter, plus a few extras, access **WOW! ONLINE** from www.peachpit.com/cs6wow, and enter the password **19952013**.

The default new dark interface (shown here with Preferences open to the new User Interface section to adjust this) makes screenshots more difficult to read in print, so throughout this book we're using the Light interface setting

Where's the Welcome screen?

Illustrator no longer starts with a Welcome screen, but you can access default (and your custom-saved New) Document Profiles in the Profile list when you choose File> New. From this dialog you can also still access the Template menu. Use the Help menu for online resources, and find a list of recent files from the File menu.

Windows WOW! Glossary

and essential Adobe Illustrator shortcuts

Ctrl	Ctrl always refers to the Ctrl (Control) key
Alt	Alt always refers to the Alt key
Marquee	With any Selection tool, click-drag over object(s) to select
Toggle	Menu selection acts as a switch: choose once turns it on, choosing again turns it off
Contextual menu	Right-click to access contextual menus

The Mac and Windows WOW! Glossaries cover basic keyboard shortcuts for commands you'll frequently use

While everyone is welcome to be inspired by the fabulous work showcased in this book, please keep in mind that this **Adobe Illustrator CS6 WOW! Book** has been designed and tested for intermediate through professional-level users of Adobe Illustrator. That means that you'll need to be familiar enough with the basics of Illustrator to be able to create your own art to follow along with the lessons. Unlike some books that do all the work for you, this book encourages experiential learning; as you follow along with the lessons, you'll not only be mastering the techniques, but you'll be creating your own art along the way. And to help you figure things out and inspire you further, this icon ⊕ tells you to look for the featured artwork within that chapter's folder at **WOW! ONLINE** (see Tip "Look for the **WOW! ONLINE** icon" at left for details).

Shortcuts and keystrokes

Please start by looking at the **WOW! Glossary** in an appendix at the back of the book for a thorough list of power-user shortcuts that you'll want to become familiar with. The **WOW! Glossary** provides definitions for the terms used throughout this book, always starting with Macintosh shortcuts first, then the Windows equivalent (⌘-Z/Ctrl-Z). Conventions covered range from simple general things such as the ⌘ symbol for the Mac's Command or Apple key, and the Cut, Copy, Paste, and Undo shortcuts, to important Illustrator-specific conventions, such as ⌘-G/Ctrl-G for grouping objects, and Paste In Front (⌘-F/Ctrl-F)/Paste In Back (⌘-B/Ctrl-B) to paste items copied to the clipboard directly in front/back of the selected object, and in perfect registration. Because you can now customize keyboard shortcuts, we're restricting the keystroke references in the book to those instances when it's so standard that we assume you'll keep the default, or when there is no other way to achieve that function (such as Lock All Unselected Objects).

Setting up your panels

Illustrator initially launches with an application default that could inhibit the way Illustrator experts work. One of the most powerful features of Illustrator is that, when properly set, you can easily style your next object and choose where it will be in the stacking order by merely selecting a similar object. But in order for your currently selected object to set all the styling attributes for the next object you draw (including brush strokes, live effects, transparency, etc.), you must first disable the New Art Has Basic Appearance setting from the pop-up menu in the Appearance panel (✓ shows if it's enabled). Your new setting sticks even after you've quit, but needs to be reset if you reinstall Illustrator or trash the preferences. Throughout the book we'll remind you to disable it when necessary, and also, at times, when it's helpful to have it enabled.

HOW THIS BOOK IS ORGANIZED...

You'll find a number of different kinds of information woven throughout this book—all of it up-to-date for Illustrator CS6: **Introductions, Tips, Techniques, Galleries,** and **References.** The book progresses in difficulty both within each chapter, and from chapter to chapter. If you've not done this yet, please see the previous section "Important: Read me first!" about the user level of this book.

1 Introductions. Every chapter starts with a brief, general introduction. In these introductions you'll find a quick overview of the features referred to in the chapter Lessons and Galleries that follow, as well as a robust collection of tips and tricks that should help you get started. In fact, there is so much info crammed in there it's likely that you'll discover new, useful information every time you take a look.

2 Tips. Don't miss the useful information organized into the gray and red Tip boxes throughout the book. Usually you'll find them alongside related text, but if you're in an impatient mood, you might just want to flip through,

✓ New Art Has Basic Appearance

New Art Has Basic Appearance

If you want your currently selected object to set all styling attributes for the next object, disable New Art Has Basic Appearance by choosing it from the pop-up menu in the Appearance panel

1

Every chapter begins with an Introduction section that focuses on overviews of features

Everything's under Window...

Almost every panel in Illustrator is accessible through the Window menu. If we don't tell you where to find a panel, look for it in the Window menu!

2 ### Tip boxes

Look for these gray boxes to find Tips about Adobe Illustrator.

Red Tip boxes

Red Tip boxes contain warnings or other essential information.

3

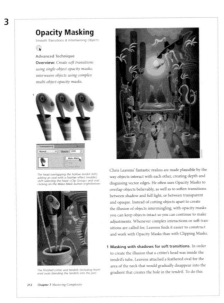

Step-by-step lessons show you how an artist or designer uses a feature to tackle a creative task

4

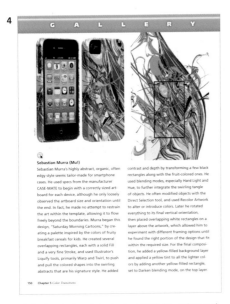

Galleries show original art projects by artists and designers from around the world

5

Access **Illustrator Help** from the Help menu, or if you have function keys, use F1

looking for interesting or relevant Tips. The red arrows, red outlines, and **red text** found in Tips (and sometimes with artwork) have been added to emphasize or further explain a concept or technique.

3 Step-by-step lessons. In these detailed sections, you'll find step-by-step techniques gathered from artists and designers around the world. Most **WOW!** lessons focus on one aspect of how an image was created, though we'll sometimes refer you to different chapters (or to a specific step-by-step Lesson, Tip, or Gallery where a related technique is further discussed) to give you the opportunity to explore a briefly covered feature more thoroughly. Feel free to start with almost any chapter, but be aware that each technique builds on those previously explained, so you should try to follow the techniques within each chapter sequentially. The later chapters include **Advanced Technique** lessons, which assume that you've assimilated the techniques found throughout the chapter. The *Mastering Complexity* chapter is packed with lessons dedicated to advanced tips, tricks, and techniques, and most will integrate techniques introduced in the earlier chapters.

4 Galleries. The Gallery pages consist of images related to techniques demonstrated nearby. Each Gallery piece is accompanied by a description of how the artist created that image, and may include steps showing the progression of a technique detailed elsewhere.

5 References. Within the text you'll occasionally be directed to *Illustrator Help* for more details; to access this choose Help > Illustrator Help. At the back of the book, you'll find a special tips supplement, plus a special list of Illustrator-related plug-ins, scripts, and other production resources, both assembled for you by Design Tools Monthly. Next you'll find **WOW! Glossary** references for Windows and Mac; followed by a listing the artists featured in this book, a General Index, and finally, on the last page, the production notes on how this book was created.

Acknowledgments

As always, my most heartfelt gratitude goes to the many artists and Illustrator experts who generously allowed us to include their work and divulge their techniques.

Special thanks to Jean-Claude Tremblay, our amazing technical editor. We are so lucky to have JC advising us on every technical detail of this project, including producing our press-ready PDFs! Thanks to Mordy Golding; as author of *Real World Adobe Illustrator* books, and now at lynda.com, he continues to champion this book and to share his expertise with the **WOW!** team. And thanks to the folks at Adobe, especially Terry Hemphill, Brenda Sutherland, Ian Giblin, Teri Pettit, and Meghan Boots. Thanks Teresa Roberts for continuing as Bay Area Illustrator User Group organizer.

This revision is the result of a major team effort by an amazing group of friends and collaborators. Thankfully Cristen Gillespie is sticking with Illustrator **WOW!** Cristen works on almost everything, including contributing the vast majority of new lessons, Galleries, and this time, all of the introductions. Also blessedly returning were veteran **WOW!** artist/writer Lisa Jackmore (who did a great job with Galleries, lessons, and the **Adobe Illustrator CS6 WOW! Course Outline**), and cartographer/writer Steven Gordon (who returned to create and update important lessons and Galleries, join me on curatorial duties, and continue to contribute dry wit when needed). Also returning was artist/writer Aaron McGarry, who continues to be our resident 3D and perspective expert. Joining us as **WOW!** writers were the wonderful artists George Coghill, Raymond Larrett, and Laurie Wigham. Thank you Eric Schumacher-Rasmussen for returning (with kindness and humor) as the master juggler of so many edits from so many of us. A special thanks goes to our stellar team of testers: Nini Tjäder, Federico Platón, David Lindblad, Brian Stoppee, Janet Stoppee, Katharine Gilbert, Darren Winder, Franck Payen, Stéphane Nahmani, Chris Leavens, and Adam Z Lein (who also helped set up and troubleshoot the database that tracks who's doing what). Thanks to Sandee Cohen (@vectorbabe) who continues to act as our official kibitzer. Sandee also introduced me to Bob Levine (@idguy), and together they helped me try to figure out GREP answers to cryptic InDesign flow issues. Thank you Jim Birkenseer and Peter Truskier (of Premedia Systems), for taking on the difficult task of updating your **WOW!** scripts for our Illustrator lessons. Thank you Jay Nelson for continuing to nurture Design Tools Monthly and **WOW!** collaborations. And I look forward to previewing and expanding **WOW!** book materials for Mike Rankin at CreativePro.com, and Nick van der Walle at Astute Graphics. Thanks to Laurie Grace for screenshot updates, and making me laugh, Jack Lewis for being such a patient and fast indexer, and Darren Meiss being the best proofer we've ever had. Peg Maskell Korn helped me ten of the past eleven editions, and she was missed this time.

Thank you CDS for the fabulous printing. Thanks to Doug Little and Mike Mason at Wacom for keeping us up to date with their great products. And thanks to everyone at Peachpit Press for everything you do to make sure this book happens, *especially* Nancy Peterson, Tracey Croom, Nancy Davis, Nancy Ruenzel, Mimi Heft (for the gorgeous cover design again), Alison Serafini, Glenn Bisignani, Eric Geoffroy. Thank you Linnea Dayton for spearheading the **WOW!** series and for sharing Cristen. And last but *not* least, thanks to all my wonderful family and friends.

1

Your Creative Workspace

Your Creative Workspace

OK, this might not seem like sexy **WOW!** stuff, but to save time and stay focused on being creative, you need to work efficiently. In this chapter you'll find tons of things you might have missed or overlooked. You'll find tips for customizing your workspace and in-depth coverage of newer organizational features such as working with multiple artboards and the multi-functional Appearance panel, which can take the place of several panels.

ORGANIZING YOUR WORKSPACE

You can save time and frustration in the long run if you spend a few minutes setting up custom workspaces and creating your own document profiles. The panels you want handy in order to create a Bristle Brush painting are probably different from what you need when creating a technical illustration or the layout for a series of brochures. Not all panels are needed for every job, but by organizing all that you definitely need—eliminating all you'll rarely need or won't need at all—you'll be able to locate quickly just what you need when you need it. In addition, the Control and Appearance panels often contain the same information found in the special-purpose panels, permitting you to close some of those panels and streamline your interface even more than you might think possible (see the "Using the Appearance Panel" section later in this chapter).

In deciding which panels you want on your desktop for any given project, you'll probably first want to cluster panels that you will frequently use in sequence, such as Paragraph and Character Styles or Transform and Align. You'll also decide where each panel or group of panels should live, and whether, when you collapse them to get them out of your way, you want them to collapse to their icon and label, or all the way down to their icon. When you have everything arranged to your liking, choose New Workspace from either Window> Workspace, or from the

---

Tabbed docs & the App Frame

- Change whether documents are tabbed (the default) or not through Preferences> User Interface.
- If more documents are open than are visible on tabs, a double-arrow at the tab bar's right will list them.
- Drag documents away from the tab to make them free-floating.
- Drag an object from one document into another by dragging over that document's tab. The tab will spring open to let you drop the object in place.
- On a Mac, you can also turn on the Application Frame (disabled by default) from the Window menu. The frame contains all the panels and documents, and everything you can do in AI takes place within the frame.

Note: *You should turn off the Application Frame when using an extended monitor setup (or during video projection).*

Magically appearing panels

If you have used Tab or Shift-Tab to hide your panels, mouse carefully over the narrow strip just before the very edge of the monitor where the panels were and they'll reappear, then hide themselves again when you move away.

pop-up menu in the Application bar. Once you've created and saved a custom workspace, its name will show up in the Window> Workspace submenu and on the Application bar (by default at the top of your working area). Switch between different workspaces by choosing a name. Note that any changes to a workspace, such as a panel opened or moved, are temporarily saved when you quit Illustrator so that you can always open Illustrator right where you left off. To restore a workspace to its original configuration, open the list of workspaces and choose Reset. Following are some tips for arranging your panels:

- **Dock panels** to the edges of your screen or, if you want them closer to your work, drag them around freely. (The Control panel docks to the top or bottom of the screen.)

- **Resize most panels** once they're open. Look for the double-headed arrow when hovering over an edge to see if the panel can be dragged in that direction.

- **Collapse and expand free-floating or fully expanded columns to their title bar** by double-clicking the panel name. (If the open panel is one in a column of icons that has been temporarily opened by itself, it can't be reduced to its title bar.) Double-click on the top gray bar to collapse a free-floating panel to an icon. Experiment with expanding and minimizing open panels in your workspace to get used to how the panels work, and you'll save time and frustration later when you want to get a panel out of your way quickly.

- **If you need multiple panels open at once**, place each panel you want open in a separate column (drag to the side of an existing column until you see the vertical blue bar). Only one item in a column of panel icons can be open, but one from each column can be open simultaneously and will remain open until you manually close it by clicking on its double arrow in the upper right corner. The exception is if you have enabled Auto Collapse Icon Panels in Preferences> User Interface. In that case, clicking anywhere outside a panel that was opened from an icon will close it for you. Since panels are "spring-loaded," you can still drag items into them even when they're closed.

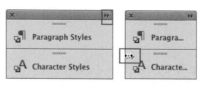

When you click the double arrow in the upper right, open panels will cycle through contracted and expanded states, which will vary depending on how you've customized the panel; customizing the width manually when the cursor turns into a double-headed arrow allows you to click-drag to resize the panel

Dock and stack panels with different results by watching where the blue highlight shows up

A double-headed arrow in the upper left (next to the panel name) indicates that you can display more, or fewer, options in the panel; the fewest options will be shown by default

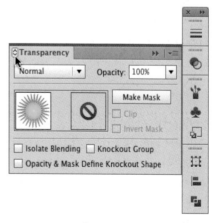

To minimize a panel opened from a column of panels that have been reduced to icons, click the double arrow in the upper right (you can't minimize it by double-clicking the dark gray bar)

Using New Document Profiles

When you create a New Document Profile, you can establish not only the size, color mode, and resolution of your document, but also whether or not that document includes specific swatches, symbols, graphic styles, brushes, and even what font is chosen as the default. By saving this to the New Document Profiles preset folder along with your other user Library presets, the document appears in the New Document dialog.

Rulers, Guides, Smart Guides, and Grids

Now that Illustrator offers multiple artboards, you can choose to display the ruler (⌘-R/Ctrl-R) as a Global ruler that extends across all your artboards, or as an Artboard ruler, one for each artboard with its own x,y coordinate system. The rulers look the same, but if you Control-click/right-click on a ruler, or press ⌘-Option-R/Ctrl-Alt-R, the Change to (Global/Artboard ruler) command reveals which ruler is active, and you can switch rulers here. In order to be consistent with other Adobe programs, new documents by default use Artboard rulers and set the origin point at the upper left corner, instead of the lower left. Documents created in older versions will still open with Artboard rulers active and the origin point in the upper left, but if you switch to the Global Ruler, the origin point will be at the legacy lower left corner, as it was when the document was originally created. If you need to work with legacy positioning, switch to Global Rulers with your legacy documents to see the old x,y coordinates. You can still change the location of the origin point by dragging from the upper left corner of the rulers to the desired location, but you can give each artboard its own origin point when you choose Artboard Rulers.

You can apply guides globally or to individual artboards. To place a non-global guide with the Artboard tool selected (Shift-O), drag a guide from the ruler to the active artboard, being careful to drag right over the board, not between it and another. If you drag a guide in between the artboards, it will place the guide across all artboards.

If you intend to use more than a couple of guides in a project, you should probably create separate layers for specific sets of guides. By keeping guides on named layers, you'll not only be able to easily control which guides are visible at any time, but also how the global locking, visibility, and clearing of guides is applied.

You can also create guides by selecting an object and defining it as a guide by choosing Object> Make Guides (⌘-5/Ctrl-5, or via View> Guides). By default, guides are unlocked, but you can lock them using the Lock/Unlock toggle (in the context-sensitive or View menus); the Lock/Unlock Guides toggle is global, and affects all guides in all documents. Any unlocked guide can be changed into a regular, editable path by targeting the guide and, again in the context-sensitive menu, choosing Release Guides. Guides not targeted will not be converted.

Smart Guides, which can be powerful aids for constructing and aligning objects as you draw, are helpful enough to become an essential part of your workflow. Try keeping them on (the toggle is ⌘-U/ Ctrl-U). Enable or disable viewing options in Preferences> Smart Guides.

MASTERING OBJECT MANAGEMENT

Take control of the stacking order of objects right from the beginning, and become familiar with the different ways to focus on just the necessary objects at one time.

Although probably the easiest and most important thing that you can do to keep your file organized is to name your layers as you create them, it's easy to get lazy and just click the New Layer icon. To avoid amassing a stack of ambiguously numbered layers, try to get in the habit of holding Option/Alt when you click the New Layer icon to name it in the Layer Options dialog, or double-click on the layer name itself to rename it. (Of course you can double-click to the right of the layer name at any time to access Layer Options and edit the name or other settings.) Both the Layers and the Appearance panel are designed primarily to help you locate, select, and modify your artwork objects, so you want to take full advantage of

Changing Constrain Angle

If you adjust the X and Y axes in Preferences> General> Constrain Angle, it will affect the drawn objects and transformations of your grid, as they will follow the adjusted angle when you create a new object. This can be helpful if you're working in isometrics or another layout requiring alignment of objects at an angle.

Hide/Show Edges

The shortcut for Hide/Show Edges is ⌘-H/Ctrl-H (or choose View> Hide/Show Edges). Once you hide the selection edges (paths and anchor points), all path edges in that file will remain hidden until you show them again—and that hidden state is saved with your file! Get in the habit of toggling it off when you're done with the task at hand. And, if you open a file and can't decode the mystery of why things don't appear selected, remember to try ⌘-H/Ctrl-H.

Three grids

View Illustrator's automatic grid using View> Show Grid (⌘-"/ Ctrl-"). Illustrator also offers a Perspective Grid and a Pixel Grid that serve special functions. For details on the Perspective Grid, see the *Reshaping Dimensions* chapter, and for information on using the Pixel Grid, see the *Creatively Combining Apps* chapter.

Layers panel and isolation

When you enter isolation mode, only the artwork in the group or layer that's isolated will be visible in the Layers panel. Once you exit isolation mode, the other layers and groups will once again appear in the Layers panel.

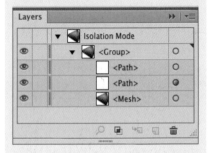

Isolation ins and outs

To enter isolation mode:

· • Double-click on an object or group
• Select an object or group and click on the Isolate Selected Object button on the Control panel
• Choose Enter Isolation Mode in the Layers panel menu

To exit isolation mode:

• Press the Esc key
• Click on any empty spot on the gray isolation bar
• Double-click an empty spot on the artboard
• Click on the Back arrow on the isolation bar until you're out
• Choose Exit Isolation Mode from the Layers panel menu
• ⌘-click/Ctrl-click to back out to the next level of isolation

Illustrator's changing interface to know just where you are and what you'll be affecting.

Using Isolation Mode

Isolation mode is a quick way to isolate selected objects so you can work on them without accidentally affecting other objects. The next time you want to edit an object, group, or layer, use isolation mode instead of locking or hiding things that are in the way. In addition to *you* choosing to enter isolation mode, Illustrator will also at times automatically place you into a special form of isolation mode, such as when editing symbols, creating patterns, or working with opacity masks. Isolation mode focuses your attention as you create and edit various types of objects.

See the Tip at left for a summary of how to enter and exit isolation mode. Once you enter, a gray bar appears at the top of your document window, indicating that you're now in isolation mode, and the gray bar displays the hierarchy that contains the isolated object. Everything on your artboard *except* the object(s) you've just isolated will be dimmed, indicating that those other objects are temporarily locked. If you have isolated an object or group, you can expand the isolation to the sublayer or layer that the object is on by clicking on the word for that layer in the gray bar. As long as isolation mode is active, anything you add to your artboard will automatically become part of the isolated group. (Disable "Double-click to Isolate" in Preferences> General to prevent a double-click from putting you in isolation mode.)

Isolation mode isn't limited to objects you've grouped yourself. Remember that other types of objects—such as blends, envelopes, or Live Paint objects—exist as groups, and isolation mode works for them, too. In addition to using isolation mode on groups, you can also use it on almost anything—layers, symbols, clipping masks, compound paths, opacity masks, images, gradient meshes, and even a single path. The next time you think you have to enter Outline mode, or lock or hide objects to avoid grabbing other objects, try isolation mode instead.

Select Behind

To select objects from the document window that are hidden by other objects without first having to lock or hide those objects, ⌘-click/Ctrl-click to Select Object Behind (toggle it on/off in Preferences> Selection and Anchor Display). The first click brings up the Select Behind cursor and selects the topmost object, and each subsequent ⌘-click/Ctrl-click targets the Fill for the next objects in the stacking order. You can't target Strokes in this manner, but if the object has a Fill, you can target the object and use the Appearance panel to change the Stroke.

Selecting & Targeting Indicators in the Layers Panel

Many seasoned Illustrator artists have missed the introduction of targeting versus selecting. When you simply select objects and apply effects or adjust opacity, the effects might not be applied as you expected, and in order to remove or edit the effects you'll have to carefully reproduce this level of selection (see "Decoding appearances" on the next page). If instead you apply an effect to a targeted group, layer, or sublayer, then the effects are easy to remove (simply target that level again).

To know for sure whether you have successfully targeted a layer, look in the Layers panel, where you should see the double-circle as the target indicator for that layer, and a large square box indicating that you've selected all objects within that layer (a small square means you have only some objects on that level selected). In addition, in the Appearance panel you should see the word "Layer" listed first as the thumbnail name (as opposed to "Group," "Path", or "Mixed Objects"). When a group, layer, or sublayer has an effect applied to it, any new objects placed into that level will immediately acquire those effects.

Copy and Paste Techniques

When you copy an object, Illustrator offers a number of power options for how the objects are pasted, including Paste in Front, Paste in Back, Paste in Place, and Paste on All Artboards. Note that none of these are affected by

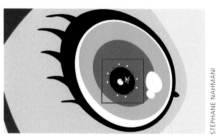

⌘-click/Ctrl-click on the topmost object to bring up the Select Behind cursor

STEPHANE NAHMANI

Selection and target indicators (from left to right): 1) target indicator for any layer or subcomponent, 2) selection is also currently targeted, 3) target indicator for any targeted component with effect applied, 4) selection indicator for a container layer, 5) selection indicator when an object is selected, 6) selection indicator when all objects on a layer are selected

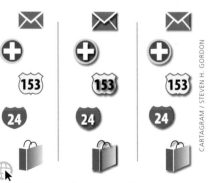

CARTAGRAM / STEVEN H. GORDON

Steven Gordon at Cartagram applies drop shadows to his map icons: (left) original, (middle) after selecting ungrouped objects (or all objects on a layer) and applying an effect (it applies to each object separately); (right) after targeting the layer or selecting the group and applying the effect (it applies to the bounding paths only)

A basic appearance does not include multiple fills or strokes, transparency, effects, or brush strokes. More complex appearances are indicated by a gradient-filled circle in the Layers panel. When you need to modify artwork created by others (or open artwork you created earlier), it's essential to have both the Appearance and Layers panels visible. Unless an effect is applied at the level of a layer or a group, you might not see the filled circle icon until you expand your view of the layer to locate the object that has the effect applied.

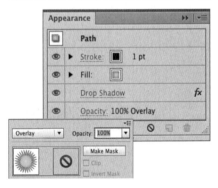

Many functions reside in the Appearance panel

Duplicating fills/strokes/effects

To duplicate a fill or stroke: select the object and click on the Add New Stroke or Add New Fill icon at the bottom of the Appearance panel, from the panel menu, or select one or more strokes, fills, and effects in the panel and drag them to the Duplicate Selected Item icon at the bottom of the panel.

the ruler origin, but are positioned in the same relative position to the upper left corner of the artboard. Here are some of the distinctions:

- **If you choose Paste in Front or Paste in Back with nothing selected,** Illustrator pastes the cut or copied object at the extreme front or back of the current layer.
- **If you choose Paste in Front or Paste in Back with an object selected,** Illustrator pastes the object directly on top of or behind the selected object in the stacking order.
- **Paste in Place** is the same as Paste in Front with nothing selected, but it pastes to any selected artboard.
- **Paste on All Artboards** pastes the object in the same relative position onto each artboard.

Using the Appearance Panel

You probably know by now that many functions can be handled in the Control panel instead of individual panels. The Appearance panel also can replace a number of separate panels, making it an indispensable hub for a productive and efficient workflow. Here you can view or edit a selected object's stroke, fill, or transparency; check to see if it's part of a group; or adjust an effect or named graphic style applied to it.

In the Appearance panel with a group or layer targeted, double-clicking on Contents reveals object-level attributes. With a text object, double-click on Characters to see the basic text attributes. You can also add additional strokes or fills to the object, apply effects and access effect dialogs, choose whether or not the next object you draw will have the same appearance, or construct a new graphic style to save for future objects. Important concepts for using the Appearance panel include the following:

- **The basic appearance** consists of a stroke and fill (even if set to None), and its transparency (0%–100% Opacity).
- **Apply an appearance** to any path, object, group, layer or sublayer.
- **The stacking order of attributes** affects the final appearance, and can be changed simply by dragging the attribute up or down in the list.

- **The visibility of attributes** can be toggled on or off by clicking the Eye icon, and multiple selected items can be unhidden with Show All Hidden Attributes from the panel menu. The visibility of thumbnails can be toggled on or off with Show/Hide Thumbnail in the panel menu.
- **Click on underlined words**, such as Stroke, Opacity, or Drop Shadow to open their respective panels; Shift-click on a swatch icon to open the Color panel.

Graphic Styles and the Appearance Panel

A graphic style consists of all the attributes applied to an object, group, or layer. To see a larger thumbnail preview when you have a single object selected, Control-click/right-click on the style (this doesn't work with more than one object selected). Save a current appearance by clicking the New Graphic Style button (you can also drag the thumbnail from the Appearance panel, or drag the object itself to the Graphic Styles panel). Option-drag/Alt-drag the thumbnail on top of an existing graphic style in the Graphic Styles panel to replace it.

To add a graphic style to an object that already has a graphic style without removing any of the existing attributes, Option-click/Alt-click on the graphic style in the Graphic Styles panel. When you look at the Appearance panel, you'll see the new attributes stacked on top of the original attributes.

MANAGING MULTIPLE ARTBOARDS

Having multiple artboards allows you to organize work within and across projects in a single document, whether you need to create multi-panel storyboards, set up elaborate character stagings for animations, organize many elements within a single complex project, or even keep multi-sized, collateral business material (such as cards, stationery, envelopes, postcards, and brochures) within one document. And then, of course, you can print or export to PDF any combination of the artboards that you want into one multi-page PDF, even one with multi-sized pages. To help you set up, organize, and work with

Drawing with Appearances

Whether or not your new object will have the same attributes as your last-drawn object depends upon settings in the Appearance panel menu.

- **If New Art Has Basic Appearance is enabled,** you'll be drawing with only the current Stroke, Fill, and Opacity. Any other attributes from your last-drawn object are ignored.
- **If you have disabled New Art Has Basic Appearance,** your new art will have the exact same Appearance as your last object, but you can choose Reduce to Basic Appearance in the panel menu to remove all attributes except the Stroke, Fill, and Opacity.
- **To eliminate even the Basic Appearance,** click on the Clear Appearance icon at the bottom of the panel, which reduces the selected object to None for Stroke and Fill, and the Default (100%) Opacity.

Control-clicking/right-clicking shows enlarged thumbnail of a graphic style applied to the selected object

Choose Window> New Window to display different aspects of your current image simultaneously. You can view the same art separately, and in different View modes (Preview, Outline, Overprint, or Pixel), or with different Proof Setups (including for color blindness), or Zoom levels. Use Arrange Documents on the Application bar to organize them or to make edges hidden or visible. Most choices from the View menu are saved with the file along with the new windows.

Design to the edge

By default, artwork that extends beyond an artboard won't print, making it important to watch not only for artwork left off the artboard, but for artwork that has been manually positioned on the page in the Print dialog. If your artwork extends beyond the edge of an artboard, make sure you add a bleed setting value; if the artwork gets placed in InDesign or saved as EPS, it's all still visible.

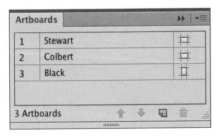

Artboards panel with reorder arrows, orientation icon (double-click to enter the Options dialog), and New Artboard and Delete Artboard icons

artboards, both the Artboards panel and the Control panel options with the Artboard tool selected provide the access and features you'll need. To manage the artboards themselves, make sure you're familiar with basic artboard functions:

- **Set up artboards** when you're configuring a new document, or later on using the Artboards panel or the Control panel with the Artboard tool active. Artboard configurations can be saved as part of a New Document Profile.

- **To add an artboard** using the same properties as the currently highlighted artboard, click on the New Artboard icon. It will be added to the same row as the current artboard, but you can rearrange the artboards later.

- **Modify artboard settings in the Artboard Options dialog** by choosing Artboard Options from the Artboards menu; double-clicking on the artboard orientation icon in the Artboards panel (single-click if the artboard is already active); double-clicking on the Artboard tool; or clicking the Artboard Options icon on the Control panel when the Artboard tool is active.

- **Create and manage artboards manually** and interactively by selecting the Artboard tool (Shift-O) instead of invoking the dialog, dragging artboards to scale and position them, and using the Control panel options. Enabling Smart Guides can help with precise manual alignment.

- **Name your active artboard** by double-clicking on the Artboard name and renaming it directly. Or select the Artboard tool and change its name in either the Control panel or in the Artboards Options dialog. The name is listed in the Artboards panel and in the list of artboard panels in the status bar (Artboard Navigation, located at the bottom right of the document window).

- **Rearrange artboards** through the Artboards panel menu or Object> Artboards> Rearrange, choose rows, columns and spacing; whether or not to move your artwork with the artboard; and the last-used settings persist.

- **Reorder the list of artboards** in the Artboards panel using the up and down arrow icons. Reordering artboards within the Artboards panel doesn't change the way the actual artboards are arranged in your workspace. However, be aware that the order of artboards in the panel determines the order in which artboards print or are ordered when saved as a multi-page PDF.

- **Use Shift-Page Up or Shift-Page Down to navigate** the Artboard panel layers, which will fill the window with your selected artboard as you navigate.
- **Artboards have a reference point**. In the Position area of Artboard Options, choose the reference point from which artboards get resized.
- **Overlapping art across multiple artboards, or overlapping artboards onto one piece of art,** allows you to develop multiple versions of the same image without duplicating elements. Each artboard will print only those portions of the art wholly contained within its borders, allowing you to print or export duplicates, and/or portions of an art piece, from the one instance of the art (this is a useful technique for storyboarding and comic strips).
- **Convert a non-rotated rectangle** to an artboard by choosing Object> Artboards> Convert to Artboard.
- **Use Fit to Artwork Bounds and Fit to Selected Art** commands (in the Preset list on the Control panel when the Artboard tool is selected, or under Object> Artboards), for resizing artboards according to their contents.
- **To locate an artboard visually** when another artboard fills your view, choose View>Fit All in Window (⌘-Option-0/Ctrl-Alt-0). To activate it, click on the artboard with the Selection tool or click on its name in the Artboards panel.
- **When zooming,** the commands Fit Artboard in Window (⌘-0/Ctrl-0) and Actual Size (⌘-1/Ctrl-1) affect the active artboard. Double-clicking in the Artboards panel to the right of an inactive artboard's name or on its number on the left (single-click if it's active), also zooms that artboard to Fit Artboard in Window size.
- **Export artboards as separate TIFF, JPEG, PSD, or PNG files** when you need a rasterized version of every artboard in your document.

Tracing a Template

Manually Tracing a Template Layer

Overview: *Place a scan on a template layer in Illustrator; manually trace over the template using the Pencil, Pen, and Arc tools; modify paths with the Direct Selection tool; use geometric objects for ease and speed.*

SELLERS

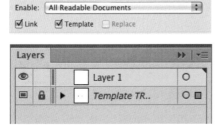

Part of the high-contrast scan of Seller's pen sketch from photographs of Atlanta's skyline

Creating the template and a drawing layer by choosing File> Place

Using the Direct Selection tool and repositioning two anchor points after tracing (left) to reshape the drawing of a building (right)

Rachel Sellers used Illustrator's basic drawing tools to build this skyline for Thirty-Third Latitude Properties. Using a scanned sketch as a template, Sellers relied on Illustrator's Pencil, Pen, and basic geometric tools to draw the skyline and artwork in the logo.

1 Placing a scanned image as a template. Scan your source image at a high enough resolution and contrast to see the detail you need for tracing and save it as a PSD, TIFF, or JPG. In a new Illustrator document, choose File> Place, select your scan, enable the Template option at the lower-left of the dialog, and click Place. Your scan is now on a Template layer beneath the original layer. Template names appear italicized in the Layers panel and are automatically set to be non-printing and dimmed to 50% opacity (to adjust opacity, double-click the Template thumbnail in the Layers panel).

2 Tracing straight lines and corners, and repositioning points. With the template as a guide, select Layer 1 (the default layer in the Layers panel) and with the Pen tool, using the scan as a guide, click to place anchor points that will connect with straight lines. To draw horizontal, vertical, or diagonal lines while you trace, hold down the Shift key as you click with the Pen tool. Once you've drawn a basic path, zoom in close and use the Direct Selection tool to adjust positioning of anchor points. Instead of being more precise, Sellers used her rough sketch as a guideline for a stylized interpretation of the Atlanta skyline.

3 Tracing and adjusting curved paths. Illustrator has several options to create curved paths. To create curves using the Pen tool, instead of clicking to place a corner point attached to a straight line, you click and drag in the direction that the curve is heading, then click-drag on the other side of the bump of a curve (this takes practice!). To adjust the curves, use the Direct Selection tool to drag its direction handles. Click the Convert icons in the Control panel to convert anchor points between corners and curves, and grab a direction handle with the Convert Anchor Point tool to hinge a smooth curve.

Another option is to draw with the Pencil tool. Double-click the Pencil tool icon to change its Fidelity and Smoothness numbers. You can also control how smooth or detailed your paths are by zooming in or out before drawing or editing with the Pencil or Smooth tools. Zoom out to create smoother lines (fewer anchor points) or zoom in for a path with more points. You can also redraw any selected path by drawing close to it with the Pencil tool (controlling how close you need to be in Options).

If your curve is a simple arc, consider the Arc tool (located behind the Line Segment tool). To use it, click and drag a curved path. After drawing the arc, you can reshape its path like any curve, by using the Direct Selection tool to adjust handles and anchor points.

4 Using basic objects to help build your image. To speed up drawing, use ready-made geometric objects like rectangles and ellipses. Create triangles using the Polygon or Star tool by clicking the desktop and changing Sides to 3 in the tool's dialog. Add paths and filled objects with the Pen or Pencil tools, or use the Pathfinder panel or Shape Builder tool to combine objects (find out more about these tools in the *Rethinking Construction* chapter).

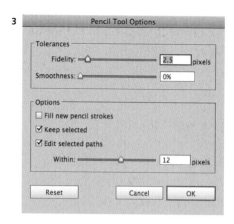

The Pencil Tool Options dialog showing the Fidelity and Smoothness controls

(Top) The path created by the Pencil tool with zoom at 300%; (bottom) the path drawn with zoom level at 50%

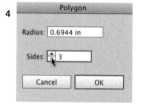

(Left) Creating a triangle with the Polygon tool by clicking the desktop and editing the Polygon menu's Sides value; (right) the resulting triangle

Stop drawing!

If you've drawn an open (not-closed) path and don't deselect it, your next click with the Pen tool will continue the same path. To draw a new path, click on the Pen tool icon, or hold ⌘/Ctrl (to temporarily access a Selection tool) and click on the artboard away from your object.

Basic to Complex

Starting Simple for Creative Composition

Overview: *Start with simple elements to build complexity; create layers to keep elements separated for easy modifications; use a Live Paint group to organize many small details.*

1

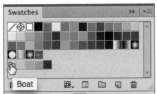

Rudmann's initial sketch to organize placement of his forms and their proportions, cropped to the artboard

Creating diamonds and the color group

When Andrew Rudmann set out to create the art piece "And Then I Swam," he began with a simple outline and a very few basic elements. He defined a color group, created clusters along with the basic elements, and then layered all of them to form more complex imagery. He also created a Live Paint group in order to draw forms without having to draw each path as a closed object. By slowly building complexity from very simple beginnings, he was able to control the results he sought to capture his vision.

1 Beginning with a simple sketch and simple objects.
Rudmann began with the Pen tool (P), sketching the structure that would tell the story. Since he was going to create the water from a single diamond shape he would modify, he only needed to sketch the proportions and placement of his elements. He used the Artboard tool (Shift-O) to adjust the artboard to fit the composition.

He next auditioned his basic elements, coloring them, and combining some of them into larger elements. To determine the colors for the piece, he first chose the background color: "My base color is usually very obnoxious, acidic, or uncomfortable so I tend to dull down the other colors in the piece," he said. He selected his final choice of four colors and saved them as a color group (Boat) by clicking the New Color Group icon in the Swatches panel.

To keep the process of building up the art from basic elements as fluid as possible, he found a method that minimized working with panels, and allowed him to keep his attention on the artboard. Selecting a diamond (or cluster of diamonds) that he wanted to duplicate and modify, he copied, used Paste in Front (or Back), and then used the Free Transform tool (E). He often ungrouped his clusters to freely modify and randomize a cluster by transforming some of the individual diamonds.

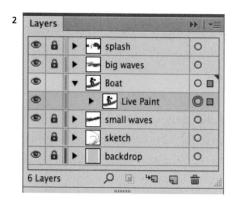

Using layers to lock and hide areas in the artwork in order to concentrate on a single area

2 Using layers to organize complex objects. Despite working freely, Rudmann needed to be able to access portions of the image for modifications. The illusion of organic chaos and randomly placed elements requires some control, and separating sections with just a few layers, descriptively named, made all the difference as he worked. He could lock all the layers to prevent moving artwork already in place, and turn off visibility for some layers in order to concentrate on just one region without distraction. He created the illusion of depth and distance by placing small waves behind the big waves, yet kept each set of waves accessible by putting the smaller waves on a layer beneath the big waves. Rudmann sandwiched the man and his boat on a layer between the large and small diamond-shaped waves, and the big splash came last.

3 Using Live Paint to quickly fill the man with dripping water. After Rudmann drew the outlines for the boat and the man, he used the Pen tool to freely draw open paths for the dripping water on the man, and a few stripes to signify his bucket. So that he could fill the interior (white) areas where these paths overlapped, he turned them all into a Live Paint Group. He didn't have to draw fully enclosed objects before filling them, as long as the outlines overlaped and formed enclosed areas. (See the *Rethinking Construction* chapter for more on using Live Paint.)

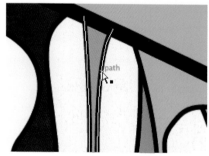

A Live Paint Group allows for coloring objects without having to draw each of them as separate objects made from closed paths

Navigating Layers

Creating, Organizing, and Viewing Layers

Overview: *Customize Layers panel defaults; create layers and sublayers; move layers in the Layers panel's hierarchy; change layer colors; hide layers to view artwork.*

1

The completed layer structure showing master layers for web pages and their sublayers

Option-clicking/Alt-clicking the Create New Sub-layer icon to bring up the Layer Options dialog

Running on empty

To easily spot an empty layer in the Layers panel, make sure to disable the Show Layers Only option in the Layers Panel Options dialog. A layer name without a black triangle in front of it is empty.

Madison Alabama
The Map and Guide Web App

| FAQ | Get Set | Get Going | Go Shop |

© Copyright 2011-2012 Cartagram, LLC

Layers are a great way to create and organize artwork as you work and view finished artwork when you're done. To design a mock-up of a web app for www.cartagram. com/MadisonAL, Steve Gordon created the artwork for each page on its own layer. He was able to hide and show layers to see how the design of different pages looked when viewed in different sequences.

1 Changing the Layers panel defaults and creating sublayers. For his mock-up Gordon planned on creating a "master" layer for each page with separate sublayers for the artwork comprising the page header, navigation bar, content container, footer, and page background. To see more layers at once, he changed the default row height and turned off thumbnail display in the Layers panel. To set up layer options to look like Gordon's, select Layers Panel Options from the panel menu and choose Small from the Row Size list (if you prefer larger row sizes, simply disable the choices in the Thumbnails list). You can change the default layer name, "Layer 1," as Gordon did by double-clicking the layer name in the Layers panel.

To create sublayers within this first master layer, select the layer in the panel and Option-click/Alt-click the Create New Sublayer icon at the bottom of the panel. In the Layer Options dialog, name the sublayer. Repeat this for each of the sublayers you need. Gordon completed the mock-up of the Home page by creating artwork on each of the sublayers.

2 Duplicating and moving master layers, and changing the Layers panel display. With the first master layer completed, Gordon created master layers for other pages in his mock-up. If your design uses common artwork, like Gordon's page elements, consider duplicating a layer and then editing the artwork unique to that layer. To duplicate a layer, drag it to the panel's Create New Layer icon or select Duplicate from the Layers panel menu.

To change the order of your master layers or sublayers, select a layer (Shift-click to select contiguous layers or ⌘-click/Ctrl-click for non-contiguous layers) and drag it to the desired position in the Layers panel (watch the bar icon in the panel as you drag to make sure it's going between layers, not within another layer).

To make the Layers panel easier to navigate at a glance, give each master layer and its sublayers a unique color in the panel. For the master layer, double-click to the right of its name in the Layers panel and pick a color from the Color menu in the Layer Options dialog. For the sublayers, Shift-select them and choose Options for Selection from the panel menu.

3 Using the Visibility layer control to mimic user movement between pages. After Gordon completed mock-ups for each of the pages, he made all master layers visible in the Layers panel by choosing Show All Layers from the panel menu. Then Gordon clicked each layer's visibility (Eye) icon to hide its artwork, displaying the artwork of the page on the layer below it. This provided a preview of what users would see moving from one page to another, assuring that the design of the pages were compatible.

2 *Selecting and dragging the FAQ layer above the Get Set layer*

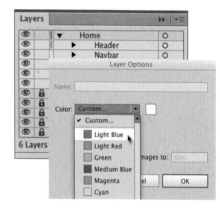

Top, selecting all sublayers; bottom, the Color menu in the Layer Options menu

3 *Left, all layers hidden except the Map layer; right, the Map web page artwork*

Let Illustrator do the walking

Illustrator can automatically expand the Layers panel and scroll to a selected object within hidden layers. Just select an object in your artwork and click the Locate Object icon in the Layers panel.

Basic Appearances

Making and Applying Appearances

Overview: *Create appearance attributes for an object; build a two-stroke appearance, save it as a style, and then draw paths and apply the style; target a layer, create a drop shadow effect, create symbols in the layer, and then edit layer appearance if needed.*

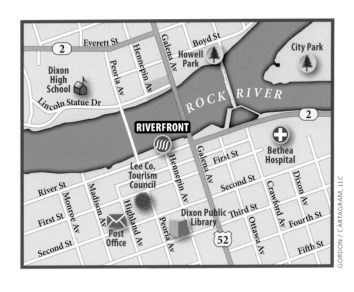

1

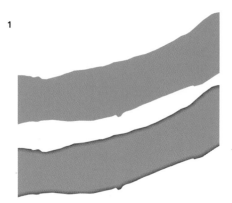

(Above) The river with blue fill; (below) the river with the Inner Glow effect added to the appearance attribute set

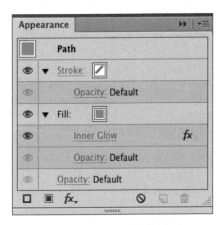

Appearance panel displaying the finished set of attributes with an Inner Glow effect applied

Complexity meets simplicity when you use Illustrator's Appearance panel to design intricate effects, develop reusable styles, and simplify production workflow. For this map of downtown Dixon, Illinois, cartographer Steven Gordon built complex appearances and applied them to objects, groups, and layers.

1 Building an appearance for a single object. Gordon developed a set of appearance attributes that applied a soft vignette and blue fill to a shape representing the river. To begin building appearance attributes, open the Appearance panel and click the panel's Clear Appearance icon to clear all attributes in the shape you're about to draw (including Illustrator's default black stroke and white fill attributes). Gordon first drew the outline of the water with the Pen tool and then gave the path a medium-blue fill. To accentuate the shoreline, he applied a dark Inner Glow effect. To do this he opened the Appearance panel and clicked on the Fill attribute. Then from the *fx* icon in the Appearance panel he chose Stylize> Inner Glow. In the Inner Glow dialog, he changed the Mode to Multiply, set Opacity to 70%, and adjusted the Blur to 0.05 inches (for the width of the vignette edge), making sure the Edge option was enabled. To finish the glow, he clicked the dialog's color swatch and chose black for the glow color.

2 Creating a style for your street paths. To create "cased" or outlined streets, make a multi-stroke style that you can apply to all streets. Gordon started by deselecting all objects and clicking the Clear Appearance icon to eliminate the attributes for the river he had created previously. To build cased streets like Gordon's, click the Stroke attribute and choose a light color swatch and a 2-pt width. Next, add a second stroke by clicking the Add New Stroke icon in the Appearance panel. Because the new stroke has the same attributes as the first stroke, select the bottom of the two strokes and change it to a darker color and a 3-pt width. In order to reuse this set of appearance attributes, open the Graphic Styles panel and Option-click/Alt-click the New Graphic Style icon at the bottom of the panel and then name your new style.

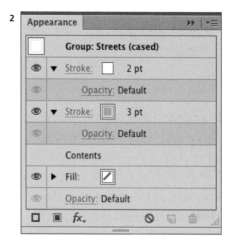

Appearance panel Gordon used to create the map's cased streets

3 Assigning a style to a group. If you apply a style like the cased streets to a selection of paths, the outline of a path will overlap and interrupt the outlines of paths below it. If you apply a style to a group of paths instead, the style will surround the group, merging strokes where they overlap. To do this, select the paths you wish to merge, then select and Group (⌘-G/Ctrl-G). Now make sure that Group is highlighted in the Appearance panel and apply your new cased streets style.

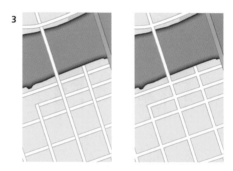

(Left) The streets with the style applied to the individual paths; (right) the style applied to street paths after they were grouped

4 Assigning appearance attributes to an entire layer. Instead of applying styles to individual objects, like the iconic "map symbols" on the map, Gordon applied a style to the layer itself and then added symbols to that layer. To do the same, create a layer for the symbols and click the layer's target indicator in the Layers panel. From the *fx* icon in the Appearance panel, select Stylize> Drop Shadow. Now each "map symbol" you draw or paste on that layer will be painted automatically with the drop shadow. You can modify the drop shadow by clicking the layer's targeting icon and then clicking the Drop Shadow attribute in the Appearance panel and changing values in the pop-up Drop Shadow dialog.

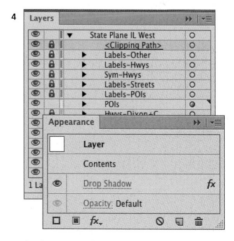

(Top) Targeting the layer in the Layers panel; (bottom) the Appearance panel showing the Drop Shadow attribute (double-click the attribute to edit Drop Shadow values)

Guides for Arcs

Designing with Guides, Arc, and Pen Tools

Overview: *Create guides on one side of the artboard; reflect and copy guides to the other side; create an arc with the Arc tool; cut and extend the arc with the Pen tool; reflect and copy the arc and join with the two arcs using the Pen tool; print templates using the Tile option.*

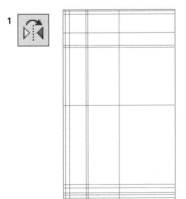

Reflect tool icon on the left; on the right, select-ed guides (colored magenta) that will be reflect-ed and copied to the other side of the artboard

Tasked with building a garden gate as a functional sculp-ture for an outdoor exhibition on the grounds of the Nor-man Rockwell Museum, artist Stephen Klema sat down with Illustrator to create life-sized drawings that would serve as templates for cutting the sculpture's wood pieces.

1 Creating the document and positioning guides. To start, Klema made a new document with the same di-mensions as those of the constructed gate (80" tall by 44" wide). Next, he turned on rulers (⌘-R/Ctrl-R) and dragged guides from the rulers. To position a guide more precisely, first make sure that guides are unlocked (go to View> Guides and choose Lock Guides if it has a check mark before its name), and select the guide and use the Control Panel's Transform fields to enter values for the X or Y position of the guide on the artboard.

If your artwork will be symmetrical, like Klema's, you can create guides on one side of the document and then select and copy them to the other side. Start by creating a guide in the exact middle of the document. An easy way to do this is to drag a new guide from the ruler and, making sure that Guides are still unlocked, click the Hori-zontal Align Center icon in the Control panel to center it horizontally on the artboard (be sure that you've chosen Align to Artboard in the Control panel). Next, activate

Smart Guides from the View menu (this will help position the cursor over the exact middle of the document). Finally, select all of the guides you've created, choose the Reflect tool (it's hidden under the Rotate tool icon) and Option-click/Alt-click on the guide you created in the middle of the document. From the Reflect dialog, choose Vertical as the Axis and click on the Copy button.

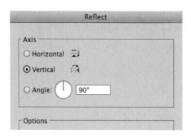

Clicking Vertical in the Reflect tool dialog

2 **Drawing an arch.** Klema turned to the Rectangle, Arc, Ellipse, and Pen tools to draw the different objects in his illustration. For the inner arch, Klema selected the Arc tool (hidden under the Line Segment tool) and double-clicked its icon to bring up the Arc Segment Tool Options dialog. Because he planned on drawing from the center guide outward to the left, Klema clicked on the dialog's Base Along menu and selected the Y Axis option. Next, he clicked on the center guide and dragged down and to the left until the arc was shaped the way he wanted. Depending on the shape of the arc you need, you may have to draw it wider or longer. If that's the case, you'll need to cut the arc with the Scissors tool as Klema did so that it fits the width of the arch shape you want. Next, extend the arc downward as a straight line by selecting the Pen tool, clicking the bottom endpoint of the arc, and then Shift-clicking below to complete the straight line. Duplicate the extended arc using the Reflect tool and the center guide, just as you did in the previous step with the guides. Klema connected the bottom endpoints of the two extended arcs with the Pen tool, creating a single object.

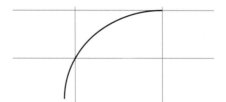

On the left, the Arc tool icon; on the right, choosing Y Axis in Arc Segment Tool Options

The arc and the guides

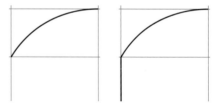

The arc after being cut with the Scissors tool on the left; on the right, the arc extended after drawing a vertical path with the Pen tool

3 **Printing templates for construction.** After drawing all the objects in his design, Klema printed the full illustration and separate illustrations of each of the gate parts (he used the Tile option in the Print dialog because the pieces were bigger than his printer paper). The prints served as templates that he traced on the wood so that he could precisely cut out the individual pieces of the gate. He used the full-sized illustration as a guide for assembling the gate parts into the finished sculpture.

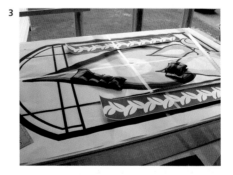

Printed template pages assembled on wood

Auto-Scaling Art

Apply Effects and Graphic Styles to Resize

Overview: *Draw using picas and points to easily approximate feet and inches; calculate units to work with and amounts to scale by; apply a Transform effect to duplicate, scale, and move artwork in one step, and duplicate the effect to apply different settings; use a Graphic Style to save effect settings.*

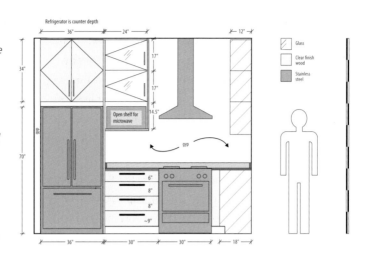

Kitchen West Elevation

WIGHAM

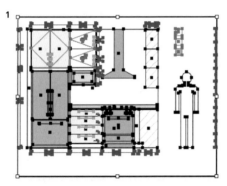

The "master" drawing nearly complete before adding the Transform Effect

Getting targeted to move

To target the master layer for an effect, be sure to click directly on the layer's target (circle) and note that the square is large and the Appearance panel shows "Layer" as the selected item. If you're not really careful you might accidentally apply an effect to an object or sublayer, instead of applying it to the master layer.

As she was designing a kitchen, Laurie Wigham learned she needed to provide others with the same model at different sizes: She worked at 1 pica to the foot, but the builders needed plans at 1/2" to a foot and the city wanted large prints. She chose the Transform Effect to duplicate and scale her art so that changes made to her original plan would automatically be updated in the scaled version.

1 Setting the scale for the architectural drawing. To create and visualize objects in their real-world inches and feet, Wigham set Illustrator's measurement units to picas—there are 12 points per pica, so each point represented one inch and each pica one foot. She drew most of the artwork, including the keys, selected it all, and chose Object>Artboards>Fit to Artwork Bounds. When she needed to submit rough plans to her contractor, she needed to figure out how to get from this small version to the 1/2"= 1' scale. She first changed her ruler to inches and noticed that 1/2" (which would represent 1' in the larger scale) = 3 picas. Therefore if 1 pica = 1', she would need to multiply by 3 (300%) to get 3 picas to equal 1'. She then noted the width of her artboard (2.63 inches), so that plus a bit more for space gave her an approximate distance to use for moving the copy she was going to make.

2 Targeting for the Transform effect. In order for the Transform Effect to duplicate art to other artboards as new objects are added to it, all the art has to be within a master layer, and the master layer itself must be targeted. Once an effect is properly applied to a targeted master layer, any objects added to the layers within will automatically inherit that effect (see the warning Tip at left).

3 Applying the Transform effect. With the layer targeted, Wigham clicked the *fx* icon at the bottom of the Appearance panel and chose Distort & Transform> Transform. Wigham anchored the transformation reference point to the upper left corner (an easy reference point to work from), set the distance for the move and the amount to scale it by—300%, and entered 1 for copies. To check everything was working properly for the transform, she enabled Preview. Once Wigham saw that her artwork duplicated and scaled properly, she clicked OK. To preserve the effect to apply it any time in the future that she needed this same transformation, she created a Graphic Style (Option-click/Alt-click on the New Graphic Style icon in the Graphic Styles panel to name it while adding it). Now she could freely edit, add, and subtract objects in her kitchen's West Elevation. The objects on this artboard weren't selectable or directly editable, but would print. When her plan was finished, she drew an artboard around the scaled artwork and printed it.

To make a version for the city permits, she duplicated the effect in the Appearance panel by dragging it to the Duplicate Selected Item icon. She turned off the visibility for the first instance. She next drew an 11"x17" artboard roughly 20 points to the left from the other side of her master artboard (so the master was now between the two scaled versions). She double-clicked on the Transform effect to open the dialog, and this time played with the settings in the dialog until her drawing filled the page. She saved this as another Graphic Style. With both Transform Effects in the Appearance panel, she toggled their visibility each time she needed one scaled version or another.

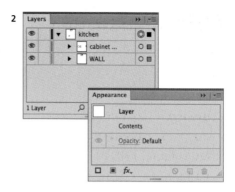

Indicators in Layers and Appearance panels showing the master layer targeted (not just objects)

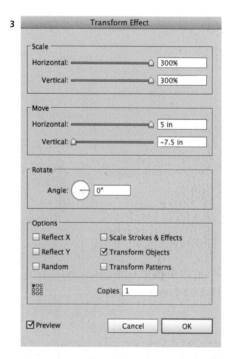

Setting up to duplicate, scale, and move artwork with the Transform Effect—the Vertical setting is for viewing on the monitor only, serving no other practical purpose

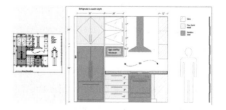

Artboards after creating the 1/2" to 1' scaled model of the elevation

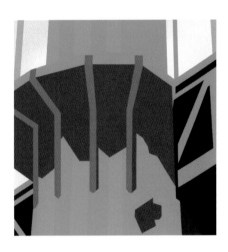

KIMBALL

Mike Kimball

Commissioned by the Golden Gate National Parks Conservancy to create a poster for the 75th Anniversary of the Golden Gate Bridge, Mike Kimball produced an illustration that focused on the bridge's streamlined Art Deco design. He simplified the detail in the bridge to eliminate construction details that distracted from its design lines, and restricted the number of colors in keeping with posters of that period. Critical to achieving the strong perspective favored by the client were the hand-drawn perspective guides Kimball placed on a layer above the artwork. To make them, he drew a line along the left and right cables (the extreme right was cropped from view later), created intermediate lines with Object> Blend> Make, then chose View> Guides> Make Guides. A second set of guides marked the cable width. He organized the illustration with separate layers for the bridge itself, the highlights, shadows, and the sky. He made extensive use of blending modes, opacity, and gradients to create highlights and shadows, while Gaussian Blur softened the clouds. When finished, Kimball's poster echoed a style from the day the famous bridge opened.

2

Designing Type & Layout

Designing Type & Layout

This chapter focuses on tips and tricks related to working with the type tools, as well as design and layout. While Chapter 1 covers the basics of working with multiple artboards, you'll find some of the more advanced issues of working with multiple artboards later on in this introduction, and in lessons in this chapter.

TYPES OF TYPE

There are three kinds of type objects in Illustrator: *Point type*, *Area type*, and *Path type*. The Type tool lets you click to create a Point type object, click-drag to create a box for an Area type object, or click on a path to create Path type. Click within any existing type object to enter or edit text. To exit type editing mode, press the Esc key; to be poised to start creating or editing another type object, hold down the ⌘/Ctrl key (temporarily turning your cursor into a Selection tool) and click outside the text block, or reselect the Text tool. Some features for manipulating type include the following:

- **Point type never wraps** to a new line. To add another line of text without also adding a new paragraph (so your paragraph style applies to all the lines), press the Shift-Return/Enter key. To add another line that is also a new paragraph (useful when you want to use separate paragraph styles), use just the Return/Enter key.

  To scale Point type, use the Selection tool to select the type and drag on one of the handles of the bounding box. Both the type and the bounding box scale together. Use modifier keys as you would with any object to constrain proportions or scale from the center.

- **Area type automatically wraps** to the next line. Use the Return/Enter key to start a new paragraph within an Area type object.

  To scale Area type, use the Selection tool to scale just the bounding box itself; the type will reflow inside the area, but remain the same size. To scale the bounding box

DONAL JOLLEY

Hovering the cursor over the edge of an object reveals the Area Type cursor, then click to enter the desired text; the object can be easily re-shaped, causing the text to reflow

and the type, choose the Free Transform tool (E) before dragging on the bounding box handles.

Create a custom container for Area type by constructing a path with any tool. With a closed path, choose either of the Area Type tools and click on the path (not inside the object) to place text within the confines of the path. Hold down the Option/Alt key to create Area type with an open path when the Area Type tool is not selected.

Use the Direct Selection tool to distort a container object for Area type by grabbing an anchor point and dragging on it, or reshape the path by adjusting direction lines. The text within your Area type object will reflow to fit the new shape of the confining object.

Use the Area Type Options dialog (Type> Area Type Options) to gain precise control over a number of important aspects of Area type, such as numerical values for the width and height, precise values for rows and columns, offset options, the alignment of the first baseline of text, and how text flows between rows or columns (by choosing one of the Text Flow options).

- **Path type flows text** along the path of an object. Create Path type by clicking on a path with the Type tool; the path become unstroked and unfilled, and is ready to receive text.

A Path type object has three brackets—the beginning bracket, which has an *in port*; a center bracket; and an end bracket, which has an *out port*. Use the ports to thread text between objects (see the Tip "Ports defined" later in the chapter). Use the center bracket to control positioning the type along the path.

To position type on a path, hover your cursor over the path until the cursor turns into an upside down **T**. Dragging the center bracket along the path moves the type toward the beginning or end. Dragging across the path flips the type to the other side of the path. For example, type running outside of a circle will flip to the inside.

To automatically reflow type along a path, use the Direct Selection tool to reshape the path. Set or adjust Path type attributes with the Type on a Path Options

---

Scale text frames only

By default, Illustrator's Scale tool scales both the text frame *and* its contents. To scale the text frame alone, Direct-Select it first. Then use the Scale tool, or scale it manually using the bounding box.
—*Jean-Claude Tremblay*

Turning the corner—Path type

When type on a tightly curved path is squeezed together or spread apart, choose Type> Type on a Path> Type on a Path Options and choose Center from the Align to Path menu. Set Baseline Shift to 0 in the Character panel, and move the path until the type is where you want it on the page.
—*Steven H. Gordon*

DONAL JOLLEY

Type on a Path graphic by Donal Jolley

Path type and closed paths

Even though the feedback you get from the Type tool cursor seems to indicate that you can only apply Path type to open paths, you actually *can* apply Path type to both open and closed paths (hold Option/Alt and watch for the cursor to change from the Area Type icon to the Type on a Path icon).

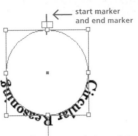

start marker
and end marker

If you try to set Path type on a circle, and the text is set to Align Center, the text will be forced to the bottom of the circle. That's because each Path type object has two handles (the start marker and the end marker) between which the type is centered. When you first draw the circle and apply the Path type to it, those two handles appear together at the top of the circle, due to the fact that the circle is a closed path.

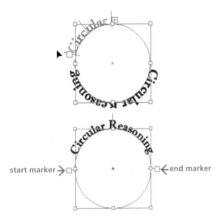

start marker → end marker ←

To position the text on top of the circle, grab the start marker handle and drag it to the 9 o'clock position, and then drag the end marker handle to the 3 o'clock position. Your text will now be centered between the two handles, on top of the circle.

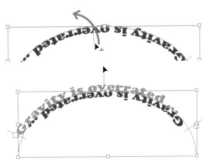

To manually flip type on a path to the other side of the path, select the type and drag the center handle (the thin blue line perpendicular to the type) across the path, as indicated by the red arrow above. Note the tiny T-shaped icon that appears next to the cursor as you position it near the handle; you can also flip type by choosing Type> Type on a Path> Type on a Path Options, enabling the Flip box, and clicking OK.

dialog (Type> Type on a Path> Type on a Path Options). Choose different Type on a Path effects (such as Rainbow or Stair Step), enable Flip to automatically flip type to the other side of the path, set the alignment of type relative to the path, and use a Spacing control to adjust the type as it moves around a curve. You can also access Type on a Path effects through the Type> Type on a Path submenu.

WORKING WITH THREADED TEXT

If an Area type or Path type object contains more text than it has room to display, you'll see a red plus sign indicating a loaded *out port* (see the Tip "Ports defined" on the next page).

To enlarge an Area type object or a Path type object on an enclosed path, allowing for more text, use the Selection tool to grab the object by a bounding side, and drag to resize it. To lengthen a path for Path type, use the Direct Selection tool to select the last anchor and drag the path longer, or use the Pen tool to start drawing more of the path from the last anchor, then drag the end bracket to the new end of the path. Following are more techniques for dealing with threaded text:

• **To add a new text object to receive overflow text,** use the Selection tool to select the first text object. Next, click on the *out port*; your cursor changes to the "loaded text" cursor. Click on the artboard to create a new text object the same size and shape as the original (this works nicely for custom shapes), or drag to create a rectangular text object of any size. The new text object is *threaded* (linked) to the original, flowing text into the second.

• **To link existing text objects together,** click the *out port* on the first object, and then click on the path of the object that will receive the overflow text. (Keep your eye on the cursor, which will change to indicate valid "drop" locations.) You can also link objects using a menu command: Select both objects and choose Type> Threaded Text> Create, and the objects become linked.

• **To disconnect one object from another,** select the object and double-click its *in port* to break the thread to a preceding object, or double-click its *out port* to break the thread to a subsequent object. Alternatively, you can select the object and click once on either the *in port* or the *out port*. Then click on the other end of the thread to break the link.

- **To release an object from a text thread,** select it, then choose Type> Threaded Text> Release Selection. Or, to remove the threading from an object while leaving the text in place, select it and choose Type> Threaded Text> Remove Threading.

WRAPPING AREA TYPE AROUND OBJECTS

Text wrapping is controlled as an object attribute and is set specifically for each object that will have Area type wrapped around it. These *wrap objects* affect only Area type objects that are both within the same layer, and directly beneath it in the Layers panel, and do *not* affect Point type or Path type. To make a selected object into a wrap object choose Object> Text Wrap> Make. To change options for the wrap object, keep it selected and choose Object> Text Wrap> Text Wrap Options. Here, you'll choose the amount of offset; you also have the option to choose Invert Wrap, which reverses the side of the object that text wraps around.

FORMATTING TEXT

While the Character and Paragraph panels let you format text by changing one attribute at a time, the Character Styles and Paragraph Styles panels allow you to apply multiple attributes simply by applying the appropriate style.

An open document always has a paragraph style applied to it even before there's any text, so if you select the Type tool, then modify its attributes in the Control panel, Illustrator thinks you're intending to modify the default, [Normal Paragraph Style]. A plus sign next to the style name in the Paragraph Styles panel indicates you've applied extra formatting, or *overrides*. To avoid unneeded overrides, work with styles wherever possible, and see the Tip "Avoiding formatting overrides" on the next page.

Ports defined

Your text *in port* and *out port* indicators will change to reflect different situations:

- A red plus sign in the *out port* means the object contains *overflow text*.
- An arrow in the *in port* means the object is threaded to a preceding text object, and text is flowing into the object.
- An arrow in the *out port* means the object is threaded to a subsequent text object, and text is flowing out of the object.

Making one text block of many

To join separate Area text boxes or Point type objects, select all the text objects with any Selection tool and copy. Then draw a new Area text box and paste. Text will flow into the box, in the *stacking order* in which it had appeared on the page. (It doesn't matter if you select graphic elements with your text—these elements won't be pasted.) *—Sandee Cohen*

When handling ducks you must always wear protective arm and hand covering. Many unwary duck trainers have lost fingers and even hands and suffered deep puncture wounds from careless handling methods or even brief inattention.

Some of the as the Hookbill, Orpington will and have been burns from the feathers of important that only expert close handling.

more docile breeds such Bali, Muscovy and Buff allow some minor handling even known to cuddle. Acid ducks can be serious so it is handlers attempt such

One particularly nasty Welsh Harlequin. Aptly this uncommon bird has unusual characteristic of itself behind curtains of grass only out and deliver lines in a from Shakespeare's unsuspecting animal

breed is the named, the hiding to jump melodramatic style sonnets whenever an approaches

DONAL JOLLEY

Artist Donal Jolley wrapped Area text around this duck by placing the duck above the text and choosing Object> Text Wrap> Make

- **To create a style based on existing formatting,** format the text as you want it to appear, select it, and click on the New Style button (Option-click/Alt-click to name the style). The selected attributes define the new style.
- **To create a new style based on another,** highlight the style you want to copy and click the Create New Style icon. To name the style as you create it (and modify the style if you wish), hold Option/Alt when you click.
- **To rename a style,** double-click on the name in the panel for inline editing.
- **To apply a paragraph style to text,** just insert your cursor into the paragraph you want to format and click the name of the style in the Paragraph Styles panel. When you first apply a paragraph style, it won't remove overrides. To remove all overrides, click again on the plus beside the Paragraph style name.
- **To apply a character style,** select letters you want to style and click a style name in the Character Styles panel.

CONVERTING TYPE TO OUTLINES

You can now keep type live and perform many effects that once required you to outline type. Using the Appearance panel you can apply multiple strokes to characters, run type along a curve, use envelopes to distort type, and even mask with live, editable type. Following are some cases where you still might need to outline your type:

- **Convert to outlines to graphically transform or distort type.** If Warp Effects and Envelopes don't create the effect you need (see examples in this chapter and in the *Reshaping Dimensions* chapter for examples of warps and envelopes), then outlining your type will allow you to edit the individual curves and anchor points of letters or words. Your type will no longer be editable as type, but instead will be constructed of standard Illustrator Bézier curves that are editable just like any other object. Type converted to outlines may include compound paths to form the "holes" in the outlined letter forms (such as the see-through centers of an **O**, **B**, or **P**. Choose Object> Compound Path> Release to fill the "holes" with color.

- **Convert to outlines to maintain your letter and word spacing when exporting type** to another application, as many programs don't support the translation of custom kerning and word spacing.
- **Convert to outlines if you can't distribute the font to your client or service bureau,** when you don't have permission to embed the fonts, or your service bureau doesn't have its own license for a font.

USING THE EYEDROPPER WITH TYPE

The Eyedropper tool lets you copy styling and appearance attributes from one type object to another. Double-click the tool to specify in Eyedropper Options which attributes will be picked up or applied with the Eyedropper tool. In addition to specifying whether you'll be picking up character styles and/or paragraph styles, the Eyedropper tool can also copy type *object* Appearance attributes (see the next section, "Using the Appearance Panel with Type" for more about Character versus Type level attributes).

For a one-step method, select the type object with appearance attributes you want to change, and then move the Eyedropper tool over the unselected type object that has the attributes you want and click on it.

Alternatively, the Eyedropper tool works in another mode: *sampling* and *applying*. A small **T** means it is in position to sample or apply text attributes. To copy text formatting from one object to another using the Eyedropper tool, position it over an unselected type object. When it angles downward to the left, click the type object to pick up its attributes.

Now position the Eyedropper tool over the unselected text object to which you want to apply the attributes, and hold down the Option/Alt key. In applying mode, it angles downward to the right, and looks full. To apply the attributes that you just sampled, move the cursor to the text you want to change and click. (A simple click will apply the sampled attributes to the whole paragraph; you can also drag the cursor to apply the attributes only to the specific text you dragged over.)

The Every-line Composer

Illustrator offers two composition methods for determining where line breaks occur in lines of text. The Single-line Composer applies hyphenation and justification settings to one line of text at a time, but this can make multiple lines look ragged. The Every-line Composer determines the best combination of line breaks across an entire paragraph of text.

Control tabs and leaders

Use the Tabs panel to control tabs and leaders. As you pan or zoom, you'll notice the Tab ruler doesn't move with the text box. If you lose your alignment, just click the little Magnet button on the Tabs panel, and the panel will snap back into alignment.

DONAL JOLLEY

*Artist Donal Jolley had to convert type to outlines in order to reshape the **U** and **N** type characters*

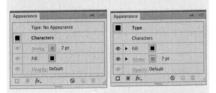
 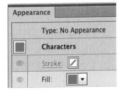
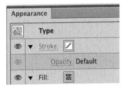
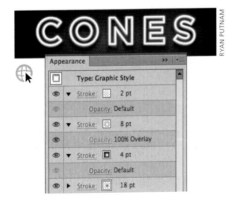
USING THE APPEARANCE PANEL WITH TYPE

When you work with type, you work with the letter characters or with the container that holds the characters—or both. Understanding the difference between characters and their container (the "type object") will help you access and edit the right one when you style type. To help understand the difference, you'll need to watch the Appearance panel as you work. (See the previous chapter for more details about working with the Appearance panel.)

Type characters

By default, Type characters entered with the Type tool are styled with a Black Fill and No Stroke. To edit a character's fill and stroke, drag across the text with the Type tool or double-click "Characters" in the Appearance panel.

You can't do the following to type *characters* (although in the section "Type Objects" following you *will* be able to do these things to a type *object*): move the stroke under the fill or fill above the stroke; apply a live effect to the fill or stroke; apply a gradient fill; add multiple fills or strokes.

Type objects

The Type object contains all the text in a Point, Area, or Path type object. You are working with the type "object" when you select the text with the Selection tool and then move the object around on your page.

With the text object you can add another fill (click on the Add New Fill icon in the Appearance panel). Now there is another listing of Stroke and Fill, in the Appearance panel, but this time they are positioned above the Characters line in the panel. If you reveal the Stroke and Fill for the type by double-clicking the Characters line in the panel, you return to character editing; reselect the type object with the Selection tool to return to editing the type object rather than its characters.

When you add a new Stroke or Fill to the type object, its color and effects interact with the color of the characters. All the strokes and fills applied to type are layered on top of those listed below (including on top of the stroke and fill you see listed when you double-click Characters in the panel). So if you add a new fill to the type object and apply white to it, the type appears white (the white fill of the type object is stacked above the black default fill of the characters).

THE GLYPHS PANEL

Illustrator's Glyphs panel (Window> Type> Glyphs) provides quick access to a wide variety of special characters (like ＊ or ❣), including any ligatures, ornaments, swashes, and fractions included with a given font. Use the list box to narrow your search of a font for the type of letterform you're seeking. With the Type tool, click to place the insertion point, then double-click the character you want in the Glyphs panel to insert it in the text.

WORKING WITH LEGACY TEXT

Adobe periodically updates Illustrator's type engine, partly in order to maintain compatibility between applications. If you open a file created in an older version and see a warning about using legacy type, you'll need to update the type to the new engine *if* you want to edit the type. However, this action could cause the type to reflow, so you might want to keep a copy of the original handy as a reference if you need to edit the type. If the file is very old, updating legacy type might be a multi-step process. Adobe first updates type to be compatible with the changes that were made in CS, and then updates for any changes thereafter—for example, updating Type on a Path created prior to CS4 to the current behavior of Type on a Path. By following the prompts, you'll get your old file updated to the latest type engine, permitting you now to edit it.

ADVANCED FEATURES OF MULTIPLE ARTBOARDS

You can find basic information on artboards in the chapter *Your Creative Workspace*. Following in this section are some of the more advanced features of artboards, which will help you work productively and maintain consistency within a project.

The warning message that appears when you open an older Illustrator file containing text

You can use the Show pop-up menu to restrict the visible character set in the Glyphs panel

SMALL CAPS

SMALL CAPS

SMALL CAPS

Illustrator's Small Caps option (in the Character panel menu) converts all selected characters to small caps (top). However, if true-drawn small caps aren't available in a font, Illustrator creates the fake, scaled-down version (middle), which is a typographic taboo. To prevent Illustrator from creating fake small caps, go to File> Document Setup> Type> Options, and change the Small Caps percentage from 70% to 100%. This option is *only* used when Illustrator is faking small caps, so when your small caps are the size of capital letters, you'll instantly recognize it (bottom). This option doesn't persist between documents, so you'll have to choose it each time. (Go to **http://www.creativepro. com/blog/typetalk-small-caps-illustrator** to read the full article.) —*Ilene Strizver, The Type Studio*

Starting with CS6, you can rename artboards inline by double-clicking on their name in the panel.

Duplicating elements to artboards

Among the more common functions you'll need when you're working in a multiple artboard document is the duplication of elements on multiple pages. Although there isn't currently a built-in "master page" function, there are a number of ways to accomplish this task:

- **To duplicate elements when adding another artboard,** select the Artboard tool, enable "Move/Copy Artwork with Artboard," and hold down the Option/Alt key while dragging an active artboard to a new location.
- **Turn artwork created on one artboard into a symbol,** then drag that symbol from the shared Symbols panel to any other artboard. Now just update the symbol to update all instances of it used on any artboards.
- **To move or copy the artwork a specified distance,** measure the distance between the artwork and where you want it on another artboard. Then use Transform> Move and enter the measurement in the Distance input.
- **To copy "instances" of artwork to another artboard,** use the Transform effect.
- **To copy objects to all other artboards** in the same relative location, use Paste on All Artboards.

Managing artboards

Many features are available to help you work with artboards according to more specialized needs. If you select the Artboard tool to accomplish these tasks, use the Esc key to return to the tool you were using.

- **To renumber artboards using the Artboard panel,** either drag artboard names to rearrange them, or highlight one artboard and click the up or down arrow icons. Renumbering artboards can be very helpful if you're using them for presentations and storyboarding.
- **Rearrange artboard positions** using either the Artboard panel menu, or Object> Artboards> Rearrange. A dialog lets you determine the order they repeat in both across the monitor and down (their layout), how far apart they are placed, how many columns they're in, and whether or not the artwork is moved with them.

- **Convert any rectangle to an artboard** using Object> Artboard> Convert to Artboard. Or use Object> Path> Split Into Grid to create several rectangles from one before converting them all to artboards.
- **To save artboards as separate files,** choose Save As, then in the Illustrator Options section select "Save each artboard to a separate file," and choose All or enter a range of artboards.

Exporting and printing multiple artboards

All artboards in a file share the same print options, including color mode, bleed settings, and scale, and you can choose to print either to a PDF file or to a printer. In the Print dialog, print artboards as separate pages (the default), or ignore artboards and tile the artwork.

- **Print to PDF** always flattens the file. But you can choose the media, such as screen or slide, ignoring the actual artboard size—this is useful for presentations. Or you can scale the artwork to fit your media, among many other features found in the Print to PDF dialog.
- **Save As PDF** preserves transparency, editing capabilities, and top-level layers, and you can set a level of security.
- **Print only some artboards** using the Range setting. Scale them to fit your print media if desired.
- **Print artboards with landscape orientation, or a mix of landscape and portrait,** with Auto-Rotate when portrait is selected for the media. If your media is landscape-oriented, Auto-Rotate is disabled.
- **Print artwork that is larger than your media** by using artboards instead of the Print Tiling tool. The Split Into Grid command (followed by Convert to Artboard) can divide the artwork into media-sized rectangles for you.
- **The boundaries of each artboard are cropped** if your artwork overlaps artboards and you print each artboard as a page.
- **When printing pages in which two or more artboards are overlapping the same artwork,** each artboard will print with whichever portions of the artwork are visible within that artboard.

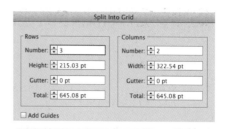

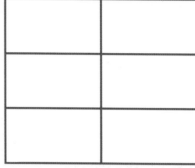

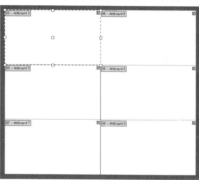

After drawing a rectangle, choosing Split into Grid (original purple stroke is preserved), and Convert to Artboard

Print to PDF dialog, including Auto-Rotate enabled by default when printing landscape artboards to media oriented to portrait

Graphic Novel Cover Design

Illustrator as a Stand-Alone Layout Tool

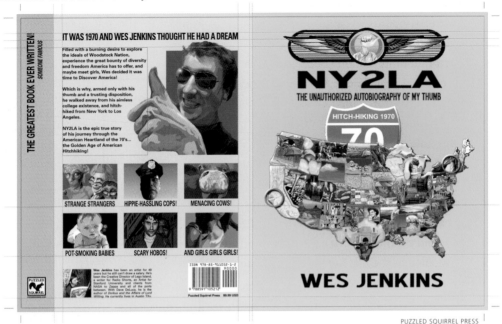

Overview: *Set your document's dimensions and bleeds; make custom guides; place vector and raster art; make Area type for columns.*

Changing the name, setting the number of Artboards to 1, changing Units to picas, setting Orientation to landscape, entering dimensions, and entering bleed measurements

Print On Demand (POD), a printing technology and business process in which new copies of a book are not printed until an order has been received, is an increasingly popular print option for independent and self-publishers, particularly those who create documents intended for both print and ePub. Raymond Larrett of Puzzled Squirrel Press finds that using Illustrator allows him to easily create cover designs that integrate vector art with raster art elements, like the ones for this graphic novel. After setting up page dimensions, bleeds, and guides for text elements, the Illustrator document can be exported as a JPEG file for ePub or web comics, and as a PDF for POD publications.

1 Setting up the page. Larrett created a new document (File> New). While in the New Document dialog, he changed the Name of the file, set the Number of Artboards to 1, chose Picas under Units, clicked the Landscape icon under Orientation, and entered the dimensions of his book cover (including front, back, and spine elements) in the Width and Height fields. He also entered his bleed measurement in the Top Bleed input field and clicked the "Make all settings the same" icon to populate the other Bleed fields with the same measurement. After entering all his settings, he clicked OK.

2 **Customizing your guides.** To make it possible to set up guides for the back cover, spine, and front cover, Larrett chose View> Show Rulers. To create the initial guide, he first checked to make sure that guides were unlocked (View> Guides), and then click-dragged from the left-side ruler to roughly his first position. With the guide still selected, he numerically adjusted the positions of a selected guide by relocating the X (or Y) axis positions in the Transform panel. To create a rectangular guide (rather than a linear one), he could convert a selected rectangle into a guide using ⌘-5/Ctrl-5. With his guides in place, Larrett chose View> Guides> Lock Guides. He used the context-sensitive menu to access Lock, Hide, and Release guide functions as needed.

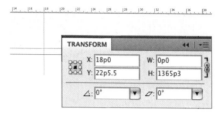

Choosing View> Show Rulers and dragging a guide into position

Selecting guide and numerically positioning from the Transform panel

3 **Placing and refining the elements.** When the page was set with the correct dimensions, bleeds, and guides, Larrett added artwork to the design. He dragged and dropped some existing vector elements, like the barcode and logo, from other Illustrator files. Larrett's design also contains raster artwork, which he imported into the document by choosing File> Place. Larrett then created rectangles with the Rectangle tool to define areas for columns of text. With the Area Type tool, he clicked on each of these rectangles, making it possible to type or paste text directly into the box. He then double-clicked on the Type tool from the Tools panel to open the Area Type Options dialog. Within the dialog, Larrett changed the Offset in the Inset Spacing field to inset the text from the edge of the text box. You can also use the Area Type Options dialog to change the Dimensions, Rows, Columns, and Text Flow Options. As an alternative to using the Area Type tool, you can use the Type tool to create type for titles, headlines, and other individual type elements.

Placing artwork

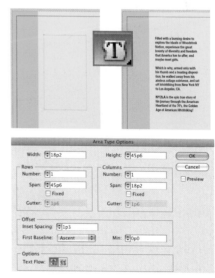

Creating rectangles with the Rectangle tool, using the Area Type tool, and setting Inset Spacing

Create an Identity

Working Efficiently with Multiple Elements

Overview: *Create artboards for each type of content; use the Artboards panel to resize the artboards and duplicate some of them; use symbols for logos; optionally, duplicate artboards with artwork for multiple variations.*

1

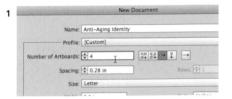

Setting up multiple artboards

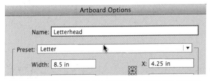

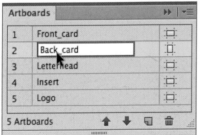

Customize, name, and reorder artboards using the Artboards panel and Artboard Options dialog

Customizing the layout using the Artboard tool and Smart Guides to help align the artboards

A company's typical identity package may contain several types and sizes of materials, such as letterhead, business cards, web pages, and ad inserts. Instead of needing to keep track of multiple files, Ryan Putnam can rely on multiple artboards and symbols to create the collateral materials in a single file, making additions or updates much simpler and less prone to errors and omissions.

1 Setting up the artboards. Putnam began by setting up four artboards using the default settings in the New dialog plus a standard bleed. Opening the Artboards panel, he double-clicked the first artboard icon, entered the dimensions of the business card, named it "Front_card," and clicked OK. He then customized the sizes and names of the other three artboards: the letterhead, an insert, and the logo design. Since he needed the same size artboard for the front and back of the business card, he used the Artboards panel to duplicate the business card by dragging "Front_card" to the New Artboard icon. In the Artboards panel he double-clicked the copy's name and typed "Back_card," and reordered the artboards (which renumbered them) by dragging "Back_card" to just below "Front_card." Because duplicate artboards automatically get added in a single row to the right of the last artboard drawn, Putnam selected the Artboard tool (Shift-O), to drag the artboards into a custom arrangement. Using

Smart Guides (⌘-U/Ctrl-U) he could easily line them up in a well-organized fashion.

2 Making symbols for replication and quick updates.
Putnam began by designing the logo. He then dragged it into the Symbols panel to save it as a symbol, named it, and clicked OK. If he modified the logo, he only had to alter the one symbol to automatically update all instances of it throughout the document. If he needed a variation of the logo, he could break the link to the original symbol to create a new symbol (see the *Expressive Strokes* chapter for more about creating and modifying symbols). Using multiple artboards with symbols adds appreciably to productivity. Artboards in one file share the same libraries, so if there were any changes in the future, Putnam wouldn't have to open separate files for each item in the identity package, and then open the library containing the modified symbol. One file would always contain all the libraries and correctly-sized artboards ready for modifications.

3 Copying and duplicating artwork with artboards.
Putnam created the design for each element of the identity package, placing the logo symbol on the artboard and adding text and artwork as needed. He linked the photo to the insert, making it easy to replace for the next event. Although the letterhead and insert only required a single version, he needed to create a business card that could be duplicated and personalized later for each employee and different events. When he needed to create another business card for a different employee and/or event, he could either duplicate the front and back cards in the Artboards panel as before, or, with the Artboard tool selected and Move/Copy Artwork enabled in the Control panel, he could hold down the Option/Alt key while dragging a selected artboard. With everything in place, Putnam only had to select the text, graphic, or linked image that needed changing and quickly replace it. Because he could add up to 100 artboards in a single file, Putnam was now able to stay organized with just one file.

Sharing artboards and libraries

Any project that shares artwork for different elements—whether they share the same color theme, graphic and type styles, symbols, brushes, etc.—might benefit from using multiple artboards. That way you only need to maintain the libraries belonging to any single document, sharing them among all of the project pieces.

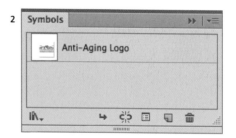

Using symbols for logos to maintain consistency, to make updates a snap, and to modify or place symbols from a shared library onto different artboards as needed

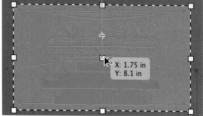

Duplicating the artboard with the artwork by enabling the Move/Copy Artwork with Artboard icon and holding down the Option/Alt key

Really Organized
Streamlining File Output with Artboards

Overview: *Create an artboard template that automates the output process; label and name each artboard; export each artboard as a file for the application coders to use.*

1

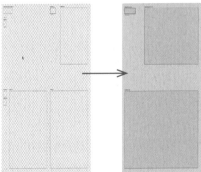

Using Simulate Colored Paper to create a non-printing gray background in order to see the white border on some elements

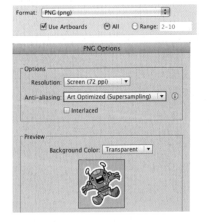

Exporting multiple files to separate artboards

Illustrator's multiple artboards and flexible output options made it easy for Dacosta! of Chocolate Soop® to produce all the elements coders need to create custom, sticker-style wallpapers. Stikalicious™ is a character-based wallpaper application for the iPad that Dacosta! created to showcase the work of artists from around the world. The user selects a background and desired characters, then layers, rotates, and scales them for a unique, shareable wallpaper. Each character requires four versions—the smallest and largest version of both the active and placed states.

1 **Using a template for artboards.** Dacosta! began by creating artboards at the size needed for the Collection icons, backgrounds, and the four states for each character (~100 artboards per file). In order to clearly see the versions with a white border, Dacosta! changed the artboard color. To do this, click on the Document Setup button on the Control panel and enable Simulate Colored Paper; then double-click on the top swatch beside the Transparency preview and select a light gray in the color picker. To associate each artboard with its role in the application, he both named it in the Artboard panel and labeled each artboard on the canvas. Dacosta! saved the file in .ait (Illustrator template) format, and when he received artwork, opened the template to place each state for every character on its correct artboard, creating a complete Stikalicious™ character set. For each artboard in the Artboard panel, he used a predetermined naming convention, which the coders would use to identify the role each element played in the application. Dacosta! saved the .ai file for backup, then exported it to PNG format, enabling Use Artboards in the Export dialog. Use Artboards saves each artboard to a separate file with the artboard name as its filename. Now the coders could finish the work on the separate elements.

1	Collection_Icon	
2	Collection_header	
3	BGicon_BotBG00	
4	BG_BotBG00	
5	BGicon_BotBG01	
6	BG_BotBG01	
7	BGicon_BotBG02	
8	BG_BotBG02	
9	BGicon_BotBG03	
10	BG_BotBG03	
11	BGicon_BotBG04	
12	BG_BotBG04	
13	BGicon_BotBG05	
14	BG_BotBG05	
15	OBJicon_Bot018_Norm	
16	OBJicon_Bot018_Shdw	
17	OBJ_Bot018_Norm	
18	OBJ_Bot018_Wht	
19	OBJicon_Bot06_Norm	
20	OBJicon_Bot06_Shdw	
21	OBJ_Bot06_Norm	
22	OBJ_Bot06_Wht	
23	OBJicon_Bot013_Norm	
24	OBJicon_Bot013_Norm	
25	OBJ_Bot013_Norm	
26	OBJ_Bot013_Wht	
27	OBJicon_Bot04_Norm	
28	OBJ_Bot04_Shdw	
29	OBJ_Bot04_Norm	
30	OBJ_Bot04_Wht	
31	OBJicon_Bot02_Norm	
32	OBJicon_Bot02_Shdw	
33	OBJ_Bot02_Norm	
34	OBJ_Bot02_Wht	
35	OBJicon_Bot05_Norm	
36	OBJicon_Bot05_Shdw	
37	OBJ_Bot05_Norm	
38	OBJ_Bot05_Wht	
39	OBJicon_Bot016_Norm	
40	OBJicon_Bot016_Shdw	
41	OBJ_Bot016_Norm	
42	OBJ_Bot016_Wht	
43	OBJicon_Bot07_Norm	
44	OBJicon_Bot07_Shdw	
45	OBJ_Bot07_Norm	
46	OBJ_Bot07_Wht	
47	OBJicon_Bot01_Norm	
48	OBJicon_Bot01_Shdw	
49	OBJ_Bot01_Norm	
50	OBJ_Bot01_Wht	
51	OBJicon_Bot015_Norm	

Artboards

99 Artboards

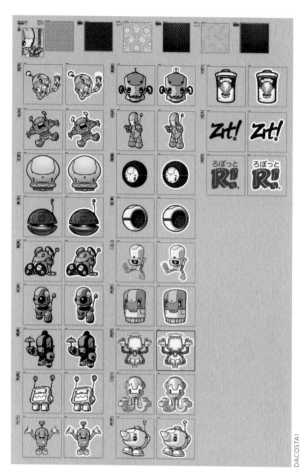

DACOSTA!

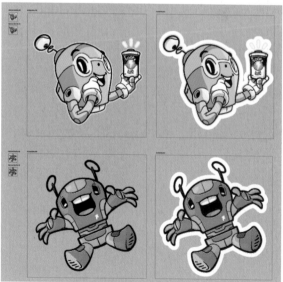

Approximately 100 artboards with one artboard each for the four states of each character, plus backgrounds and icons for the set

Moving Your Type

Setting Type on a Curve and Warping Type

Overview: *Create banners that will go behind curved labels; type label text on a curved path and adjust its alignment on the path; warp text and adjust its tracking; modify the kerning of the space between words.*

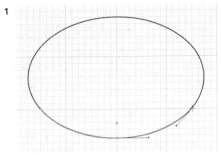

The ellipse with the left and right endpoints of the banner path cut by the Scissors tool

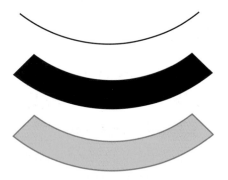

Thickening the banner path's stroke, then outlining the path and giving it stroke and fill colors

Greater Bridgeport Transit hired Jack Tom to design a T-shirt supporting its new campaign to raise public awareness of the local bus system. Tom's design combined the campaign's taglines—"Go Green," "Go GBT.com," and "Go Public"—with artwork illustrating birds, butterflies, and flowery vines.

1 Creating the background art and the two banners.
After drawing the floral, bird, and butterfly figures, Tom created the banners that would serve as backgrounds for the curved "Go Green" and "Go Public" labels. You can make a symmetrical banner by first selecting the Ellipse tool and drawing an ellipse. Then cut the ellipse with the Scissors tool to make the curved path that will form the banner. Using the grid (View> Show Grid) and positioning the ellipse over a horizontal grid line will help you cut the ellipse at the same vertical position on its left and right sides, keeping the curve symmetrical. Next, make a copy of this path; you'll use it later for curving the text of the label. Now give the joined path a thick stroke (Tom used 35 pt) and then outline the path by selecting Object>

Path> Outline Stroke. You can now give the stroke a width and color the stroke and fill.

2 Curving a label. To make the curved labels for "Go Green" and "Go Public," Tom used the path he had copied in the previous step. If you use Paste in Front (⌘-F/Ctrl-F), the path will overlay the banner you created previously. After pasting the path, select the Text tool, click on the path, and type your label text. With the path still selected, click the Align center icon in the Paragraph section of the Control panel. That centers your text horizontally across the banner. Before adjusting the vertical position of the type, realign the position of the type to the path by choosing Type> Type on a Path> Type on a Path Options. From the Type on a Path Options dialog, change Align to Path from the default Baseline to Center. Also, set the baseline shift to 0 in the Character panel. This will minimize any pinching or expanding of space between the letters of the label. Now you can move the path up or down to better center the label against the banner.

3 Arcing and bending a label. Tom wanted the main label, "Go GBT.com," to bend backwards in a gentle arc. To bend type, start by typing your text (you can use an Area- or a Point-type object). With the text object selected, choose Effect> Warp> Arc Lower. In the Warp Options dialog, make sure Horizontal is still active and change Bend by moving the slider or entering a number in the Bend field. A negative number will bend the type backwards (Tom entered –17% for Bend).

When you warp type, the spacing between letters and words may change more than you'd like. Consider resetting or adjusting Tracking or Kerning from the Character panel. Tracking controls the distance between all letters in the selected text, while kerning requires you to adjust the distance between each pair of letters. Also, to tighten the space between words, click on the space between words and narrow the kerned space between words by holding Option/Alt and pressing the left arrow key.

2

The Align Center icon in the Control panel

The Type on a Path Options dialog with the Align to Path changed to Center

The finished label

3

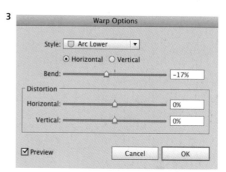

Above, the Warp Options dialog; below, the type before warping (top) and after warping (below)

Above, the text with a space between words; below, negative kerning inserted between the **O** and **G** characters

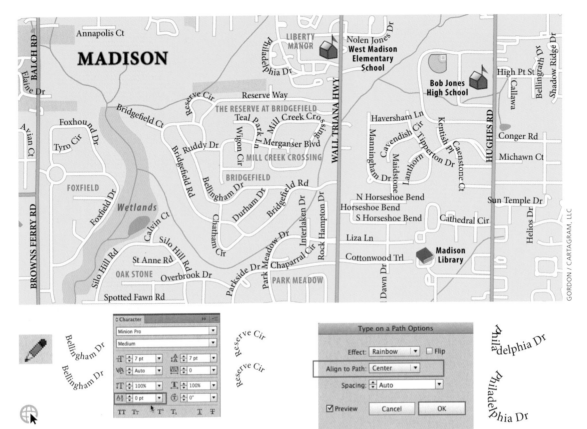

GORDON / CARTAGRAM, LLC

Steven Gordon/Cartagram, LLC

To label curving features like rivers and roads on his maps, cartographer Steve Gordon relies on type on a path. Gordon copies and pastes the river or road paths on a separate layer before applying type to them. He sets the Baseline Shift to 1 pt in the Character panel in order to move the type away from the underlying road or river path. In this map of Madison, Alabama, Gordon encountered paths with sharp turns and tight curves that pinched letters together or spread them apart with unsightly gaps. He smoothed the kinks from some paths by clicking to select a path with type, selecting the Pencil tool, and then dragging it over

or near the path. For paths that couldn't be smoothed solely with the Pencil, Gordon reset the path's Baseline Shift to 0 and then dragged the path away from the street path so that its lettering was the same distance away from the street as the labels with the 1-pt Baseline Shift. Some of the type paths required another adjustment: Gordon chose Type> Type on a Path> Type on a Path Options, and in the dialog box changed Align to Path from the default value of Baseline to Center. Gordon employed these techniques, separately or in various combinations, as he worked with hundreds of type objects in the map.

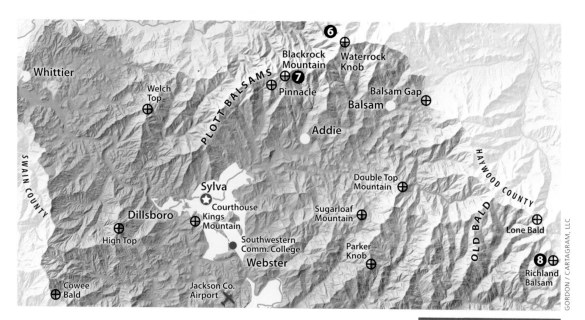

GORDON / CARTAGRAM, LLC

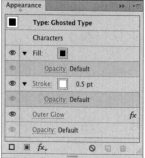

Steven Gordon/Cartagram, LLC

When cartographer Steven Gordon creates a map with a terrain image in the background, he has to ensure that type is not lost in the mountains of the image. For this map of North Carolina's Jackson County, Gordon received directions to create a bold, colorful terrain image by his client, *The Sylva Herald*. He began the map by creating the terrain image in Photoshop, placing it in the Illustrator file, and positioning it on the artboard. After creating the type labels, Gordon opened the Appearance panel, chose Add New Stroke from the panel menu, and dragged the Stroke attribute below Characters in the panel. Next, he set the width of the stroke to 0.5 pt using the Stroke Weight menu and then clicked the Stroke attribute's color icon to pop up the Swatches menu and selected the white swatch. Gordon wanted to soften the contrast between the white stroke and image behind it and decided to add a white glow around the type. To do this he clicked Characters in the Appearance panel and then clicked the Add New Effect icon and chose Stylize> Outer Glow. In the Outer Glow dialog, he clicked the color picker, selected white, and changed Opacity to 100% and Blur to 0.04 inches to complete the effect.

Arcing Type

Transforming Type with Warps & Envelopes

Overview: *Create and color a title using appearances; explore the three Envelope distortions for creating an arc effect; use an Arc Warp effect to arc the type; create a graphic style and apply arc effect to other title elements.*

PUTNAM

1

Putnam's 50-point Cabaret font headline

Applying Object> Envelope Distort> Make with Warp and changing the Bend to 20%

Applying Object> Envelope Distort> Make with Mesh, setting the number of Rows and Columns to 1, and editing the anchor points with the Direct Selection tool

Creating an arc-shaped object with the Pen tool over the type, selecting the arc-shaped object and type, and applying Object> Envelope Distort> Make with Top Object

Adding an arc effect to a headline turns boring type into a dynamic engaging headline that grabs the viewers' attention. With Illustrator you can explore a number of ways to create arcing text; using effects and graphic styles, you can quickly create an arcing effect easily applicable to any other titles or subtitles! (See the *Reshaping Dimensions* chapter for more about warps, blends, and graphic styles.)

1 Creating your headline text. To create headline text, choose a font with distinct, bold characteristics. For his headline text, Ryan Putnam chose 50-point Cabaret font.

Amongst the many ways to create an arcing effect in Illustrator, there are three different Envelope distortions that you can apply to your text: Warp, Mesh, and Make with Top Object.

First, Putnam applied Object> Envelope Distort> Make with Warp. Next, he chose Arc from the Warp options, and changed the Bend to 20%. For a second option, he then applied Object> Envelope Distort> Make with Mesh, set the number of Rows and Columns to 1, and edited the anchor points with the Direct Selection tool. For the final option, he used the Pen tool to draw a separate arc-shaped object over the type, selected the type and arc-shaped object, and applied Object> Envelope Distort> Make with Top Object.

2 Applying an Arc Warp effect to arc the title. Even though using Envelope distortions created the effect Putnam was looking for, and provided significant control for customizing his warp, he ultimately decided that he wanted a quick way to add the same simple arc effect to other titles and subtitles on the cover. Putnam figured out that if he created the arc using Effect> Warp, he could save his effect as a graphic style that he could then apply to additional titles.

There are 15 standard Warp shapes you can choose from when creating a title. For the "Spiritual" title, Putnam applied Effect> Warp> Arc. With Preview enabled, he changed the Bend to 20%, then clicked OK.

3 Saving and applying a graphic style. With the title selected, Putnam clicked the New Graphic Style icon in the Graphic Styles panel. With the graphic style now saved, Putnam could easily apply that style to other titles and subtitles.

To create a variant of this style, he replaced the text with "Muscles:", changed the font to 28 points, the Rotation to 355°, and then clicked the New Graphic Style icon in the Graphic Styles panel.

4 Applying finishing touches. To custom color the individual characters in his headline, Putnam decided to outline the type (Type> Create Outlines). He then applied a custom gradient and adjusted it for each character. (For more about working with gradients, see the *Color Transitions* chapter.)

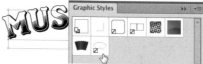

In Effect> Warp> Arc, changing the bend to 20%

Selecting the title and clicking the New Graphic Style icon in the Graphic Styles panel

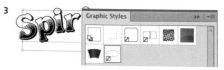

Applying the graphic style

Using Add New Effect from the Appearance panel, apply Distort & Transform, change the Rotation to 355°, and click the New Graphic Style icon in the Graphic Styles panel

Applying Type> Create Outlines to the titles

Applying a linear gradient to the titles

Applying a custom gradient

MIYAMOTO

Yukio Miyamoto

The best way to really understand how to construct complex appearances for type is to pick apart someone else's styles. Yukio Miyamoto, master of photorealism in Illustrator and author of many Japanese books on creating art with the software, has generously shared his varied collection of styles for you to you to pick apart and modify. These styles, many of which were originally created for his (Japanese) *Illustrator Appearance Book*, are downloadable in both live type and outline format, along with a PDF excerpt from his book.

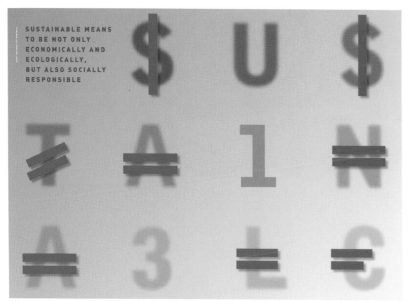

LEVY

Jean-Benoit Levy

San Francisco graphic artist Jean-Benoit Levy combined letters, numbers, and red bars to create monetary symbols in this poster about societal investment in sustainability for the "Occupy: What's Next" international poster contest sponsored by the NextByDesign organization. Levy started the poster by creating the gradient-filled background. Then he selected the Type tool and created type objects for each of the characters that spell "SUSTA1NA3LC." With the Selection tool, he selected each type object and positioned it within the layout. Next, to create the blur effect for the letters, Levy selected one of the type objects and opened the Appearance panel and clicked Fill to select a dark green. Then he clicked the Add New Effect icon at the bottom of the panel, choose Blur> Gaussian Blur, and entered 32 in the

radius field. To help save time blurring the rest of the characters, he created a graphic style that he could reuse. With the type object still selected, he opened the Graphic Style panel and clicked the New Graphic Style icon to save the appearance as a style. Next, he selected all of the remaining type objects and clicked on the graphic style he had created to blur them. To give each letter a unique color fill, Levy selected each type object, opened the Appearance panel, selected the Fill, and then Shift-clicked the Fill to access the Color panel. He adjusted the CMYK values until each character color looked the way he wanted. For the red bars, he drew paths with the Pen tool, converted them to outlines (Object> Path> Outline Stroke), and used the Appearance panel to add a drop shadow (Stylize> Drop Shadow).

BRYAN

Billie Bryan

Carib Select Watersports in Grand Cayman asked Billie Bryan to design a logo to attract cruise ship passengers to their popular Stingray City excursion. Bryan began by drawing the dark blue shape of Grand Cayman island and setting the type. She duplicated the artwork layer and then hid it by clicking its visibility icon in the Layers panel. Selecting the type, Bryan opened the Appearance panel, double-clicked Characters, filled the type with light blue, clicked the Add New Effect icon, and chose Stylize> Inner Glow. She clicked on the swatch next to the Stroke to change the color to a medium blue, clicked the Add New Effect icon, chose Distort & Transform> Transform, and changed the Move values to offset the stroke. She moved the stroke below the fill in the panel. Next, she selected the Add New Fill from the panel menu and dragged the new fill below the stroke. She changed its color to dark purple-blue and gave it an inner glow like the first fill. Finally, she selected Add New Stroke from the panel menu,

widened its stroke, and colored it with dark blue. She also used the Transform effect to offset the stroke. To complete the logo, Bryan used the island shape to add a water effect to the letters. To do this, she turned on the visibility of the duplicate layer she had hidden previously. She converted the type to outlines, selected the island, moved it in front of the type outlines, and selected the island and the type. Then she opened the Pathfinder panel and chose Intersect. She finished the logo by recoloring the resulting shapes in a light blue.

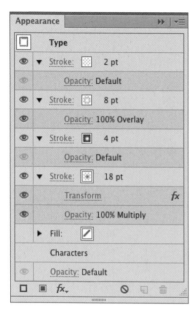

Ryan Putnam

Graphic designer Ryan Putnam turned type and paths into neon tubing using Illustrator's Appearance panel and gradients on strokes in this professional portfolio piece. Putnam began by drawing a semi-circle and setting the type for "CONES" on it. Then he selected the Type tool and double-clicked the type to select its characters. He opened the Appearance panel and changed the Fill to None. Next, Putnam clicked on the Selection tool to select the type as an object. From the Appearance panel menu, he chose Add New Stroke and set the new Stroke to 2 pt. To create the gradient for the stroke, he opened the Gradient panel, then changed the Type attribute to Radial and the Stroke attribute to "Apply gradient across stroke." Putnam modified the default gradient, making the left color stop white with 10%

opacity and the right color stop white with 0% opacity. He duplicated the stroke three times and edited each duplicate, changing the colors in the gradients. For two of the duplicates, Putnam clicked the word Opacity (below the Stroke in the Appearance panel) and changed the blending mode to Overlay on one and Multiply on the other. He offset the bottom stroke slightly from the others by clicking the Add New Effect icon, selecting Distort & Transform> Transform, and entering 5 pt in the Move> Vertical field. When he finished, Putnam made a graphic style from the type so he could apply it to the word "Frosty." To do this, he selected the type, opened the Graphic Styles panel, and clicked the New Graphic Style icon. Then he selected the type object for "Frosty" and clicked the new graphic style he had created.

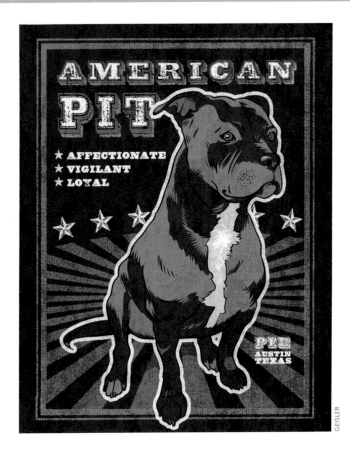

GEISLER

Greg Geisler

When Greg Geisler needed to create a poster
for an event showcasing the Pit Bull, he wanted
to emphasize the breed's American Heritage.
He created a variation on the Stars and Stripes
using a sunburst design, adding depth and perspective using Effect> 3D Bevel & Extrude. For
the stars he used Western Bullets WF, a dingbat
font. Using the star for bullets, Geisler added
adjectives describing the Pit Bull in another
slab-serif, Gatlin Bold WF. He used Clifford 8 WF
to create the main title with a white fill against
a black background to enhance the depth
he was creating in his poster. He converted
the type to Outlines (⌘-Shift-O/Ctrl-Shift-O),
and used the Blob Brush tool to paint over
part of the letters, creating a red outline that

maintained the 3D appearance of the type.
He placed all his blob brush strokes in Multiply mode in order to reveal the black texture
through the font's transparent areas, as well as
the textures he later added to the entire poster.
After adding a blue "frame" to complete the
Americana style of the poster, he used a photo
of a Pit Bull as a template and drew his stylized dog with the Pen tool. Lastly, in order to
simulate an old, rough print, he placed two
linked texture images. He clicked Opacity in the
Appearance panel; he changed the first texture
to Overlay blending mode, and then used Lumi-
nosity for the second blending mode, reducing
the opacity to 18%.

3

Rethinking Construction

Rethinking Construction

The white snap-to cursor

With Snap to Point enabled (the toggle is on by default in the View menu), grab objects with your Selection tool (from any path or point) and drag until they "snap to" a guide or another anchor point (the cursor turns white).

Modifier keys for drawing...

For a long list of modifier keys to control how you draw with the geometric tools (e.g., increase or decrease sides of a polygon or points in a star, modify the radius of a spiral, and reposition the object as you draw), search *Illustrator Help* for "keys for drawing."

To put holes into this chair, Lisa Jackmore just clicked with the Eraser tool, automatically turning the chair into a compound path, and revealing the blue underneath

The Blob Brush tool won't affect non-selected paths (left) with strokes or fill colors different from the current fill color (center), but if your current color matches the unselected path then you can add to the original path by dragging over it with the Blob Brush tool (right)

Constructing objects is at the heart of artwork in Illustrator, and nowhere has Illustrator been more innovative than in finding new ways to construct new objects from the amalgamation of simple paths and shapes. The early days of painstakingly constructing and joining every path, anchor point by anchor point, is giving way to methods of coloring shapes in ways that create new objects or that more closely simulate drawing with pencil and paper. This chapter works its way from newer methods for combining and editing shapes—using the semi-automatic methods of the Eraser, Blob Brush, the Shape Builder tools, Live Paint, and Image Trace—to older methods such as the Pathfinder panel and working with compound paths and shapes. Here also you'll find drawing assistants—such as drawing inside or behind objects, joining paths, and aligning objects and anchor points—that will help you to combine basic paths and objects.

THE ERASER TOOLS & THE BLOB BRUSH

One of the easiest ways to separate and combine objects is using the Eraser and the Blob Brush tools. With the Eraser tool you can cut an object into many parts, and with the Blob Brush you can combine multiple objects with the same fill attributes (and no stroke).

The Eraser Tools

If nothing is selected, the Eraser tool (or the eraser end of your stylus if you're using a graphics tablet) erases objects as you drag over them. To restrict the effect of the Eraser tool, select the paths you want to edit, then drag the Eraser tool through them, or enter isolation mode. If you want certain paths to be protected from the Eraser tool when nothing is selected, lock or hide those paths or their layer. You can constrain the direction of the Eraser tool by Shift-dragging, or by Option-dragging/Alt-dragging a marquee to erase a rectangular area. The Eraser tool also has the calligraphic attributes of the Paintbrush tool: Double-click the Eraser tool in the Tools panel to customize it.

The Path Eraser tool (hidden beneath the Pencil in the Tools panel) erases parts of selected paths. To remove a portion of a path, you must erase along (not perpendicular to) a selected path. Erasing a midsection of a path leaves an open anchor point on either side of the erasure.

The Blob Brush tool

In case you were wondering, the Blob "brush" is in this chapter, and not with the other brushes in the *Expressive Strokes* chapter, because it functions more like the Eraser than a brush. If you paint the same brushstroke using the Blob Brush tool and the Calligraphic Paintbrush, they might at first appear similar; if you switch to Outline mode, however, the difference becomes clear. An Illustrator vector path runs down the middle of a Paintbrush stroke, and the application of the Paintbrush remains live, which means the brushstroke can be restyled or edited like any other path in Illustrator. In contrast, a mark made by the Blob Brush is expanded as soon as you complete a stroke. Where a Paintbrush brushstroke is defined by the single path down its middle, a Blob Brush brushstroke is defined by a path around its outer edge. Following are some rules and tips for painting with the Blob Brush:

- **To paint with the Blob Brush tool,** select it, set a stroke color, and drag a brushstroke. Your stroke is automatically expanded and the fill takes the current stroke color, while the stroke itself is removed. The Blob Brush merges successive brushstrokes depending upon the options you set. As long as you keep painting with the same Fill/Stroke and Opacity, overlapping brushstrokes will merge. If you change any of these, your brushstrokes will stay separate.
- **To customize the Blob Brush tool,** double-click its icon in the Tools panel. If you enable Keep Selected, you can immediately alter the path with the Smooth tool, or make it easy to add to an existing path in a crowded illustration by enabling the "Merge Only With Selected" option. When "Merge Only With Selected" is on, the Blob Brush

If the Blob Brush doesn't merge

Can't merge objects using the Blob Brush tool? Check the following:

- Objects must be the same fill color and have no stroke
- With Merge Only with Selected Objects on, objects must be selected to merge
- With Merge Only with Selected off, objects must be adjacent in the stacking order (you can't have a differently styled object in between in the stacking order; see Layers panel below)

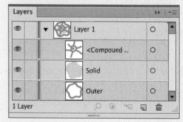

Protection from the Blob Brush

Here are three ways to protect objects from Blob Brush:

- Set the preference to Merge Only with Selected
- Enter isolation mode
- Lock or hide paths you don't want affected

Smoothing blobs...

When drawing with the Blob Brush tool, you can temporarily access the Smooth tool by holding Option/Alt as you drag along the outline of a path.

In Shape Builder Options, (double-click on the Shape Builder tool), you can choose a Gap setting, whether to fill open paths as if they were closed, and whether you want to click on a path to split an object into two or more areas.

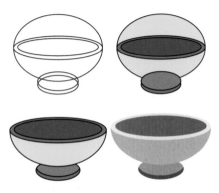

*Using Shape Builder to transform a batch of ovals into a bowl: (upper left) a series of ovals drawn with the Ellipse tool; (upper right) automatically coloring all objects using the Premedia Systems WOW! Artwork Colorizer script (**WOW! ONLINE**); (lower left) after deleting and combining objects using the Shape Builder tool; (lower right) returning to regular editing tools, shown after changing the colors and setting the stroke weight to None*

Shape Builder and holes

To merge shapes and create holes in them, hold Option/Alt and click on an area or stroke to delete it. The Shape Builder tool, like the Blob Brush, can generate compound paths.

Retain your strokes

To retain interior strokes in your drawing, click to fill the shapes separately, rather than dragging across them to join, even when you want to use the same fill on these shapes.

tool only affects the selected paths if it's selected and you drag over it using the same stroke color and opacity. Disabling this option allows the Blob Brush tool to edit paths created with the exact same Appearance, regardless of whether or not the paths are selected.

- **To modify a path that was drawn using another tool,** draw the object using any Fill and a Stroke of None. Use the Blob Brush with the same Stroke color as the object's Fill, and add your brushstrokes to the object. The Blob Brush won't edit a path with a stroke, and if you edit an open path with the Blob Brush, it will create a closed path. To add to a compound shape, first expand it.

- **To modify and combine multiple objects** that share the same Fill color with no Stroke, make sure they are on the same layer and contiguous in the stacking order.

- **To create calligraphic strokes** with a pressure-sensitive stylus and tablet (such as a Wacom) use the Blob Brush Options dialog to change brush shape and drawing angle.

- **To refine the edges of a Blob Brush brushstroke,** use the Eraser tool. You can't do this with Brush tool strokes.

SHAPE BUILDER TOOL

Although it bears some similarities to Live Paint and Pathfinder commands (discussed later in this chapter), the Shape Builder tool presents an entirely new method for constructing objects. When you initially draw, you can allow objects to overlap in the interior of the outline you want to create; e.g., drawing a three-leaf clover from three overlapping circles and an overlapping rectangle for the stem. With the Shape Builder tool, all you need to do is to first select the objects you want to combine into new shapes, then place your cursor over an area. To unite one area with others, simply click-drag across from one highlighted area to another. You can click-drag in a straight line, or Shift-drag a marquee over selected areas to unite multiple areas. Your objects don't need to reside on the same layer to start, but when they are merged with an initial shape, they will be moved to that shape's layer. To delete areas or strokes from your selected artwork using the Shape Builder tool, press the Option/Alt key while clicking on the highlighted area or portion of a stroke.

Depending on how your options are set, you can either select swatch colors as you go (with a Swatch preview cursor), or use the colors already in the highlighted object (double-click the tool to choose which method to use). If you choose "Pick Color From Color Swatches" in the Options dialog, you can enable the Cursor Swatch Preview. Now you can use the left and right arrow keys to switch the current color to the next color in any selected color group in the Swatches panel, or the up and down arrow keys to move to another color group. If you choose "Pick Color From Artwork," the first object you click on will determine the color that fills the others as you drag. Separate objects can easily become merged into a single object. The rules for filling objects can be complex, so see the Tip "Shape Builder & appearances" at right if an object's appearance isn't what you expected.

One of the most powerful aspects of Shape Builder is that you are actually reconstructing how objects are made and filled, not just how they look on the surface. When working with strokes, those you keep remain live and editable, whereas Live Paint or Pathfinder commands might result in strokes that have become unexpectedly expanded or deleted. You can continue to modify the appearance of your Shape Builder strokes. Your new objects do not become a special kind of group, either, so you can freely switch between regular editing tools and the Shape Builder tool.

WORKING WITH LIVE PAINT

Hidden under the Shape Builder tool are the Live Paint Bucket and Live Paint Selection tools. Whereas the Shape Builder tool helps you to reconstruct and combine objects, Live Paint provides you with a way to recolor objects without modifying the vector paths, ignoring the normal rules about how you define a vector object. Paint lines and spaces as if you were coloring a drawing by hand. In order to use these tools, you have to first convert your objects

Shape Builder & appearances

Changing the order and direction with which you drag to apply the Shape Builder tool can alter the appearance of the resulting objects. If you aren't getting the results you want, undo and try starting the merge with a different object.

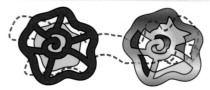

Using the Shape Builder tool to transform a duplicate of the left figure into the right figure by filling and deleting areas created by overlapping objects, and deleting strokes; once you've used Shape Builder to reconfigure objects you can simply select sections using the Direct Selection tool and continue to change the fill and stroke, adjust transparency, and more; a dashed brush beneath is shown to demonstrate transparency

Shape Builder as Paint Bucket

The Shape Builder tool can also be used like an ordinary paint bucket; click (instead of click-drag) to fill shapes without uniting them.

Adding to a Live Paint Group

Add new members to a Live Paint Group by selecting the new paths and the Live Paint Group, then clicking the Merge Live Paint button in the Control panel (or choose Object> Live Paint> Merge). Or even better, enter isolation mode with the Live Paint Group; then anything you paste or create will remain part of the Live Paint Group (see the chapter *Your Creative Workspace* for more on isolation mode).

If you choose Object> Live Paint> Expand, or click the Expand button in the Control panel, your objects will be converted into ordinary vector paths that look the same, but are broken apart into separate objects. To revert the objects in your Live Paint Group back to their pre–Live Paint, ordinary-path state, choose Object> Live Paint> Release.

GUSTAVO DEL VECHIO

Using Live Paint to both construct and color a cityscape; Intersecting open paths created enclosed areas suitable for filling with the Live Paint Bucket tool (bottom)

Stop the Preview!

In order to adjust settings without prompting Image Trace to re-trace as soon as one setting is altered, toggle Preview off after an initial trace, and back on when you want to test your settings again.

into a Live Paint Group; all the enclosed spaces, filled or empty, become areas you can potentially fill or clear of color. You can create a "hole" in your Live Paint object by filling with None, or you can fill an "empty" area made from adjacent vector objects with your selected color. All the lines become editable paths that you can keep, color, reshape, or delete, creating new shapes. To convert a selection to a Live Paint Group, choose the Live Paint Bucket tool and click on the object, or choose Object> Live Paint> Make (⌘-Option-X/Ctrl-Alt-X); like any other grouped object, Live Paint objects all move to the topmost layer that contained the original objects.

To change the way the Live Paint Bucket behaves, double-click on it and set options, such as whether the Bucket paints fills, strokes, or both; whether you want a Cursor Swatch Preview; or the color and size of the highlight you see when you position the Bucket over an editable area. Choose how Live Paint handles gaps in the Object> Live Paint> Gap Options dialog. To edit paths and reshape areas, use normal editing tools, such as the Pen or Smooth tool. To actually alter or delete segments of paths (created from intersecting paths in Live Paint), use the Live Paint Selection tool.

USING IMAGE TRACE

Previously called Live Trace, Image Trace provides you with a variety of different ways to turn raster images into vectors. To access default presets in Image Trace (such as Photorealistic or Technical Drawing), select any raster image that you've brought into Illustrator via Open or Place, and click either the Image Trace button in the Control panel or Trace in the Image Trace panel (Window menu). Use the Image Trace panel to enable or disable preview, customize your trace settings, and save your current settings as custom presets. Image Trace leaves the traced object live and re-adjustable. If you want to edit the objects with normal vector tools, you'll need to expand the trace by clicking the Expand button on the Control panel, after which the object will no longer be live.

The Image Trace panel

In the Image Trace panel, you can specify a color mode (Color, Grayscale, or Black and White) and a Palette of colors for the tracing object. The palette determines whether your trace will use a limited or unlimited number of colors, and whether to take them automatically from the object or to use a Swatch group or library (Pantone converts to global color) that is open or has been opened during the session. If you want another library, or need to create a new color group, deselect the object, open the library or create the color group, and then reselect the image and choose your new library or group from the Color drop-down list. In the Image Trace panel, select the open library in the Palette drop-down list, and then select a color group listed in Colors. Using sliders, you can modify how closely paths adhere to the original and set tolerances for when paths join with corner angles, or whether the trace should ignore pixels as noise. In Black and White Mode, you can choose to create Fills and/or Strokes.

Image Trace can create vector objects that abut one another (like puzzle pieces), or that overlap each other (stacking one on top of another). If you intend to edit the paths, you should probably choose the "Overlapping" option; with the "Abutting" option, the paths fit together precisely, so editing one path can create a gap between it and its neighboring (abutting) path. With Abutting as the Method, you can automatically remove a white background from your image by enabling "Ignore White."

ALIGNING, JOINING, AND AVERAGING
Align and distribute objects

Even though most Align and Distribute controls also appear in the Control panel, Distribute Spacing controls are found only in the Align panel. With an active selection, you can align objects to that selection, or the edges of the artboard, and you can Align to a Key Object (heavy outlines show you which object the others align to). To distribute the space between objects, designate one as the key; in the Align panel, enter an amount in the Distribute

The expanded Image Trace panel showing a custom swatch library with a set selected to limit colors, default settings in Advanced, plus Ignore White enabled

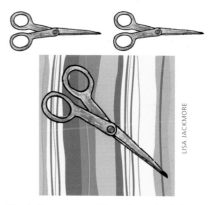

LISA JACKMORE

Lisa Jackmore scanned her scissors sketch (top left), then used Image Trace with "Ignore White" enabled (top right); the traced scissors over a striped background showing through (above)

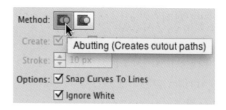

With Abutting as the Method, choosing Ignore White lets you automatically remove a white background from your tracing object

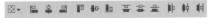

Align controls in the Align panel (top) and on the Control panel (bottom)

Path Simplify command

The Simplify command (Object> Path> Simplify) removes excess anchor points from selected paths. The higher the percentage, the more anchor points will remain, and the closer the new path will be to the original. The endpoints of an open path are never altered. The higher the Angle threshold, the more likely a corner point will remain sharp.

Resizing and stroke weight

Double-click the Scale tool to resize your selection with or without altering line weights:

- To scale a selection while also scaling line weights, enable Scale Strokes & Effects.
- To scale a selection while maintaining your line weights, disable Scale Strokes & Effects.
- To decrease line weights (50%) without scaling objects, first scale the selection (200%) with Scale Strokes & Effects disabled. Then scale (50%) with it enabled. Reverse these steps to increase line weights.

Spacing input box; then click either the Vertical or Horizontal Distribute Space icon.

Easier joins

It's now easy to join open endpoints without getting an error dialog, and you can even join multiple pairs of endpoints together at the same time. To join you must first either select one pair of points with the Direct Selection tool, or select one or more open paths with the Selection tool. Next, if a pair of points are *exactly* on top of each other, you can join them without a dialog by using ⌘-J/Ctrl-J or Object> Path> Join. Use the Control panel to change a join from corner to smooth, or vice versa. If points are not *exactly* on top of each other, choosing join will connect them with a line, or you can average them together first (see below for more on averaging). If you select multiple open objects and choose Join, one object will join to the next (paths won't close upon themselves). At any time you can convert points from corner to smooth, or smooth to corner, by selecting the anchor points with the Direct Selection tool and clicking the appropriate icon from the Convert section in the Control panel. Below are some rules about joining and averaging:

- **Endpoints that are precisely on top of one another join** with a corner point unless you choose "Smooth" in the Join dialog (⌘-Option-Shift-J/Ctrl-Alt-Shift-J).
- **Joining two or more open endpoints on separate paths that are not precisely on top of each other** connects the points with a straight segment using corner points. If your paths have different appearances applied, the path topmost in the stacking order determines the appearance of the paths as they are joined to it.
- **Average and join two endpoints that are not on top of each other** using ⌘-Option-Shift-J/Ctrl-Alt-Shift-J.
- **To average (without joining) endpoints,** select any number of points with the Direct Selection or Lasso tool on any number of objects; then use ⌘-Option-J/Ctrl-Alt-J to average the points along horizontal, vertical, or both axes. If you have the path selected, but not specific points,

then all points will be averaged together. If you use the Direct Selection or Lasso tool to select points, then the Align icons in the Control panel or Align panel will average the points, rather than align the objects.

DRAW BEHIND AND DRAW INSIDE

Illustrator has three drawing mode icons near the bottom of your Tools panel: Normal, Behind, and Inside. Once you click the Draw Behind icon, anything that you paste or draw will be the backmost object in your current layer, or, if you have something selected, will be placed directly behind the currently selected object. (Paste in Front and Paste in Back still work as expected, and ignore the drawing mode.) If the Draw Behind mode is active when you add a new layer to your file, it will add it behind the active layer. To create an object with a different appearance from the selected object, create it first, then change the new object's attributes. Or, if you want to be able to set an object's attributes before drawing it, enter isolation mode first. The object you're drawing behind doesn't need to be selected when you're in isolation mode. You can safely deselect it, and then set the attributes for each new object before you draw it.

Draw Inside is only available when one object (or compound path or text object) is selected, and will quickly make a *clipping mask* out of the selected object. When your originally-selected object is automatically converted to this special clipping mask, it loses any attributes beyond the basic stroke and a fill, so art brushes or live effects, for instance, are removed. To set up your object for Draw Inside, first select it, then click on the Drawing Mode icon in the Tools panel and choose Draw Inside. Your selected object will display the dotted corners of a bounding box. Next deselect the object (the dotted box remains); now you can choose your drawing tool or brush and its attributes. Now you only have to draw over the object to have any strokes or fills that extend outside to be clipped to the boundaries of the selected object. Your clipping mask object and whatever you have drawn inside are now a

Toggle drawing modes

You can use the keyboard shortcut Shift-D to switch between available modes. Keep an eye on the changing icon to know which drawing mode you have selected.

Using Draw Inside to restrain the Bristle Brush strokes within each object as it's selected

Compound paths or shapes?

Use compound paths on simple objects for basic combining or hole-cutting. Use compound shapes on complex objects (such as those made with additional effects) and to fully control how your objects interact. Be aware that compound shapes can become too complex to print, or to be combined within some effects, and might have to be released (returning objects to their original state) or expanded (which keeps the appearance, but breaks it apart permanently). Make/release/expand compound shapes from the Pathfinder panel menu, and make/release compound paths from the Object menu.

modern
modern
modern

LISA JACKMORE

Artist Lisa Jackmore used the Draw Inside mode to add a gradient-filled rectangle to the text, then drew with a calligraphic brush, all leaving the text live and the "clipped" object separately editable

Don't forget the drawing mode

IMPORTANT: Drawing modes are persistent! If you forget what mode you're in, you'll get unexpected results. Try to get in the habit of switching to Normal mode (Shift-D) as soon as you no longer need to be in that special drawing mode.

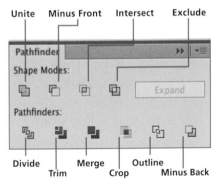

The Pathfinder panel contains two sets of icons: Shape Modes (which combine shapes), and Pathfinders (which divide paths)

Left to right: two ovals (the inner oval has no fill, but appears black because of the black fill of the larger oval behind it); as part of a compound path the inner oval knocks a hole into the outer one where they overlap; the same compound path with inner oval, which was Direct-Selected and moved to the right to show that the hole is only where the objects overlap

group. To edit any part of this new object, use the Direct Selection tool or target it in the Layers panel and edit as a regular vector object. You can even apply effects to the entire group, if you desire. You can also copy and paste artwork in Draw Inside mode, which will clip the artwork inside text, for example. Learn more about working with clipping masks in the *Mastering Complexity* chapter.

COMPOUND SHAPES & COMPOUND PATHS

There are three additional ways to create new objects by combining and subtracting objects with and from each other: compound shapes, compound paths, and by using the commands found in the Pathfinder panel. Compound paths and compound shapes are live and can easily be released to recover the original paths. Compound paths are used primarily to create holes in objects, whereas compound shapes provide more complex ways of combining objects. The Pathfinder panel icons perform operations very much like compound shapes, except that these operations are applied permanently—Undo is the only way to reverse the effects of a pathfinder operation. If you wish to apply a live version of a Pathfinder command to a layer, type object, or a group, instead of using the Pathfinder panel, apply it from either the Effects menu, or the *fx* icon from the Appearance panel.

Compound paths

A compound path consists of one or more paths that have been combined so they behave as a single unit. Compound paths can be used as a single mask, and they can create holes where the original objects overlapped (think of the letter **O**), through which you can see objects.

To create a simple compound path, draw one oval, then draw a smaller oval that will form the center hole of the **O**, and choose Object> Compound Path> Make. Apply the fill color of your choice, and the inner object remains unfilled. To adjust one of the paths within a compound path, use the Direct Selection tool; or select the compound path and enter isolation mode.

Pathfinder panel

The Pathfinder panel includes the top row of Shape Modes icons and the lower row of Pathfinder commands. The Pathfinder panel's icons alter the selected objects permanently, slicing them up if needed to achieve the icon's effect (see the "Compound shapes" section following about applying the top row as live effects). These permanent alterations to the objects allow you to, for example, apply the Intersect icon to selected objects so that you can pull apart and further edit the resulting pieces. Note that the Trim and Merge commands can be applied only to filled objects.

Compound shapes

A compound shape combines objects with, or subtracts objects from, each other, while leaving the original objects intact. You can make compound shapes from two or more paths or from other compound shapes, text, envelopes, blends, groups, or artwork with vector effects applied. To create compound shapes, hold the Option/Alt key as you click a Shape Mode icon in the Pathfinder panel; if you click without the Option/Alt modifier, original objects are permanently altered. You can also apply the Unite Shape mode by choosing "Make Compound Shape" from the Pathfinder panel menu. Compound shapes take on the attributes of the topmost object in the selection.

As long as you keep compound shapes live, you can continue to apply (or remove) Shape Modes and add a variety of effects to the compound shape as a unit, such as envelopes, warps, and drop shadows. Compound shapes can also be pasted into Photoshop as editable shape layers, although they won't retain their Illustrator appearance. To retain their appearance and keep them editable, paste them as vector Smart Objects (to edit a Smart Object, double-click its thumbnail in Photoshop and it will open in Illustrator; when you save, it updates in Photoshop). Release the Shape Mode to restore the original objects, or click Expand to permanently apply the effect to the objects, using Pathfinder Options from the panel's menu.

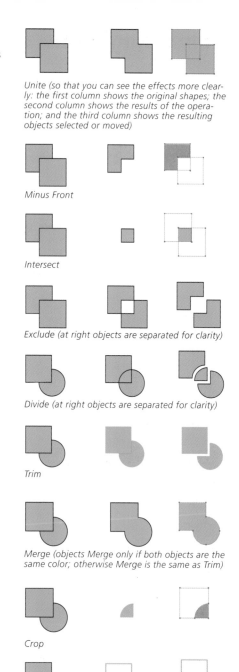

Unite (so that you can see the effects more clearly: the first column shows the original shapes; the second column shows the results of the operation; and the third column shows the resulting objects selected or moved)

Minus Front

Intersect

Exclude (at right objects are separated for clarity)

Divide (at right objects are separated for clarity)

Trim

Merge (objects Merge only if both objects are the same color; otherwise Merge is the same as Trim)

Crop

Outline (after applying Outline, Illustrator sets the stroke to 0—here, with a 2-pt stroke added)

Minus Back

Combining Paths

Basic Path Construction with Pathfinders

Overview: *Create an illustration by joining and intersecting objects using the Pathfinder panel's Unite, Minus Front, and Intersect.*

1

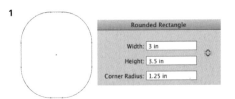

Creating a rounded rectangle by clicking on the Artboard with the Rounded Rectangle tool, setting dimensions, and increasing Corner Radius

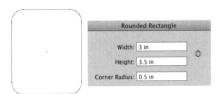

Creating a rounded rectangle by clicking on the Artboard with the Rounded Rectangle tool, setting dimensions, and decreasing Corner Radius

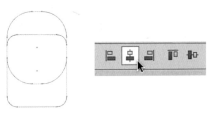

Selecting both rounded rectangles, using Horizontal Align Center, using the Unite Pathfinder command, and changing fill to cyan

To create many eye-catching stock illustrations like the one above, which are used for advertisements, websites, and more, Ryan Putnam frequently uses the Pathfinder panel. Using the Pathfinder's Unite, Minus Front, and Intersect, you too can easily create compelling character illustrations.

1 Constructing the body with the Unite Pathfinder command. Ryan Putnam created the body from two rounded rectangles. To create the first object, he clicked on the Artboard with the Rounded Rectangle tool to open the Rounded Rectangle dialog. In the dialog, he set the dimensions of the rectangle to 3 in for Width, 3.5 in for Height and increased the Corner Radius to 1.25. Putnam wanted the bottom corners of the body to be smaller, so he then created a second rectangle with the same dimensions, entered .5 for the Corner Radius, and placed the top a third of the way down from the first rectangle.

Putnam selected both rectangles, clicked the Horizontal Align Center icon from the Control panel, used the Unite command from the Pathfinder panel, and chose a Cyan swatch from the Swatches panel.

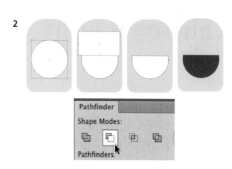

2 Constructing the mouth with the Minus Front Pathfinder command. With the Ellipse tool, Putnam drew a circle within the body object for the mouth. He then drew an encompassing rectangle halfway up from the center of the circle. He selected both, clicked the Minus Front command from the Pathfinder panel, and chose a brown swatch from the Swatches panel.

Drawing a circle, drawing a rectangle over the circle, selecting both, using the Minus Front Pathfinder command, and changing fill to brown

3 Constructing the teeth and tongue with Pathfinder commands. To create the tongue, Putnam created two overlapping circles within the mouth shape, selected both, and used the Unite Pathfinder command. To fit the tongue into the mouth, he first copied the mouth shape, and then chose Edit> Paste in Front. Selecting both the mouth copy and the tongue, he applied the Intersect Pathfinder command, and then chose a magenta swatch from the Swatches panel for the fill color.

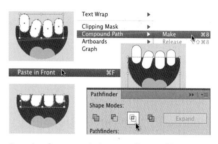

Drawing two ellipses, using the Unite Pathfinder command, Copying the mouth and Pasting in Front, selecting the mouth and tongue, and using the Intersect Pathfinder command

To create the teeth, Putnam drew four objects with the Rounded Rectangle tool. He rotated one tooth with the Selection tool by moving the cursor along the rectangle until he saw the Rotate icon and then dragged the tooth slightly to the right. He then selected all four teeth and combined them into a single compound path using Object> Compound Path> Make (for more about compound paths, see this chapter's intro). To trim off the portions of the teeth that extend above the mouth, Putnam chose Edit> Paste in Front, selected the copied mouth and teeth, and used the Intersect Pathfinder command.

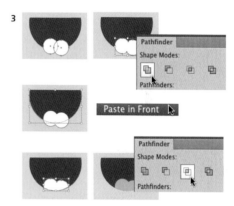

Drawing four rounded rectangles, making a compound shape, Copying the mouth and Pasting in Front, selecting the mouth and teeth, and using the Intersect Pathfinder command

4 Creating other character features. Putnam could then add character features as he needed, for instance, a 15-pt stroke for the lips, a circle for the back of the mouth, another pair of circles for eyes, and a rounded rectangle for the stick.

Adding additional features with circles and rounded rectangles

Coloring Line Art
Using Live Paint for Fluid Productivity

Overview: *Draw with the Pen tool to trace the minimum paths needed to define discreet areas; color using Live Paint tools for easy selections.*

GUSTAVO DEL VECHIO

1

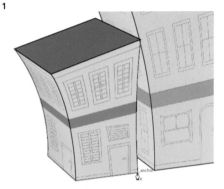

Outlining the 3D model with open paths, using the Pen tool and Smart Guides

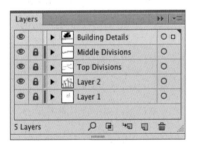

Drawing interior details with the other layers locked and Smart Guides turned off

When Gustavo Del Vechio needed an illustration for his client's urban development proposal, he used Illustrator to draw the initial concept, which he developed more fully in 3D Studio Max. He then rendered the artwork and placed it back into Illustrator as a template. Seeking to create a lively and humanistic interpretation of a crowded city environment, he used the Pen tool for tracing and Live Paint to control coloring, so he could give each building its own personality.

1 Freeform drawing with the Pen tool in preparation for Live Paint. Since he was using Live Paint, Del Vechio was able to draw open paths that would ultimately enclose the areas to be colored, instead of precisely stacking discrete objects atop one another and creating the fully closed paths that normal fills require. Paths that merely crossed over other paths created separate areas, and by drawing only enough paths to separate one area from another, he was able to draw more quickly and efficiently, using many fewer paths and layers. He kept Smart Guides turned on to help signal him as each anchor and path properly lined up with the others.

After he outlined the basic shapes of the building, Del Vechio turned Smart Guides off while he drew the doors and windows more freely on their own layer. Even though the 3D model had curved lines, in order to create the slightly off-kilter look of an illustration, he used only straight segments (except for the arched door and circular window). After tracing the artwork, he selected it all and clicked on it with the Live Paint Bucket tool (hidden under the Shape Builder tool). Once converted to a Live Paint group, the content of all the layers automatically moved into the top layer. Del Vechio next needed to select and delete a few unwanted segments. While the Selection tool selects objects and the Direct Selection tool selects paths, he was able to use the Live Paint Selection tool to select, then delete, individual faces and line segments.

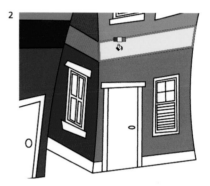

Removing unwanted intersecting edges (highlighted in red) with the Live Paint Selection tool

2 Creating Swatch groups and using Global colors makes it easy to apply, and later edit, color. Del Vechio created a small color group for each building. Using the Live Paint Bucket tool, he colored each building, cycling through colors in a group using the left and right arrow keys, and moving between color groups using the up and down keys. He also assigned all the colors he created as Global swatches. If he later wanted to replace a color, he only had to replace the swatch itself and it would automatically update that color anywhere in the document.

To ensure he wouldn't accidentally color a stroke when he only wanted to fill a face on the buildings, Del Vechio double-clicked on the Live Paint Bucket tool and disabled Paint Strokes in the dialog. After he filled the main areas of the buildings, he created a gradient for the lights in the windows. In order to paint some of the strokes (but not all), he again opened the Live Paint dialog to enable Paint Strokes and disable Paint Fills. He then selected all the Strokes and set their weight to None. With the Stroke weight set to 0.75 pt and choosing various brown colors, he selectively filled some strokes around the windows and doors. Although the strokes were now invisible, Live Paint would highlight them when his cursor passed over them.

Finally Del Vechio reset the Live Paint Bucket Options to Paint for both Fills and Strokes, then recolored some of the areas and edges to complete his whimsical cityscape.

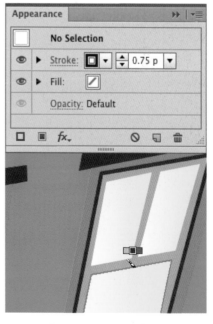

Using Live Paint, small Swatch groups, and the left and right arrow keys to select new colors while filling faces with the Live Paint Bucket tool

Painting a few of the edges with Paint Fills disabled, Paint Strokes enabled, and the Stroke set for color and width in the Appearance panel

Blob to Live Paint

From Sketch to Blob Brush and Live Paint

Overview: *Place sketch as a template; trace sketch with the Blob Brush tool; color with the Live Paint Bucket tool.*

PUTNAM

1

The original tattoo sketch

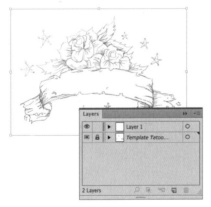

Placing sketch as a template layer

2

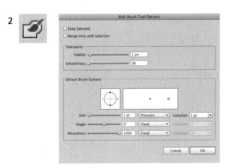

Setting up default Blob Brush tool options

Ryan Putnam has a stock illustration portfolio full of hand-drawn illustrations. Putnam found that using the new Blob Brush tool and his Wacom pen tablet, he could now easily create a hand-drawn look using Illustrator. Moreover, by using Live Paint, he could quickly fill his illustration with color.

1 Creating a sketch and placing it as a template. Putnam first created a tattoo sketch in Photoshop and placed it into Illustrator as a template. Create your own sketch, scan it, or sketch directly into a painting program (such as Painter or Photoshop). Save your sketch as PSD, JPEG, or TIF format. Next, create a new Illustrator document and choose File> Place. Locate your sketch, then enable the Template option and click Place (see the chapter *Your Creative Workspace* for more on templates).

2 Setting Blob Brush tool options and tracing sketch. Putnam wanted to create marks that were very true to his stylus gestures and had minimal smoothness. To create this effect with the Blob Brush tool, he first had to modify the default options. To do this, he double-clicked on the Blob Brush tool in the Tools panel. In the Blob Brush Tool Options, he set the Fidelity to 1, Smoothness to 0, and set Size to 5 pt. From the Size drop-down menu he selected Pressure, changed the Size Variation to 5 pt, and clicked OK. If you don't have a pen tablet, change all the same settings except the Pressure and Size Variation.

Using these custom Blob Brush settings, Putnam began to trace the scanned sketch template into the layer above, varying his stylus pressure to re-create the hand-drawn style.

Tracing sketch with the Blob Brush tool

While drawing with the Blob Brush tool, Putnam used the Eraser tool, set up to work with pressure-sensitivity, to modify brush marks and correct mistakes. To do this, Putnam double-clicked the Eraser tool from the Tools panel and changed the Diameter to 5 pt. He then selected Pressure from the Diameter drop-down menu, changed the Diameter Variation to 5 pt, and clicked OK. By setting up the Eraser tool with pressure-sensitive settings, he could move easily between the two tools by simply flipping the stylus around.

Setting up default Eraser tool preferences and erasing with the Eraser tool

3 Filling areas with Live Paint. If Putnam used the regular Brush tool to trace his sketch, he would have had to create additional paths defining fill areas to color the drawing. But Blob Brush objects can easily be converted into Live Paint Groups for quick and simple coloring. To convert the illustration to a Live Paint Group, Putnam selected the illustration with the selection tool, chose the Live Paint Bucket tool from the Tools panel, and on first click, the object became a Live Paint Group. With the Live Paint Bucket tool, he hovered over the selected illustration to highlight areas to fill. With the left and right arrow keys, Putnam cycled through the swatches from the Swatch Panel until he found his desired color (see the *Color Transitions* chapter for details on creating colors). Once he found the color, he clicked in the area to fill. He repeated cycling through the swatches and filled in the other enclosed areas of the illustration.

3

Filling areas with the Live Paint Bucket tool

Cycling through swatches with the Live Paint Bucket tool

4

4 Applying finishing touches. Putnam added additional features as needed. For instance, he warped the type and added gradients to the Live Paint fills (see the "Arcing Type" lesson in the chapter *Designing Type & Layout*, and see the *Color Transitions* chapter for gradients details).

Adding a warped type treatment and gradients

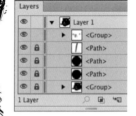

TURTON

David Turton

For a powerful, yet highly detailed drawing of a tiger's head, David Turton relied upon the natural combination of the Blob Brush tool and the Wacom® Cintiq21UX tablet computer. Because Turton could draw directly on the tablet itself, and his paths would join automatically as they overlapped, he felt he had greater control over this kind of meticulous, but still freehand, pen-and-ink drawing, without having to interrupt the flow to create a new brush or adjust his stroke width. He began a rough sketch with brush settings that most closely emulated natural pen strokes. He kept Fidelity and Smoothness at their lowest settings to be as true to his hand as possible, and used a very fine, 2-pixel point. Gradually Turton refined the tiger's features, filling in more detail, and keeping the brush tip fine and allowing his strokes to merge naturally as he drew over them, thickening the detail in some areas for greater definition. As the file size grew, he began to lock layers he was happy with and to add more detail as the drawing progressed. This prevented strokes from merging and forcing constant re-renders of the drawing. Such extensive detail is very demanding of a computer's resources. When he had completed most of the tiger, he unlocked the layers and merged them all. Lastly, he used the Eraser tool to "draw out" the whiskers by erasing next to their lines, creating an interruption in the strokes in order to enhance the illusion of whiskers overlapping the fur.

JACKSON

Lance Jackson

Lance Jackson drew this fanciful animal using a combination of the Blob Brush and Eraser tools. Here is his tale of how this unusual creature came into being: "I had the opportunity to apply to a position opening for a Google doodler. Part of the preliminary interview process was to take the Google Graphics Test. The second question was "Draw or sketch a furry animal. It can be any kind of animal, but most importantly, it should be original." I submitted three animals. The first one was the Vegetarian Cheetah. It was initially done as a pencil sketch.

After submitting my ten drawings and digital color paintings to Google (this was a timed test) I decided to create another version in Illustrator using the Blob Brush. I first started with just the merged bodies of the running cheetah with the quizzical head of a rabbit. A week later I decided to add the background. I continued on using the Blob Brush since it helps to unify the similar colors. The Blob Brush provided the best means to merge the cheetah and rabbit together without going deep into the DNA code of both animals."

STOPPEE

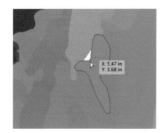
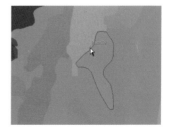

Janet Stoppee

As a graphic designer and master gardener Janet Stoppee combined her two favorite activities to create a seed packet for a Flowering Maple. She used a photo of a maple she had grown herself from seed as the basis for her illustration. Experience has shown her that prepping a photo before tracing it helps produce the desired results. In Illustrator, choosing a palette to use in Image Trace both simplifies and colorizes a photo, but Stoppee has traditionally simplified first with a favorite third-party filter (Topaz Simplify) in Photoshop. In this case, she chose the preset Painting Harsh-

Color to intensify the natural colors. In Illustrator, she opened the file, selected it, and opened the Image Trace panel. There she enabled Preview and experimented with the different presets. Stoppee chose High Fidelity with the default settings. After tracing her image, she expanded it and zoomed in to 1200%. Unavoidably, even when using the Overlap method, complex tracings can still have small holes where edges don't meet. A solid background in a matching color might solve the problem, but if not, you can do as Stoppee did and manually repair the holes with the Direct Selection tool.

MARKIEWICZ

Danuta Markiewicz (Danka)

Danuta "Danka" Markiewicz is a Polish artist who lives in Italy and creates wonderful illustrated books using Illustrator and a bit of Photoshop. She scans in her sketches, then runs them through Image Trace in black and white with "Ignore White" enabled. Danka converts these traced illustrations into Live Paint objects and colors and recolors the elements. She brings in textures from Photoshop and changes the blending mode to Overlay. She brings in her texture a second time and uses Image Trace in color mode. To create the bowing she applies Effect> Warp> Arc to the image, and to both an image and a drop-shadow. Opening the images and textures in Photoshop, she combines some layers with Soft Light blending mode, while on others she runs her favorite filter: Minimum. She integrates text in either English or Polish using fonts that simulate handwriting. Though her characters are vector-based and graphic in style, her final books end up rather painterly and richly textured.

GILBERT

Katharine Gilbert

Katharine Gilbert used Illustrator and Photoshop to produce "Vintage," an image of the
multiverse of a rusting truck as it appears in
many dimensions. She used Image Trace to create her black and white version of the truck
because Photoshop's Threshold filter doesn't
retain as much detail. She reduced the Threshold setting for this dark photo in order to bring
out a maximum range of contrast in the 2-color
image, and she set Paths to their maximum
accuracy. To keep the grungy, angular detail
throughout, she also set Corners to their high-
est for the least amount of smoothing, and
moved the Noise setting to a minimum so the
finest detail would be traced. After running
Image Trace, she clicked on the Expand button
in the Options bar, resized the image to 6 x 4
inches, and reduced the layer's Opacity to 20%.

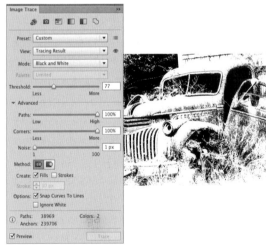

From there, Gilbert opened the .ai file in Photoshop (saved with PDF compatibility, it opens
as a PDF), and began layering different versions
of the truck. She made extensive use of Photoshop's blending modes, as well as the 3D Postcard feature, in order to reproduce the truck
with varying color, tonality, and perspective.

Cheryl Graham

Cheryl Graham drew this self-portrait based on a reference photo she simplified with Image Trace. After placing the photo in Illustrator, she opened the Image Trace panel and, from Preset, chose Shades of Gray. Graham enabled Preview to see the effects as she adjusted settings until paths and corners were simple and there were just a handful of grays. With Preview selected, her setting was automatically applied when she closed the Image Trace window. Graham placed this version in a locked layer as a template to trace over; she also kept a copy of the original photo on her artboard as an additional reference. She created a dark global color so she would be able to specify various tints of the color as she drew. Graham double-clicked on the Blob Brush tool and, in the Blob Brush Options, she set the Fidelity to 0.5 px, Smoothness to 0%, specified an 8-pt brush size with an 8-pt variation and selected Pressure. In the Color panel, Graham specified a 10% tint of the global color and with the Blob Brush drew in the lightest values. She repeated the process using progressively darker tints, making a separate layer for each tint and gradually building the portrait (some of the layers shown at right). Occasionally she increased or decreased the Blob Brush size with the [ ] keys. While Graham drew, she kept an enlarged Navigator panel open (Window> Navigator). When she zoomed into an area, either drawing with the Blob Brush, or adjusting a path with the Direct Selection tool, she could refer to the Navigator panel and easily see how the changes she made in a particular area affected the entire portrait,

GRAHAM

without having to constantly zoom in and out of the drawing. Although the low fidelity Blob Brush setting creates too many anchor points, Graham prefers to start with this setting and later apply Object> Path> Simplify (specifying 95% for Curve Precision). To finish the portrait, Graham made custom Art Brushes with tapered ends (directly above) for the details such as the eyelashes and eyebrows. She used a Round Curve Bristle Brush to create the shadows behind the head.

KLEMA

Stephen A. Klema

Stephen Klema uses Illustrator's Live Paint to assist him in the conception and construction of his sculptures. For "Wood's Revenge," he scanned his pencil sketch of the tree and saw blade, then opened it in Illustrator. To keep the outline distinct as he filled in the parts, he used the Pen tool to create a contour shape with a white fill and no stroke, and used it as a mask on the top layer. He selected the Paintbrush with a 1pt stroke to begin tracing (Live Paint converts brushstrokes to basic strokes, so the Pen or Pencil tools will also work here). After tracing some of the key lines that would become his wood shapes, Klema selected them and chose Object> Live Paint> Make. To get a clear view of the relationship between the shapes, he used the Live Paint tool (K) to fill the shapes with colors that clearly delineated

the separate pieces (above right, middle figure). Where necessary, he used the Pen tool to add and subtract anchor points, and the Direct Selection tool to adjust the paths. Klema then traced another section of his scan. To move this set of paths into the Live Paint group, he selected both the new paths and the Live Paint object, and chose Object> Live Paint> Merge. In this way, he developed all the filled shapes for his sculpture. To recolor the shapes so they more closely approximated wood and saw, he created a custom swatch group and used the Live Paint tool to refill the shapes with their final colors. Klema then removed the strokes to see how well the colors and contrast worked. With his concept finalized as a Live Paint object, he could move on to creating the template files needed to make the sculpture itself.

 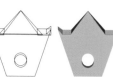

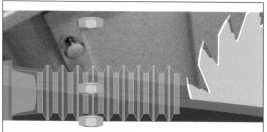

Stephen A. Klema

Stephen Klema found that the Shape Builder tool helped him to save time when creating some of the tool illustrations in his art animation and interactive design piece entitled "100 Days." To construct the drill bit, for instance, Klema began by drawing basic 4-sided objects with the Rectangle tool, and 3-sided objects using the Star tool (reducing it to three sides using the down arrow key). He then added points with the Add Anchor Point tool, and shifted the points using the Direct Selection tool (holding the Shift key to constrain movement). When the basic shapes were in the proper position, he selected them all and then used the Shape Builder tool to start combining some objects by click-dragging from one to the other (e.g., from the bottom orange object to the top triangle), and deleting others and even making holes by holding Option/Alt when clicking (or click-dragging). When the drill bit was properly combined he marquee-Direct-Selected the top anchor points and Shift-dragged the points upwards to elongate the point. Finally, he recolored the newly configured objects. See Klema's "100 Days" project at www.StephenKlema.com/100days.

Rapid Reshaping

Using Shape Builder to Construct Objects

Overview: *Create overlapping objects, color them with a Premedia Systems script, and use the Shape Builder tool to unite some parts and delete others; recolor, use drawing modes and the Bristle Brush to add a background, shading, and textures; resize artboards with another Premedia script.*

1

Drawing the oval objects and using the Premedia WOW! Artwork Colorizer script to give each object a different color

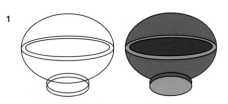

Dragging to unite the shapes that make up the bottom of the bowl; then deleting side pieces on foot and top shape (cursors magnified)

STEUER

Sharon Steuer created this piece for a user group demo highlighting how some newer features in Illustrator—the Shape Builder tool, drawing modes, and the Bristle Brush—make constructing objects quicker and easier.

1 Constructing the bowl from overlapping objects.

Since the Shape Builder can both unite objects and delete parts of intersecting objects, using it can be much simpler and quicker than either drawing precisely with the Pen tool, or using Pathfinder commands. To follow along with the figures in this lesson, set the fill and stroke to the default (press the D key), then set the fill to None (X toggles focus between fill and stroke; the / key sets the style to None); then, with the Ellipse tool (L), draw a series of ovals that align at the center. (To help you do this quickly and efficiently, make sure that Smart Guides are on (⌘-U/Ctrl-U), use the modifier keys Option/Alt to draw from the center, and use the spacebar key to adjust the position of the oval as you draw.) It's easier to control your use of the Shape Builder tool if each object you'll be working with is a different color. A quick way to do this is to use the Premedia Systems WOW! Colorizer script (install instructions and scripts are on **WOW! ONLINE**). With the script installed, select everything and choose File> Scripts> WOW! Artwork Colorizer. In the script dialog, enable "No colors" to let the script select colors and save the used colors as a swatch group (your colors may differ from the ones shown here). For the next step, you'll be using the Shape Builder tool (Shift-M) to hover over the selected shapes, looking at the highlighted areas to see how they will connect. If the areas that you wish to maintain aren't visible (for instance, the purple oval needs to be on top in order to form the foot of the bowl), then adjust the stacking order by cutting and using Paste in Front/Back. With Pick Color From Artwork enabled (double-click on the Shape Builder tool for options), drag from the red bowl through the upper half of the purple oval. To delete the side pieces of the foot and the top of the bowl, hold down Option/Alt while clicking on them.

Recoloring the bowl with the Grays swatch group; then choosing None for the objects' stroke

Draw Normal, Draw Behind, Draw Inside

2 Completing the composition. You can select each shape (which is now a separate object) and recolor the bowl, and you can even marquee-select all the objects and set the Stroke to None. To quickly place a background behind all objects, select the Draw Behind drawing mode, either by clicking its icon in the Tools panel, or by pressing Shift-D until you see the icon. Draw rectangles for the background objects. (Steuer drew one rectangle filled with the Plaid 2 Pattern, and another with blue.)

Using Draw Inside to constrain the Mop Bristle Brush to a single, selected object, denoted by the dotted corners

3 Finishing touches on the bowl. Select one bowl object (you can only select one at a time), along with the Brush tool, and choose Draw Inside mode (Shift-D), which places dotted corners around the object. Deselect the object and load the Bristle Brush library. Choose a Bristle Brush and paint on the object; Draw Inside constrains your brush strokes within the selected object. When you want to paint another object, you must first exit Draw Inside mode (Shift-D, or double-click with a selection tool). Select the next object and choose Draw Inside again (you can even draw inside a pattern, like the bowl's shadow). When Steuer was done, she wanted to crop the image for the demo she would output to PDF. The easiest way was to resize all the artboards by 72% using the Premedia Systems WOW! Artboard Resizer. This script (also on **WOW! ONLINE**) resizes any or all artboards from the center.

Using the WOW! Artboard Resizer by Premedia Systems to resize selected artboards smaller

Easily view drawing modes

You can see (and therefore easily click) each drawing mode if your Tools panel is in double-column view; click the double-arrow in the title bar of the Tools panel to toggle the view between single and double-column. Check your drawing mode if your objects are not going where you intended.

Drawing Inside
Building with Multiple Construction Modes

Advanced Technique

Overview: *Create varying types of shading, texture, and detail within objects using Draw Inside mode; alter basic shapes and prepare them for masking using Shape Builder; add soft shading by using Blob Brush in conjunction with Draw Inside mode.*

The intial blocked-in artwork

When in Draw Inside mode, new objects added into the cliff object are clipped

Building and shading complex artwork in Illustrator can be a daunting task. Thankfully, there are clipping masks. Chris Leavens employs a combination of construction methods in his artwork, "The Gardener," including harnessing the artistic and organizational capabilities of both the Draw Inside mode (to quickly create clipping masks) and the Shape Builder tool (to combine objects).

1 Creating masks using Draw Inside, and beginning to add detail. Using the Pen tool, Leavens blocked in the composition by drawing basic, flat, colored forms. He then selected the large cliff object (which spans the width of the artwork's background) and changed the drawing mode to Draw Inside (Shift-D). Upon entering Draw Inside mode, he deselected by holding ⌘/Ctrl and clicking outside of the artboard and then added form-defining objects within the cliff object using the Pen tool. He freely plotted new anchor points outside the boundaries of the cliffs, allowing the mask created by Draw Inside mode to keep the edges clean and precise. After finishing the cliffs, Leavens repeated the same steps on the other objects, adding both shading and detail.

2 Preparing objects for Draw Inside mode with Shape Builder. To speed up the drawing process, Leavens used the Pen tool and drew the large, swooping tree in multiple pieces. In order to employ the same shading method he used for the other objects, he selected the various overlapping pieces of the tree. He then chose Shape Builder (Shift-M) and click-dragged over the overlapping objects, quickly combining them into one large object, which he shaded using the method mentioned in step one.

In creating the cactus, Leavens used Shape Builder again, but did so subtractively. To make the cactus look broken and parched, he used the Pen tool to draw jagged forms on top of a pair of the cactus's branches. He then selected the cactus and the new, jagged shapes and switched back to the Shape Builder tool. While holding the Option/Alt key, Leavens click-dragged over the area he wanted to remove, leaving behind a couple of newly-broken branches.

3 Adding fast shading with Blob Brush and Draw Inside mode. In order to add soft, feathered shading to the puffy purple foliage on the large tree, Leavens decided to use the Blob Brush. To maintain smooth strokes, he first double-clicked the Blob Brush tool in the Tools panel, and in Options he increased the Fidelity and Smoothness settings. He then predefined a graphic style for the shading by mixing a shade of violet using the Color panel, switching the blend mode to "Multiply" (by clicking Opacity in the Appearance panel), adding a 3-point feather effect (Effect> Stylize> Feather), and saving the style by clicking the New Graphic Style button in the Graphic Styles panel. To ensure that this style would be properly maintained once he selected and began working with it, he disabled "New Art Has Basic Appearance" from the Appearance panel menu. He selected one of the purple foliage objects, changed to Draw Inside mode (Shift-D), deselected, and chose the Blob Brush tool (Shift-B). Before adding the shading, he clicked on the newly-defined Graphic Style swatch. Finally, Leavens brushed in the shading, using the Blob Brush additively to build up larger masses of darker shading, painting solitary strokes where he wanted lighter shading, and using the Eraser tool to make corrections.

2

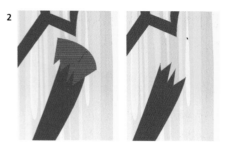

Before and after: using the Shape Builder tool to subtractively alter the cactus branch

3

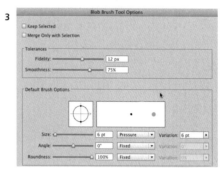

Leavens increased the Fidelity and the Smoothness settings in the Blob Brush Tool Options panel

Final, enlarged version of the composition

COGHILL

George Coghill

Cartoon logo and character artist George Coghill uses the Shape Builder tool to quickly add interior colors to his line art illustrations. In Illustrator, Coghill places a .PSD sketch as a template layer and uses the Pen tool to trace the contours of each pencil-drawn outline with black-filled objects (as opposed to stroked paths). He then selects all the objects and uses the ShapeBuilder tool to fill the main interior (white) areas with color. (If you create outlines using stroked or brushed paths, you'll have to first expand the paths into black-filled objects using Object> Path> Outline Path.) Coghill creates a global color group for his illustration to allow him to later edit a swatch and have it update the art instantly (for help with global colors and color groups see the *Color Transitions* chapter). Double-clicking the Shape Builder tool icon to customize options, he chooses Color Swatches from the Pick Color From drop-down menu, enables Cursor Swatch Preview, and clicks OK. Coghill then selects all objects on that layer (⌘-A/Ctrl-A) and clicks on the new custom color group's folder icon in the Swatches panel. Hovering the Shape Builder tool over the interior areas and using the left and right arrow keys, he cycles through the color swatches he created earlier in his custom color group and chooses a color for each area. The center color swatch preview under the cursor indicates which swatch is the current color. He clicks on the highlighted area to fill it with the color and continues until he has colored all the interior areas. Because he used global colors, if he double-clicks a swatch and edits the color, when he clicks OK, every object filled with that swatch will also update.

4

Expressive Strokes

Expressive Strokes

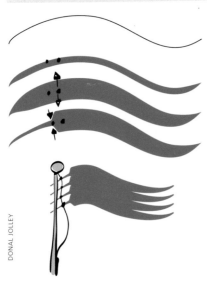

DONAL JOLLEY

Creating discontinuous curves from continuous curves with the Width tool when creating a flag

New features in Illustrator give the user more control over Strokes than ever before. You can manually adjust the contours of a path with the Width tool to emulate calligraphy, and save its form (profile) in the Stroke panel to apply to another path. You can specify precisely where the middle section of an art brush will stretch along a path, and where the ends (such as arrowheads) will be protected from distortion. You have control over how pattern brushes and dashed lines fit around corners. You can use "natural media" bristle brushes to make complex and painterly marks, emulating airbrush, pastel, and wet paint, and using traditional brush shapes like flat or fan. And symbols can be sprayed and manipulated using a special set of Symbolism tools.

WIDTH TOOL AND STROKE PROFILES

The Width tool (Shift-W) varies the width of strokes created with the drawing and geometric shape tools, or art and pattern brushes. The path doesn't have to be selected; hover over it with the Width tool and the path will highlight, along with hollow diamonds indicating existing width points that were either set automatically, such as the end points of a path, or that you have set. As you move your cursor over the path, still hovering, a hollow diamond moves with your cursor, ready to become a width point at whatever location along the path you click on. You can modify paths between two existing width points, and can create either a flowing, *continuous* curve, or a *discontinuous* one with a sharp break between sections.

If width points are spaced apart, the path gradually gets wider or narrower from one point to the next in a continuous curve. If width points are placed on top of each other, you create a sharp break between the two widths, causing the curve to abruptly widen or narrow, much like adding an arrowhead to the path. Modify strokes on either side of the path either by adjusting the stroke weight evenly along the path, or placing more weight on one side of the path than the other. Your custom stroke profile is temporarily stored in the Stroke panel, making it possible to apply the same stroke to as many paths in the document as you wish. An asterisk in the Appearance panel beside Stroke denotes a width profile. You can also save a custom profile as part of a Graphic Style and/or to the Profiles list using the Save icon at the bottom of the Stroke panel list. The Reset icon restores the default width profiles, replacing any custom profiles you've saved, so be careful about choosing to restore the default width profiles. You can modify width points in a variety of ways with the Width tool:

- **To open the Width Point Edit dialog,** double-click on a path or existing width point. Numerically input the stroke weight for each side of the path, and/or choose to have adjoining width points adjusted at the same time.
- **To interactively adjust the width point,** click-drag on a handle to symmetrically adjust the stroke width.
- **To adjust one side of a stroke,** press Option/Alt while dragging on a handle.
- **To adjust or move multiple width points,** Shift-click to select the points (not anchors) you want to alter, then drag on one point or handle to adjust the others with it.
- **To adjust or move all adjoining width points** (up to the next corner anchor point), hold Shift while dragging.
- **To copy selected points,** hold Option/Alt as you drag.
- **To delete a selected width point,** press the Delete key.
- **To deselect a width point,** click on an empty space away from the path, or press the Esc key.

THE EXPANDED STROKE PANEL

The Stroke panel controls settings for the many different types of strokes, from how they align to the path of an object to how they join at corners. Dashed lines, end caps, and arrowheads all are part of the Stroke panel, as well as stored width profiles, from a normal even width to a fully calligraphic profile. Here you can also customize and save your carefully crafted stroke profiles after creating a

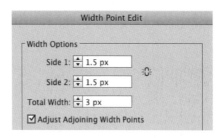

To numerically adjust one or more selected width points, double-click on one to open the dialog and make adjustments; select just one point before entering the dialog if you want to enable Adjust Adjoining Width Points

---

Width points vs. anchor points

It's difficult to distinguish between the shape of Width points and normal points. The tip says "path" when you hover over a Width point, while the tip for other points says "anchor."

(Top) The starting stroke with width points already added and adjusted; (middle) the width point at the right end adjusted again to make the end wider and Adjust Adjoining Width Points disabled; (bottom) with Adjust Adjoining Width Points enabled when adjusting the same original right-end width point—starting stroke shown for clarity in red on top of both adjusted strokes

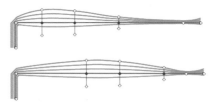

Shift-selecting just some contiguous (shown) or non-contiguous (not shown) width points on a pattern brushstroke, releasing Shift, then moving them all at once

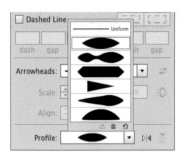

With the Stroke panel width profiles list, save or delete one custom width profile at a time (resetting defaults removes all custom width profiles)

A path shown first in Outline, then in Preview with a Miter join, Round join, and Bevel join

SALLY COX

(Top) When Dashes with round caps are added to art by Sally Cox, the default option in the Stroke panel preserves dash size but are unevenly distributed around the frame; (bottom) changing the option to Align to corners dash size varies the size of dashes but evens spacing

variable-width stroke, and preview how your path joins to an arrowhead. Adjust the way dashes follow a path, and scale arrowheads to suit.

Making ends meet

Sometimes stroked lines seem to match up perfectly when viewed in Outline mode, but they visibly overlap in Preview mode. You can solve this problem by selecting one of the three end cap styles in the Strokes panel. The default Butt cap causes your path to stop at the end anchor point and is essential for creating exact placement of one path against another. The Round cap is especially good for softening the effect of single line segments. The Projecting cap extends lines and dashes at half the stroke weight beyond the end anchor point. Cap styles also affect the shape of dashed lines.

Corners have joins that serve a similar purpose to end caps. The Join style in the Stroke panel determines the shape of a stroke at its corner points; the inside of the corner is always angled. The default Miter join creates a pointy corner, with the length of the point determined by the width of the stroke, the angle of the corner (narrow angles create longer points), and the Miter limit setting on the Stroke panel. The default Miter join (with a miter limit of 10x) usually looks fine, but can range from 1x (which is always blunt) to 500x. The Round join creates a rounded outside corner with a radius of half the stroke width. The Bevel join creates a squared-off outside corner, equivalent to a Miter join with the miter limit set to 1x.

Dashes behave like short lines, and therefore have both end caps and, potentially, corner joins. End caps work with dashes exactly as they do with the ends of paths—each dash is treated as a very short path. However, if a dashed path goes around the corner, it can make that turn in one of two ways: The spacing between the dashes can be precise and constant, so the dash won't necessarily bend around a corner, or even reach to it, or you can click the "Aligns dashes to corners and path ends, adjusting lengths to fit" icon. Dashes won't be precisely spaced, but will look tidy at the corners. The command affects dash spacing for other shapes, from circles to stars, as well.

One more "end" to a path is an arrowhead, and the Stroke panel now offers a choice of both the types of arrowheads and how they are affixed to the ends of the paths. Click on the Arrowheads pop-up list to choose to attach an arrow or feather to the start or end of the path. You can then scale it proportionally or disproportionally, reverse the start and end, or align the arrowhead so that either the tip or the end of the arrow meets the end of the path. To remove an arrowhead (or feather), choose None from the list. You can add custom arrowheads to the list without removing any of the default arrowheads (you'd have to reinstall Illustrator to make them available again if you removed them). Both dash alignment options and arrowheads can be modified again at any time.

BRUSHES

Illustrator's calligraphic, art, scatter, bristle, and pattern brushes can mimic traditional art tools, create photorealistic imagery, or provide pattern and texture to your art. You can either create brushstrokes with the Paintbrush tool, or you can apply a brush to a previously drawn path.

Calligraphic brushes create strokes that mimic real-world calligraphy pens, brushes, or felt pens. You can define a degree of variation for the size, roundness, and angle of each "nib." You can also set each of these attributes to respond to a graphics tablet and stylus (like the Wacom) with a variety of different pen characteristics (with a mouse, you can only use Fixed or Random).

Art brushes consist of one or more pieces of artwork that get fitted to the path you create with them. You can use art brushes to imitate traditional painting media, such as drippy ink pens, textured charcoal, spatter brushes, dry brushes, watercolors, and more. Or an art brush can represent real-world objects, such as a petal, a leaf, or a ribbon, a flower, decorative flourish, or train. You can modify art brushes and their strokes using a number of different parameters, including variables affected by pressure using

Creating custom arrowheads

Illustrator Help provides directions for locating the Arrowheads file on your computer. The file contains instructions for customizing and saving arrowheads without overwriting the original file.

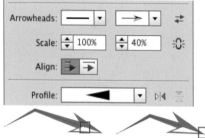

Using the Arrowheads section of the Stroke panel to align the arrowhead so the tail of the arrowhead joins the end of the path with the head extending beyond (left and as shown in the dialog), or to align the arrowhead so the tip of the arrowhead joins the end of the path (right)

Deleting arrowhead presets

To make custom arrowheads, be sure to modify only the file holding the default presets. If you delete any arrowheads in that file, you'll have to reinstall Illustrator to get them back again.

Graphics tablets & brushes

Bristle brushes, which mimic painter's brushes, respond to hand gestures when using a tablet and pen, such as the Wacom. The "Wacom 6D Art" or "Art" pens also easily retain the appearance of the individual bristles, while allowing full rotation to create unique strokes that imitate real brushes. A mouse is much more limited.

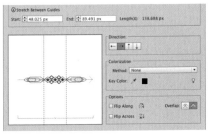

Using the Width tool to alter an Art brushstroke modified by Stretch Between Guides option

The Scatter Brush dialog varies how the artwork is scattered along a path

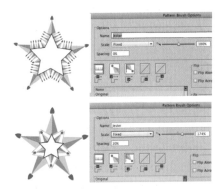

Altering Pattern Scale and Spacing to create a very different look to the brush

a Wacom tablet and stylus). Art brush marks can be made to scale proportionately to fit the length of your path, or stretched to fit. You can also scale your brush non-proportionally by restricting the area of the art brush that can stretch, using two guides to create a segmented brush (choose Stretch Between Guides for the Scale option). Either or both ends of the brush are then protected from being stretched, and the middle portion is stretched to fill in the remaining length. This allows you to stretch the stem of a rose, for instance, without stretching the blossom itself. You can further modify an art brush with colorization methods, such as choosing to vary a key color by tint or hue. Modify the way the art brush follows a path by flipping its direction, and use the Overlap option to determine whether or not to allow it to overlap itself when turning a corner. You can also use the Width tool to modify an art brush.

Use scatter brushes to scatter copies of artwork along the path you create with them: flowers in a field, bees in the air, stars in the sky. The size of the objects, their spacing, how far they scatter from the path, and their rotation can be set to a Fixed or Random amount or, with a graphics tablet, can vary according to characteristics such as pressure or tilt. You can also align the rotation of the scattered objects to the direction of the path, or to the edges of the page. Change the method of colorization as you would with a calligraphic or pattern brush.

Use pattern brushes to paint patterns along a path. To use a pattern brush, first define the tiles that will make up your pattern. For example, a train has an engine, rail cars, links, and a caboose. Each of these constitutes a tile where you have the start of the path, the middle (the side tile), the tiles that turn either an inside or outside corner, and the end of the path. The tiles must be made as individual art and stored in the Swatches panel before you can make your pattern brush. Afterwards, however, you can delete them from Swatches. In the Pattern Brush Options dialog, select a tile, then click on the swatch name below the tiles that you want assigned to that tile. You can customize settings for how the tiles fit to, or flip along, the path, and to alter their color. You can also vary the appearance of the pattern brush, how it fills sharp angles (by altering the Scale in both Fixed parameters and those affected by tablet features), and the spacing between tiles.

Bristle brushes emulate traditional paint brushes, showing both the texture of the bristles and the tip shape, which can be round, flat, fan-shaped, etc. To create a bristle brush, select it as the New brush type and, in the Bristle Brush Options dialog, choose a tip shape. From there, modify the brush's bristle length, density, and thickness; whether or not the bristles are stiff or soft; and how opaquely it applies the paint. By default, these brushes use a Paint Opacity of less than 100%, so you'll see some opacity in your strokes even when you have set Opacity in the Control panel to 100% opaque. Because calculating transparency for printing often takes a long time, a dialog warns that if you have more than 30 bristle brushstrokes, you may want to select some or all of the bristle brushstrokes and choose Object> Rasterize to set raster settings for them before you attempt to print.

Working with brushes
The following describes functional features that apply to most or all brushes:

- **To create art, scatter, and pattern brushes,** create the artwork for them from fairly basic artwork, including compound shapes, blends, groups, and some live effects such as Distort & Transform or Warp. You *can't* create brushes from art that uses gradients, mesh objects, raster art, and advanced live effects such as Drop Shadow or 3D.
- **To modify the art that makes up a brush,** drag it out of the Brushes panel, edit the object, then drag it back into the Brushes panel. Use the Option/Alt key as you drag to replace the original art with the new art.
- **To set application-level preferences for all brushes,** double-click the Paintbrush tool. (The new preferences will apply to work you do with the brushes going forward, but won't change existing work.)

Bristle brushes are a good candidate for the Draw Inside mode (see the *Rethinking Construction* chapter). You can add the bristle texture to a vector shape while retaining some or all of the original color; Draw Inside also constrains the strokes inside the object, ensuring stray bristle marks are automatically masked.

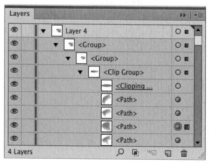

Using a bristle brush (the Footprint brush showing) to draw inside a selected path, and the Layers panel showing the Clipping Paths created by Draw Inside

Because it's easy to edit symbols, using symbols can be preferable to using scatter brushes, whose attributes will be applied to the whole set. The ability to delete individual symbols within a set is another potential advantage over scattering objects with a brushstroke, which must be expanded before individual objects can be deleted from it.

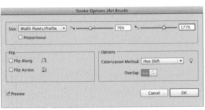

Modifying based on Width Points using Options of Selected Object for an Art Brush that has already been modified with the Width tool

Bristle brush opacity

Set bristle brush opacity:

- In bristle brush Options under Paint Opacity.
- With the Paintbrush tool active, the 1-0 keys change the opacity for selected strokes, or, with no strokes selected, the setting affects the next brushstroke.
- With the Opacity slider in the Appearance or Control panels.

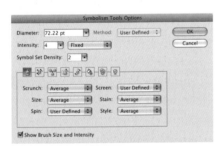

Symbolism Tools Options dialog

Quick access to Symbol features on the Control panel when a symbol object is selected in the artwork; the Reset button not grayed out indicates the symbol has been transformed and the Replace pop-up gives immediate access to the loaded Symbols library

- **To modify the properties of a single brushstroke,** select it, then choose Options of Selected Object in the Brush panel's menu. If you've used the Width tool to modify the stroke, your options include using the width points to calculate the profile for your next strokes.
- **To choose how to apply modifications** to existing brushstrokes, in the brush's Options dialog choose Leave Strokes to create a duplicate brush, or Apply to Strokes to modify every use of the brush in the document.
- **When Keep Selected and Edit Selected Paths are both enabled,** the last drawn path stays selected; drawing a new path close to the selected path will redraw that path. Disabling either of these options will allow you to draw multiple brushstrokes near each other, instead of redrawing the last drawn path.

SYMBOLS

Working with symbols in Illustrator saves file size (since objects converted to symbols aren't duplicated in the file), provides consistency whenever the same artwork needs to be used more than once, and makes it easy to update objects in your artwork simply by editing the symbol to change it wherever it has been used. Symbols can be made from almost any art you create in Illustrator. The only exceptions are a few kinds of complex groups, such as groups of graphs, and placed art (which must be *embedded*, not linked). Symbols are edited and stored using the Symbols and Control panels, and are manipulated like other objects, or with the Symbolism tools:

- **To store selected artwork as a symbol,** drag it into the Symbols panel (or click on the New Symbol icon in the panel). Use the Libraries Menu icon to save the current symbols to a new library, or to load other libraries.
- **To add a single instance of a symbol to your document,** drag it into your document or, with it selected, click on the Place Symbol Instance icon. Drag a symbol instance into your document as often as you like, but you can only use the Place Symbol Instance icon once. It's most useful for modifying the symbol (see below).

- **To modify a symbol without modifying the original symbol** in the Symbols panel, click either the Break Link button in the Control panel or the "Break Link to Symbol" icon in the Symbols panel.
- **To modify a symbol and all instances of it** already in the document, place or drag it into your document, then click on the Edit Symbol button in the Control panel. Your symbol will be placed in isolation mode. After you modify it and exit isolation mode, all instances of the symbol, including the symbol in the Symbols panel, are updated.
- **To modify a symbol in the Symbols panel when you have already broken the link,** Option/Alt-drag the modified symbol on top of the symbol in the Symbols panel. This will replace the original symbol with the modified artwork and update all instances of the original symbol.
- **To restore a symbol to its original size and orientation** after transforming it, click the Reset button in the Control panel.
- **To quickly find all instances of a symbol** in your artwork, select the symbol either in the Symbols panel or in your artwork and choose Select All Instances from the Symbol panel's menu.
- **To replace one symbol with another without opening the Symbols panel,** select the symbol in the artwork and click on the Replace list arrow in the Control panel. A miniature Symbols panel opens, which allows you to swap out symbols.
- **To add a sublayer to a symbol's artwork,** in isolation mode click on the topmost layer with the symbol's name, and then click on the New Sublayer icon. (You can't add sublayers to a <Group> or <path>.)
- **To add a new layer above a group or path sublayer at the same hierarchy level,** target the layer, then Option-click/Alt-click on the New Layer icon. If the layer remains a normal layer (not a group or a path), you can continue to add new layers at that level merely by clicking on the New Layer icon.

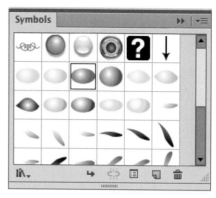

Storing symbols in the Symbols panel, with access to other symbol libraries, editing commands, and the Symbol Options dialog

Transforming symbols

When creating symbols, Illustrator has two features that are important whenever a symbol might be scaled or transformed any other way: If you use Flash, these features also affect symbols taken into Flash for animating:

- Apply 9-slice scaling to symbols in Illustrator. Doing so reduces distortion when transforming objects, especially noticeable with elements such as buttons that have custom corners. All nine areas of the symbol can be scaled independently.
- Assign a Registration point to the symbol in Illustrator. The point appears as a crosshair both in Symbol Edit Mode and when the symbol is selected in normal mode. Use the Registration point to affect any transformations applied inside Illustrator.

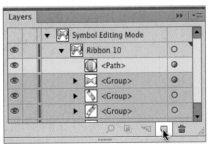

Create New Layer

Adding a new layer at the same level as a path sublayer by Option-clicking/Alt-clicking on the Create New Layer icon

LISA JACKMORE

Artwork by Lisa Jackmore created with symbols

Using the Symbolism tools to modify the original set (top) for greater variety (bottom)

Working with the Symbolism tools

There are eight different Symbolism tools. Use the Symbol Sprayer tool to spray selected symbols onto your document, creating a symbol set. You can't select individual instances inside a set with any of the selection tools. Instead, modify them with any of the other Symbol tools. To display a ring of tools in your document in order to select a new one, press Control-Option/Ctrl-Alt while clicking and holding in an empty spot in your document, then drag to a new icon before releasing your mouse. (In the CS6 1.0 release, the HUD doesn't appear, but you can still see the Symbolism icons for the tools change in the Tools panel.) Add symbols to a selected set by selecting a symbol in the Symbols panel—the symbol can be the same as or different from the symbols already present in the instance set—and spray. To add or modify symbols in a set, make sure you've selected *both* the set and the corresponding symbol(s) in the Symbols panel that you want to affect. The Symbolism tools will only affect those symbols in a selected set that are also selected in the Symbols panel, thus making it easy to modify just one of the symbols in a mixed set.

To adjust the properties of the Symbolism tools, double-click on one to open Symbolism Tools Options. Vary the diameter (the range over which the tool operates), the rate at which it applies a change, and the density with which it operates on a set. If you're using the default Average mode, your new symbol instances can inherit attributes (size, rotation, transparency, style) from nearby symbols in the same instance set. For example, if nearby symbols are 50% opaque, symbols added to the set will also be 50% opaque. You can also change the default Average mode to User Defined or Random. (See *Illustrator Help* for more information about choosing User Defined.)

To remove symbols from an existing instance set, use the Symbol Sprayer tool with the Option/Alt key, and click on an instance to delete it (or click-drag your cursor over multiple instances—they're deleted when you lift your cursor).

WATERCOLOR STROKE 03

BRISTLE BRUSH STIPPLER

WATERCOLOR STROKE 06

BRISTLE BRUSH MOP
(NOTE STROKE POSITION TO STYLUS ANGLE)

GRUNGE BRUSHES 03

HAND DRAWN BRUSHES 01
(OVERPRINT)

SPIKEY

HAND DRAWN BRUSHES 06

ARTISTIC_CHALKCHARCOALPENCIL
SCRIBBLE

give me
jellybeans

JOLLEY

Donal Jolley

This sampler by Donal Jolley, using his 6D Art Pen, demonstrates the tremendous variety you get from brushes that ship with Illustrator. When you add a Wacom pressure-sensitive pen and tablet to these out-of-the-box brushes, you can introduce even more variety into your strokes; the standard Grip Pen registers pressure, tilt, and bearing, and the optional, more sensitive Art Pens (6D Art for Intuos3, or Art Pen for Intuos4) add the ability to vary each stroke with rotation. The bristle brush responds particularly well to the Art Pens, adding a new dimension to painting. You can manually transform some of your strokes (but not those made with the calligraphic, scatter, or bristle brushes), by modifying its profile with the Width tool (such as Spikey above), and then saving that profile to apply to other strokes.

Stroke Variance
Creating Dynamic Variable-Width Strokes

Overview: *Place sketch and trace with Pen tool; modify strokes with Width tool; save width profile and apply to other strokes.*

1

The original sketch

Traced sketch

2

Width tool (Shift-W) adjusting middle of stroke

PUTNAM

Ryan Putnam creates many character illustrations for websites, branding projects, and more. Putnam now uses the Width tool to add depth and variance in the strokes of the illustrations. Moreover, he can save the stroke adjustments to Profiles in the Stroke panel to easily apply to other strokes in current and future projects.

1 Placing a sketch template and tracing with Pen tool. Putnam first created a character sketch in Photoshop, chose File> Place in Illustrator, enabled Template, and clicked OK. Putnam then traced basic paths of the sketch with the Pen tool in the layer above.

2 Adjusting strokes with the Width tool. Putnam wanted his strokes to have some variance compared to the uniform strokes created by the Pen tool. He created two distinct stroke widths to use on the majority of the paths in the illustration. For the first stroke adjustment, Putnam created a stroke with a thicker middle and tapered ends. To do this, he used the Width tool to click in the middle of the desired path and drag a width point to the desired width. For the second custom width, Putnam created a stroke with a thicker end and a tapered end. Again, he used the Width tool, but this time clicked on the far right side of the desired path and dragged a width point to the desired width.

Width tool (Shift-W) adjusting end of stroke

If you like to be precise with your adjustments, you can double-click a width point to open the Width Point Edit dialog, allowing you to numerically adjust the width of the stroke in the Side 1, Side 2, and Total Width fields.

3 Saving stroke profiles and applying to other paths.
Instead of adjusting every path in the illustration to match the two custom widths he created with the Width tool, Putnam saved time and ensured consistency by saving his two custom stroke profiles. To save each profile, he selected the modified stroke and clicked the Add to Profiles icon in the Stroke panel. With both of his strokes saved as custom profiles, Putnam could select a uniform stroke, click the saved Variable Width Profile at the bottom of the Stroke panel, and select the saved profile from the drop-down list. These custom profiles will then be available in other new Illustrator files.

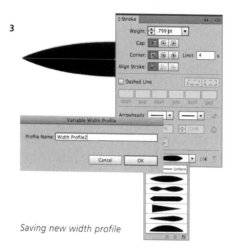

Saving new width profile

After Putnam applied the custom profile to all the desired paths, he utilized specific keyboard commands with the Width tool to further adjust individual paths. For example, holding down the Option/Alt key when dragging width points creates non-uniform widths, the Delete key deletes selected width points, and holding the Shift key while dragging adjusts multiple width points. Other keyboard modifiers with the Width tool include holding down Option/Alt while dragging a width point to copy the width point, holding down Option-Shift/Alt-Shift while dragging to copy and move all the points along a path, Shift-clicking to select multiple width points, and using the Esc key to deselect a width point.

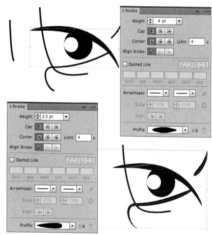

Applying a saved width profile

4 Applying finishing touches. Putnam added additional elements as needed. For instance, he create simple shapes with the Pen tool and filled them with grayscale colors.

Adjusting a path with Width tool and keyboard commands

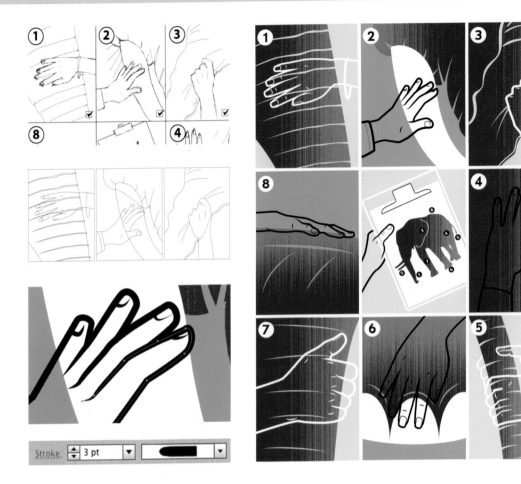

MCKIBILLO

MCKIBILLO (AKA Josh McKible)

For a commissioned piece on different management styles, MCKIBILLO used the parable of the Blind Men and the Elephant as the basis for his illustration. He began with a sketch created in Alias SketchBook Pro that he traced in Illustrator using the Pen tool. While the image was in progress, he used a fine, uniform line, bright Magenta so it wouldn't visually disappear. When it came to finessing his linework, MCKIBILLO frequently applied a couple of the default width profiles from the Profile pop-up in the the Stroke Panel to create many of the lines. If he needed even more control over the shape of his strokes, however, he used the Width tool to modify both width and anchor placement along a curve. In this illustration, he manually delineated the hands and fingernails with the Width tool. Most of his strokes used a rounded cap, but he occasionally varied the cap according to the way the lines joined. Using the Width tool, and then saving and reusing profiles (from Profile in the Stroke panel), MCKIBILLO was able to quickly develop a style that appears completely hand-drawn, yet has the advantage of remaining easily edited throughout the course of a project.

JOLLEY

Donal Jolley

To create his "Rubber Ducky," Donal Jolley began by drawing the basic lines with the Pencil tool. Then with the Width tool, he adjusted each stroke so it curved gently and came to a sharp angle at the end (his custom profiles are shown above). To finalize the line work, he used the Scissors and Eraser tools to clean up the extra anchor points that sometimes occur at the end of brushstrokes. He then locked his line work layer and created a new layer at the bottom, into which he painted the colors. He works very intuitively with the brushes, saying, "Usually I will open a brush category, choose a brush, and then make a stroke with a sharp angle and a gentle curve to see how it behaves with the color I want to use. Because many of the strokes have a certain transparent quality that does not truly mix with the underlying color (or white), I make sure of the stroke before I employ it. I check for opacity, form, and how it 'bends,' because many brushes tend to give unpredictable results at sharper angles." Then, using his chosen default bristle and calligraphic brushes, Jolley painted the ducky's colors, varying pressure and angles with his Wacom Intuos tablet and 6D Art Pen.

JACKMORE

Lisa Jackmore

For drawings as fluid as this floral design, Lisa Jackmore finds that initially drawing with the Paintbrush tool and a calligraphic brush is the most natural and intuitive way to begin. However, when she wants to create specific variations to the strokes, she then converts the brushstrokes to Basic stroked paths, so she can use the Width tool (you can't use the Width tool on calligraphic brushstrokes). To do this, she clicked on the Basic Brush in the Brushes panel (the basic stroke version is shown directly above). Jackmore then selected the Width tool (Shift-W) and clicked on the stroke itself, dragging the handle outwards to evenly widen the path. To make adjustments to one side, she held the Option/Alt key while dragging the handle. To make even further variations to the strokes, Jackmore clicked on the stroke, added new

width points, and adjusted them. She saved several profiles by selecting each modified stroke, then from the Variable Width Profile menu in the Control panel, clicking on the Add to Profile button, naming it, and clicking OK. To finish the design, she selected each of the remaining paths, applied one of her saved width profiles from the Control panel, and then increased the stroke weight on all of the paths. Jackmore's background includes a gradient mesh object and a few bristle brush-strokes drawn with the Paintbrush tool.

PAIDRICK

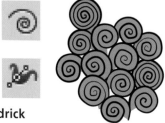

Ann Paidrick

For Ann Paidrick, the Width tool was key to creating the hand-drawn look for this pair of spiral patterns. Starting with the Spiral tool (hidden under the Line tool), she used the up and down arrow keys to vary the wind of each spiral as she drew. To begin with she chose an orange fill and black stroke. Clicking <u>Stroke</u> in the Control panel, she chose the Round Cap, and for each spiral she set a stroke weight between 5 and 8 pts. Next she used the Width tool on each spiral to thicken some areas while narrowing others. For final tweaks to the paths, she used the Direct Selection tool to move anchor points and direction lines just enough to create a hand-drawn feel. After assembling a cluster of spirals together, she entered Pattern Edit Mode (PEM), where she finished arranging the elements until the pattern worked as a whole. After saving the orange and black pattern, she remained in PEM, where she created and then saved the version at top by changing spiral fill and stroke colors, and putting a rectangle with a purple fill beneath the spirals (for more about using PEM see the *Mastering Complexity* chapter).

JACKMORE

Lisa Jackmore

To make interesting brushstrokes, Lisa Jackmore used variations of a few calligraphic and bristle brushes, painted using a Wacom Intuos4 tablet and Art Pen. In creating the variations for the brushes, Jackmore changed the parameters for Pressure, Rotation, and Tilt. When she wanted to customize a brush, she double-clicked the brush, and made changes to the options. For the tree outline, she used a 3-pt Flat calligraphic brush, set the Diameter to Pressure (with a 2-pt variation), Roundness to Tilt (34°, with a variation of 15°), and set the Angle to Rotation (with a 125° variation). For the long sweeping lines of the tree, she found the combination of using Rotation and a chisel tip of the Art Pen worked the best to vary the brushstroke. As she drew, she slightly rotated and tilted the pen and created variations in her stroke. To create

an irregular ink-like appearance in the words, she used a 1-pt Round calligraphic brush, and set the Angle to 30° (fixed), Roundness to Tilt (60°, with a 29% variation). Jackmore used several other variations of calligraphic brushes to draw the suitcases and background pattern. To make the pattern, she drew several paths with a customized calligraphic brush, grouped the brushstrokes, and dragged the pattern tile to the Swatches panel. After she drew all of the black brushstrokes, she colored the illustration with a gradient mesh object for the background, and used variations of the Fan, Round Blunt, and Round Point bristle brushes for other areas, such as the bird, suitcases, and shadows. Finally, Jackmore used the rectangle tool to make a frame, then applied a Charcoal brush to the stroke.

AHUJA

Anil Ahuja/Adobe Systems

Adobe's Product Specialist Anil Ahuja used a range of tools and techniques to create his dragonfly, and relied upon transparency methods to obtain color accuracy to closely match his reference photo. In his three levels of objects used to create the wings (shown separately at right), this is readily apparent. After drawing the wing's black-stroked vein structure with artistic calligraphic brushes of various sizes and shapes, he selected the paths and chose Object> Expand (to outline the strokes), then Merge (to create a compound path object). In the Appearance panel he clicked Opacity, and changed the Blending Mode to Darken to reduce the opacity, giving the wing its realistic brown color. With the brown and blue gradient mesh objects (residing on a layer beneath the vein structure), Ahuja used the Direct Selection tool to select individual mesh points to decrease

the opacity (ranging from 0–90%). To make the wings appear translucent instead of just transparent, Ahuja used the Pen tool to draw an outline copy of the wings which he put on a layer below the veined structure and the mesh. He filled the outline with a color similar to the background and reduced the opacity to 30%. To complete the illustration, Ahuja created a shadow on a layer between the dragonfly and the gradient mesh background. To make the shadow, he pasted a copy of the wing outline and with the Pen tool added an outline of the body. He then reduced the opacity of the shadow object to 53% and changed the Blending Mode to Darken.

Brushes & Washes

Drawing with Naturalistic Pen, Ink, Wash

Overview: *Start with a placed image as a template; create a custom calligraphic brush; create variations on the brush to apply to strokes; add a wash layer below the ink layer.*

STEUER

It's easy to create spontaneous painterly and calligraphic marks in Illustrator—perhaps with more flexibility than in many pixel-based programs. Sharon Steuer drew this sketch of Honfleur, France, using a Wacom tablet, her Art Pen for the Intuos4, and two different Illustrator brushes. She customized a brush for the thin, dark strokes and used a built-in brush for the underlying gray washes.

1

(Top) The original photo; (bottom) brushstrokes drawn over the dimmed template photo

1 Placing artwork as a template. If you want to use a sketch or photo as a reference as you draw into layers above, set it up as a non-printing template layer. For her template image, Steuer scanned a small photo of Honfleur and saved it as a JPG, then opened it in Illustrator. To place an image as a template, choose File> Place, enable the Template option, and click the Place button. If the image imports at too large a size, unlock the layer, select the image (holding down Option-Shift/Alt-Shift keys to resize proportionally from the center), and drag on a corner of the bounding box until the image is the size you want, then lock the layer again. Illustrator automatically dims images on your template layer to 50%, but you can double-click the layer icon to adjust this and other settings in Layer Options. Toggle between hiding and showing the template layer using ⌘-Shift-W/Ctrl-Shift-W, or toggle the visibility icon in the Layers panel.

2 Customizing a calligraphic brush. In order to sketch freely and with accurate detail, you'll need to adjust the default Paintbrush tool settings. Double-click the Paintbrush tool to open Paintbrush Tool Options. Drag the Fidelity and Smoothness sliders all the way to the left so that Illustrator records your strokes precisely. Disable "Fill new brush strokes," and if you want to be able to quickly draw strokes that overlap, disable Keep Selected.

To create a custom calligraphic brush, click the New Brush icon and select Calligraphic Brush. For this piece, Steuer chose the following settings: Angle=90°/Fixed; Roundness=10%/Fixed; Diameter=4 pt/Pressure/Variation=4 pt. If you have one of the newer Wacom Art Pens, try varying the Diameter with Rotation instead of Pressure, then let the pen barrel rotate between your fingers naturally as you draw. (If you don't have a pressure-sensitive tablet, only Random will have any effect on varying your stroke.) To create a variation of a brush, duplicate it by dragging it to the New Brush icon, then double-click the copy to edit it. If you create a variety of brushes—adding minor variances in Angle, Roundness, and Diameter—you can enhance the hand-drawn appearance of your ink drawing by selecting a brushed path and choosing a new brush for it.

3 Adding a wash. For this piece, Steuer added depth by introducing gray washes underneath the dark brush-strokes. To easily edit the wash strokes without affecting the dark ink strokes, create a new layer, and draw your wash strokes into this layer between the ink and template layers. To avoid altering other layers while you brush in the washes, you may want to lock all the other layers. To toggle between locking all layers except the wash layer, and unlocking all layers at once, including the wash layer, Option-click/Alt-click the wash layer's Lock icon.

For the wash, select a light color. Steuer used the Dry Ink 2 brush from the Artistic_Ink brush library (Swatch Libraries menu). In the Layers panel, click the wash layer to make it the current drawing layer, and paint away.

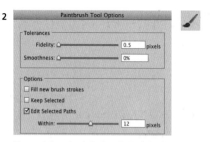

Customizing the Paintbrush Tool Options

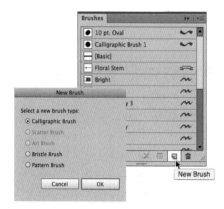

Creating a new calligraphic brush

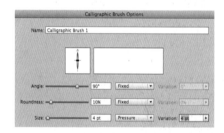

Angle, Roundness, and Size can be set to a variety of Pen characteristics (including Rotation, Tilt, Bearing), but you can only make use of these features if your tablet, and Art Pen, support them

The final ink drawing after adding a couple of people not in the original photo, and before adding the wash

WINKEL

MORRISON

PERNAL

DZIENIS

LOUKOUMIS

MARTIN

Stephen Klema's Students:
Jillian Winkel, Stephanie Pernal,
Amber Loukoumis, Jeffrey Martin,
Nicole Dzienis, Tamara Morrison
(clockwise from upper left)

As a class assignment, Professor Stephen Klema challenged his students to create expressive graphic illustrations of organic forms. The students of Tunxis Community College used a variety of default brushes from the brushes panel. They included both calligraphic and art brushes. Before drawing, the students double-clicked the Paintbrush tool and adjusted the Paintbrush tool preferences. They dragged the Fidelity and Smoothness sliders to the desired positions. The sliders moved farther to the left had more accurate brushstrokes, while those moved to the right were smoother. The "Fill New Brush Strokes" and "Keep Selected" options were disabled to allow multiple brush-strokes to be drawn near each other without redrawing the last path. Using a pressure-sensitive tablet, the students drew varying widths and angles of brushstrokes, many either on top of or close to one another, for a spontaneous, expressive look. Extra points within the brush-strokes were deleted using the Smooth tool or the Delete Anchor Point tool.

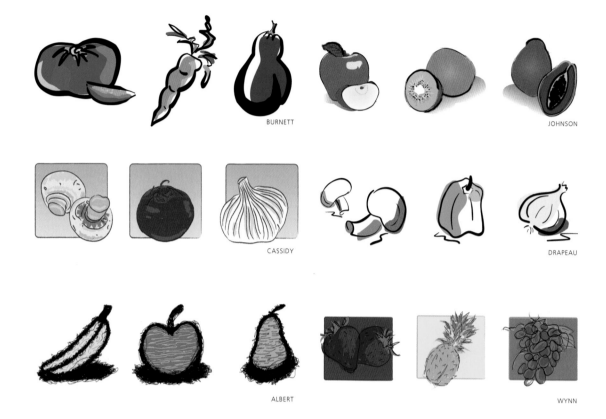

BURNETT

JOHNSON

CASSIDY

DRAPEAU

ALBERT

WYNN

Stephen Klema's Students:
Cinthia A. Burnett, James Cassidy,
Kenneth Albert, Jamal Wynn,
Suzanne Drapeau, Mahalia Johnson
(clockwise from upper left)

Using the same techniques described on the previous page, additional student creations are shown above. In some of these illustrations, artists applied art and calligraphic brushes to paths drawn with the Pencil or Pen tools, by selecting the path, and then choosing a brush from the Brushes panel. You can find many additional brushes in the Brushes library. To access

DRAPEAU

more art brushes, click on the Brush Libraries Menu icon found in the lower left corner of the Brushes panel. Select Open Brush Library> Artistic, then select the brushes you want to add to the Brushes panel. Find more artwork from Professor Klema's students on his website at: www.StephenKlema.com/wow.

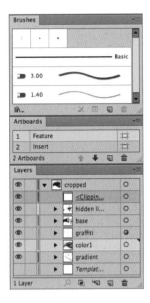

Sharon Steuer

To create this illustration for her "Good Food in the Microhood" UntappedCities.com posting, Sharon Steuer began in Photoshop, where she collaged photos she'd taken from different vantage points into one imaginary citiscape. After placing it as a JPG template in Illustrator, from another image, she copied objects styled with her custom calligraphic brushes and pasted the objects into her new file, which added the custom brushes to her current Brushes panel. She then deleted the objects and used these brushes to paint her black line drawing. In a new layer she added color using default bristle brushes and a pressure-sensitive Wacom tablet and Art Pen. To easily switch between brushes, colors, and layers, she started by selecting a path styled similarly to the one she wanted to make, then deselected (⌘-Shift-A/Ctrl-Shift-A). To draw a new, blue, wide transparent bristle brush stroke on the Color layer, she selected a blue-wide stroke on the Color layer, then deselected, and drew. Next, to draw a new calligraphic path on

the lines layer, she selected then deselected one of those. With Edit Selected enabled in Brush Options, if she kept a brush stroke selected, she could redraw the path (instead of draw a new one). After adding a few more detail layers, she created an "unwanted lines layer" and hid it, so she could then select and move unwanted lines to that hidden layer. Lastly she created two overlapping artboards: one to frame the crop when featured on the website front page, and the other sized for insertion within the post. To see this posting, which also contains a link to an article on CreativePro.com detailing how this image was created, go to UntappedCities.com and enter "CreativePro" in the search field.

Sharon Steuer

For her UntappedCities.com "Good Food in the Microhood" article on San Francisco's Tenderloin restaurants, Sharon Steuer used Photoshop to stretch, crop, and color-correct her photo of the Vietnamese soup called "phở." She placed the photo in Illustrator off the artboard (as a reference), and used the Pen tool to draw a few closed paths (filled with gradients). Locking that first layer with the objects and photo, she created additional layers, where she painted her image using two bristle brushes at default settings (one Angle and one Mop), and a custom calligraphic brush. As the image progressed

Steuer decided to modify the bowl's shape in ways that would be difficult with traditional or raster tools; she selected the bowl objects, then compressed them vertically using the bounding box. After the article posted, she reworked the image as a fine art piece titled "Vegan phở." Resizing some elements and adding others, she printed a square variation in archival materials. Coating the print with clear acrylic medium, Steuer cut and collaged it onto a 6"x6" cradled board, and then drew and painted on the surface with watercolor pencils. She applied fixative and a UV coating to the finished artwork.

Painting Inside

Painting with Bristle Brushes & Draw Inside

Advanced Technique

Overview: *Start with a placed image as a reference; create a line drawing made of closed paths; use a variety of bristle brushes and the Draw Inside mode to paint the sketch; add a rectangular background with a Charcoal art brush edge.*

1

The closed path line drawing created with the Pencil tool using a 1-pt stroke

Re-enter isolation mode

When you use the Draw Inside mode (bottom of the Tools panel or Shift-D), you're actually creating a special kind of clipping mask. Once you've "drawn inside" an object, double-click it to enter into isolation mode and automatically re-enter Draw Inside mode to add to the object. To remove a "drawn inside" clipping mask from an object and return the object to its original state, select Object> Clipping Mask> Release.

JACKMORE

Draw Inside mode makes it easy to create a painterly illustration with bristle brushes. Lisa Jackmore drew this sketch of an artichoke, using a Wacom tablet with her Art Pen, and several modified brushes. After drawing a simple outline of the artichoke leaves and the stem with the Pencil tool, she utilized the Draw Inside mode and painted with a range of bristle brushes.

1 Drawing the outlines. Jackmore used a snapshot as a basic reference, but if you prefer to draw directly on top of a photo or drawing use File> Place and enable the Template option. In order to create a fluid but accurate line drawing she double-clicked the Pencil tool to set Options for Fidelity to 3 pixels, Smoothness to 3%, and disabling Edit Selected Paths and Keep Selected. Into one layer she created a 1-pt line drawing of the artichoke using the Pencil tool, making sure that she closed each leaf and stem path so that she would later be able to add detail and color the loosely-drawn paths using the Draw Inside mode.

2 Setting up for painting using the bristle brush tool and a tablet. So she'd be able to paint freely and easily, Jackmore planned ahead and first set up her tools. She opened the Brushes panel, the Bristle Brush Library (from the Libraries menu), and the Layers panel. She also set the Wacom tablet's Touch Ring to auto scroll/zoom.

3 Painting with bristle brushes and the Draw Inside mode. To draw into a path, she selected it, pressed Shift-D to choose the Draw Inside mode, then deselected the path (so the bristle brush wouldn't be applied to the outline, but would be constrained within the path). She selected the Paintbrush tool (B), then chose a bristle brush, and a stroke color. When she finished drawing inside a path, Jackmore pressed Shift-D to switch back to Normal drawing mode. She switched between the Paintbrush tool and the Selection tool by holding the ⌘/Ctrl key to temporarily switch to the Selection tool, and toggled between drawing modes with Shift-D. Jackmore created a number of variations of the Round Point, Fan, Round, and Flat Blunt bristle brushes. To customize parameters for opacity, Bristle Length, Stiffness, and Thickness, she'd open Options by pressing the upper switch on the Intuos4 Pen (or double-clicking the Paintbrush tool). With the Paintbrush tool selected, she decreased/increased brush size with the [ ] keys, adjusted opacity with the number keys, and zoomed in or out by turning Wacom tablet's Touch Ring clockwise, or counter–clockwise.

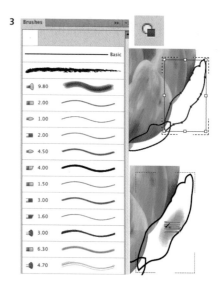

3

Some of the bristle brushes in the Brushes panel; selecting a leaf to Draw Inside; bristle brush icon while drawing inside the leaf

4

4 Organizing layers and finishing details. To reveal the correct part of the leaf as it overlapped another, as she worked, Jackmore moved each leaf into its appropriate layer. As each leaf and stem became painted enough to see the entire path, while in Normal drawing mode she set the stroke to None. To fine-tune the painted area for a particular leaf, she double-clicked on that leaf to automatically enter into isolation mode while already in Draw Inside mode, allowing her to continue to paint and modify brushstrokes. For the background, on a layer below Jackmore drew a rectangle, with the same fill and stroke color and applied a 3-pt Charcoal art brush stroke. To more fully distribute the brushstroke, she slightly rotated a duplicate of the stroke by first clicking the Add New Stroke icon in the Appearance panel (to add a stroke), and from the *fx* menu she chose Distort & Transform> Transform and entered 180° for rotation.

Double-clicking a leaf to enter isolation mode and automatically switch to Draw Inside mode

Detail of the lower right corner of the background before and after adding a second, rotated Charcoal art brush stroke

Painterly Portraits

Painting in Layers with Bristle Brushes

Advanced Technique

Overview: *Place a sketch as a template; draw with customized bristle brushes; continue to paint with custom brushes into separate layers; create frame.*

GEISLER

The template; a distorted Photoshop sketch

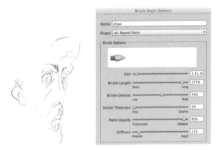

The initial bristle brush sketch made with three variations of a Round Point bristle brush; the Bristle Brush Options

Adding shadows with a wide, fairly opaque bristle brush

The myriad bristle brushes presented Greg Geisler with an infinite variety of brushes to create his expressive painterly portrait, "Blue Mirror." Commissioned by Adobe Systems, you can find this file, and a PDF ReadMe file explaining more about how he made it, on **WOW! ONLINE**.

1 Placing the initial sketch, and customizing Bristle Brush Options. Geisler placed his distorted Photoshop sketch (PSD) as a Template layer. He opened the Bristle Brush Library (from the Brush Libraries Menu in the lower left of the Brushes panel) and clicked on the 1-pt Round bristle brush, which automatically loaded the brush into the Brushes panel. Geisler next duplicated that brush (by dragging its icon to the New Brush icon in the Brushes panel) and then double-clicked on the New Brush icon so he could change several settings in Bristle Brush Options. He made changes to Bristle Thickness, adjusted Paint Opacity and increased the Stiffness, and then named it and clicked OK. On a layer above the template, he used this new brush to create the base sketch for the entire illustration. Geisler kept the Brushes panel and the Bristle Brush Library open throughout the drawing session, so he could continue to duplicate and customize brushes as his drawing progressed. For this layer, he created three different variations of the 1-pt Liner brush.

2 Adding highlights, midtones, and shadows. To make one of the many layers of highlights, such as the strokes in orange, Geisler customized copies of the 3-mm Flat Fan Brush in the Bristle Brushes Library, adjusting Bristle Thickness, Bristle Length, and Paint Opacity. He also drew highlights with a Round bristle brush customized with Pointy variations. Geisler continued to draw in separate layers, focusing in particular on midtones, shadows, highlights, or color for each layer, using variations of the Flat Fan and Round bristle brushes.

3 Working efficiently and further modifying brush characteristics. Geisler's process is very organic in that he continually defines new brushes, and creates new layers, as he draws. He rarely deletes a stroke, preferring to layer new bristle brushstrokes upon others, choosing a more opaque brush to cover the underlying strokes. As he's drawing, he presses the [key to decrease the brush size, and the] key, to increase the bristle size. To vary the opacity, he presses the keys from 1, which is completely transparent, through 0, which is completely opaque. To add texture, as in the blue background shown at right, Geisler modifies the settings to increase the brush stiffness toward Rigid, increase the brush density toward Thick, and then decrease the bristle length.

4 Finishing touches. Geisler created an irregular edged black frame that surrounded the portrait, on a layer between the blue texture and the face. He customized a wide Flat Fan brush to 100% Opacity (100% opaque bristle brushes lose their character within the stroke, but maintain a ragged edge), and then expanded the brushstrokes (Object> Expand) and clicked Unite in the Pathfinder panel, melding the brushstrokes into one frame object. He then used the Pencil tool to draw a few closed paths, delineating the area between the rectangular frame and the head. Marquee-selecting these paths and the frame, he filled them with black, and again clicked Unite in the Pathfinder panel.

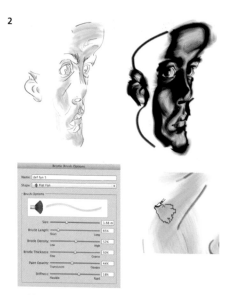

2

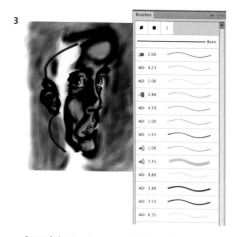

Adding highlights with a Wide Fan Brush, adding shadows; the bristle brush icon that appears when using a pressure sensitive pen

3

Part of the Brushes panel (right), and a later stage of the illustration with blue texture

4

Black frame made with expanded bristle brushstrokes and filled paths shown in Preview mode (detail at left), and Outline mode (right)

GEISLER

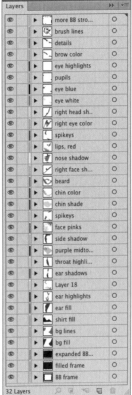

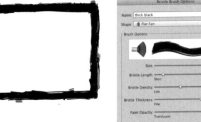

Greg Geisler

Greg Geisler created this graphic self-portrait using a customized calligraphic brush. In the Brushes panel, Geisler double-clicked the default 3-pt round calligraphic brush, and for the Diameter settings, he changed Fixed to Pressure, and set the Variation to 3 pt. Using a Wacom tablet and pressure-sensitive pen, he drew the facial outline, varying the stroke width as he changed his touch (directly above left). To block out planes of color within the face (such as the chin, beard, and cheek),

he used the Pencil tool to draw color-filled irregular paths on separate layers. Each layer contained one of the many defining areas of color (Layers panel shown above right) for highlights, shadows, or texture. To create the frame, Geisler used the same bristle brush, and a technique similar to the one developed in the previous lesson (shown below the artwork). For finishing touches, Geisler drew the bright blue squiggly lines with the Pencil tool.

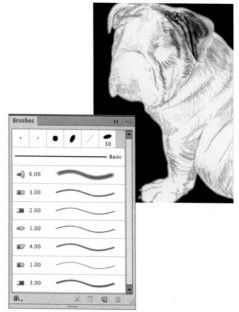

CESAR de OLIVEIRA BALDACCI

Janaína Cesar de Oliveira Baldacci

Based on a photograph taken by Tatiana Bicalho, Baldacci captured the natural undulations of the fur and folds of her pet bulldog with bristle brushes. Baldacci first drew a white outline of the dog (against the black background) with the Pen tool and applied a Gaussian Blur effect. From the Brush Libraries Menu (in the bottom left of the Brushes panel), Baldacci opened the Bristle Brush Library. She then chose a few bristle brushes that had varying characteristics in Paint Opacity, Bristle Stiffness, and Bristle Density, such as Round Fan, Flat Blunt, Flat Point, and Round Curve (a portion of her Brushes panel shown above). Baldacci then selected the Paintbrush tool (B), chose a bristle brush and a stroke color, and drew into the first of many layers (the image on the first layer is shown above in Preview and Outline modes). In layers above, she added greater definition and built the fur in stages based on color, such as white, gray, and highlights. On the uppermost layers she added the snout, eye details, and additional layers of fur until the portrait was complete.

Pattern Brushes

Building Characters with Pattern Brushes

Overview: *Create the parts that will make up a pattern brush separately; place the parts in the Swatches panel and give them distinctive names; use the Pattern Brush Options dialog to create the brushes; vary the width of the pattern brush line using the Stroke menu and the Width tool.*

Adjusting pattern brush fit

After you've applied a pattern brush to a path, you can still scale, flip, and modify its fit along the path. Modify all these settings in the Pattern Brush Options dialog, or manually reshape and scale the pattern by changing the stroke weight or using the Width tool.

LARRETT

1

Creating the various robot arm elements, oriented in the outward-facing position that pattern brushes use for their tiles

Dragging objects for pattern brushes into the Swatches panel and naming them

To create these stylized science-fiction robots, Raymond Larrett saved extensive tedious rendering by building the robot limbs using a custom pattern brush. Working this way allows him to quickly and easily make alterations to his art by adjusting the weight of the brush stroke, modifying or replacing the various brush elements, or even replacing the entire brush itself.

1 Creating the robot arm parts. Larrett's robot arm required four distinct elements: a "shoulder" piece where the arm joins the body, an "elbow" connecting the upper and lower arm, the "hand" (in this case a claw), and an "arm link" segment that replicates as it connects and forms the majority of the robot arm. He created these pieces individually, then turned each into a separate pattern swatch. These swatches become the "tiles," that together make up the robot arm pattern brush.

To create the shoulder piece, he first modified a shape made with the Ellipse tool. Using the Pen tool, he drew a lighter, unfilled path with a Round Cap for the highlight to complete the shoulder. He then dragged the shoulder art into the Swatches panel, naming it "shoulder" so he would recognize it as he built the pattern brush. In the same way he created the arm link, hand, and elbow swatches for the pattern brush tiles. He made sure that the various pieces were facing in the correct direction relative to the pattern tiles, which run at right angles to the path, before individually dragging each one into the Swatches panel (alternatively, you can select art and click the New Swatch icon, or choose Object> Pattern> Make).

2 Making and using the pattern brush. To build the pattern brush for the robot arm, Larrett opened the Brushes panel, clicked New Brush in the Pattern Brush Options dialog, and then clicked OK. He enabled the first box in the panel (the Side Tile), and when prompted selected the pattern swatch for the arm link. Next he placed the other tiles in the appropriate position: the shoulder to the Start Tile box, the hand in the End Tile box, and the elbow in the Inner Corner Tile box. He named the new pattern brush Robot Arm, and clicked OK.

To use his new pattern brush, Larrett selected the brush in the Brushes panel, then drew a path for the robot arm using the Pen tool (P). He clicked where the Start Tile (the shoulder) should go, clicked again to place a corner anchor point (necessary for the elbow tile, the Inner Side Tile, to load), and finally clicked to place the hand element (the End Tile) at the end of the path. He also sometimes drew with the Paintbrush tool or applied the brush to a drawn path.

3 Creating variations in the pattern brush. Larrett then modified the art by varying the pattern brush line weight and stroke profiles. To adjust the width of a selected robot arm, he changed the line weight in the Control panel or Stroke panel by clicking in the numeric field and using the up arrow and down arrow keys to increase or decrease stroke weight as desired (adding the Shift key alters the weight by increments of 10). To manually adjust only selected portions of the robot limb, Larrett used the Width tool (Shift-W). Placing the tool over a point on a path, he moved the diamond-shaped handles to widen or narrow a portion of the path. Lastly, he combined some old and newly-made swatches to create additional brushes for other robots' limbs.

2

Selecting the Pattern Brush option from the New Brush dialog

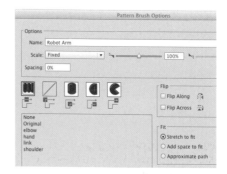

Creating a new pattern brush by placing the swatches in the appropriate tiles

3

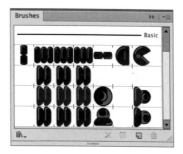

Using the Stroke panel to widen or narrow the pattern brush line weight

Using the Width tool to introduce variations in the width of your pattern brush line

Recombining and building new swatches to create new pattern brushes

MCGARRY

Aaron McGarry

For this urban portrait Aaron McGarry relied heavily upon Illustrator's Symbol Libraries and Symbols panel. He made his own panel containing only the symbols he needed using Window> Symbol Libraries> User Defined. He saved as a symbol any detail that he would need to repeat so he could easily access and apply that element. To build the roof tiles in the background building, McGarry made one tile and filled it with a solid color. He then made two duplicates and filled each with a different color. He separately dragged and dropped each into the Symbols panel, named it, and clicked OK. He was then able to quickly drag alternating tiles from the panel to lay the roof, giving it a natural look. To create the red plumbing in the foreground, he also used many duplicated parts, such as the nuts and bolts holding the assembly

together, that he had saved as symbols (see detail above right). McGarry took full advantage of Illustrator's Symbol libraries to create the greenery and curb area around the pipes. He used grass, leaves, and rocks found in the libraries accessed from the Symbol Libraries icon in the Symbols panel. To create a perspective point of view he modified some of the symbols; for instance, he used Effect> Distort & Transform to turn Rock symbols into paved concrete. He also created the oil stains on the road by modifying a Dot Pattern symbol from Illustrator's library. For the dirt on the vehicle, he drew a path around its lower side, then enabled the Draw Inside drawing mode. Using the Symbol Sprayer tool he sprayed the sand symbol within the path along the vehicle's side. Lastly, he selected the path and reduced the opacity.

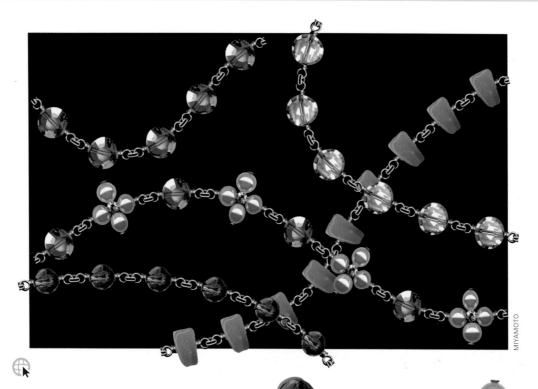

MIYAMOTO

Nobuko Miyamoto/Yukio Miyamoto

Making these intricate beaded necklaces at first glance would seem impossibly difficult, but once they carefully construct each gem, with the use of pattern brushes, the necklace virtually draws itself. Nobuko Miyamoto designed the necklace and created the bead elements (details above right) with a mixture of blended and solid filled objects. She paid careful attention to the ends of the bead to ensure that when each bead lined up with the next one there would be a seamless connection between them. Yukio Miyamoto then transformed Nobuko's designs into brushes. To make the chained ends, he selected the chain object and dragged a copy (Shift-Option/Shift-Alt) to the other side of the bead. With the chain selected, he chose the Reflect tool and clicked above and below the chain to reflect the chain vertically. He selected and grouped each bead, and then in some cases he put the beads in pairs and then grouped a pair of beads. For each bead or pair of beads Yukio clicked the New Brush icon at the bottom of the Brushes panel, selected New Pattern Brush, and clicked OK. In the Pattern Brush Options dialog, he kept the Colorization method as None, and then under Fit he chose Stretch to Fit. To make the necklace, Nobuko drew a path with the Paintbrush tool and selected the desired bead pattern brush in the Brushes panel to apply the brush. Now with the bead as a pattern brush, the necklace can be easily adjusted to any length or path.

Moses Tan

Moses Tan recreated astonishing detail and captured a precise likeness of his photographic reference using mostly meticulously-drawn filled paths, but he used custom art and scatter brushes for some of the intricate details (such as the weeded area shown across, right). He preferred to use scatter brushes for the small-sized growth and art brushes for the larger foliage. To make an art or scatter brush he first drew a weed object, then dragged it into the Brushes panel and in the New Brush Options, selected Art Brush or Scatter Brush (several are shown at right). For art brushes he specified the stroke direction (either top to bottom

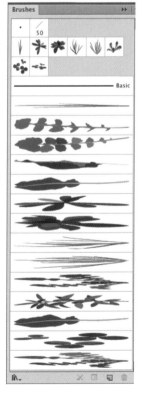

or left to right) so when he drew a brushstroke, the foliage was oriented correctly. He kept the other parameters at the default settings. For the scatter brushes he varied options for each weed (size, spacing, scatter, and rotation). For scatter brushes he used Page for "Rotation relative to," and to preserve the original artwork colors in all his brushes, he used a Colorization of None. To paint with a brush he would select the Paintbrush tool, a scatter or art brush, and draw paths to easily form the weeded detail in his drawing.

5

Color Transitions

Color Transitions

Whether your colors are black and white, ranges of grays, a limited palette, or a full spectrum of colors, taking control of color transitions or groups of colors is essential to mastering the power of Adobe Illustrator. This chapter focuses on the myriad ways of coloring and recoloring your objects in Illustrator, from using the various panels, to creating transitions of colors with gradients and gradient mesh; it also looks at the group of panels and functions that Adobe calls Live Color.

WORKING WITH THE COLOR AND SWATCHES PANELS

The main panels that help you work with color include Swatches, Color Guide, Gradient, Appearance, and Control panels. Click a Fill or Stroke color to reveal an arrow, which provides access to a version of the Swatches panel, or Shift-click to access the Color panel.

To save your current Stroke or Fill color as a swatch, drag it from the Toolbox or Color panel to the Swatches panel. You can also create swatches by dragging one or multiple colors from the Color Guide to the Swatches panel. To name a single selected color as you create it (and set is as a global color if desired), click the New Swatch icon at the bottom of the Swatches panel instead. Whenever you copy objects that contain custom swatches from one document and paste to another, Illustrator will automatically add the swatches to the new document's panels.

You can create three kinds of solid colors in Illustrator: process colors, global process colors, and spot colors. Each is easy to distinguish visually.

- **Process colors** (solid swatch) are mixed from the CMYK colors used for printing with ink. Change the percentage of each ink to change the color, or choose a color from a swatch library, such as Pantone process uncoated.
- **Global process colors** are process colors with an added convenience: If you update the definition for a global process color, Illustrator updates that color throughout the

---

No warning with Trash...

If you click the Trash icon in the Swatches panel, Illustrator does *not* warn you if you're about to delete colors used in the document; Illustrator will simply delete the swatches, converting any global colors and spot colors to non-global process colors. Instead, choose Select All Unused and then click the Trash icon.

Steven Gordon's "Kuler Colors" lesson, later in this chapter, combines Image Trace and Live Color

Access to panels

In addition to the normal versions of the Color and Swatches panels, access pop-up instances from within the multi-purpose Appearance and Control panels. In the Appearance panel, click a Fill or Stroke color to reveal an arrow that lets you access a version of the Swatches panel, or Shift-click to access the Color panel—all without leaving the Appearance panel. In the Control panel, you can simply click on the arrow next to the Fill or Stroke swatches.

document. Identify a global process color in the Swatches panel by the small triangle in the lower-right corner of the swatch in any view, and by the Global Color icon in List view. Create a global process color by enabling the Global option (it's off by default) in either the New Swatch or Swatch Options dialog.

- **Spot colors** are used in print jobs that require a premixed ink or varnish, rather than a percentage of the four process colors. Specifying a spot color allows you to use colors that are outside of the CMYK gamut, or to achieve a more precise color match to the spot color you'll be using than CMYK allows. You can specify a color as a spot color in the New Swatch dialog from the Color Type menu, or you can choose a spot color from a Swatch library, such as the various Pantone libraries (from the Swatch panel's Swatch Libraries Menu icon choose Color Books). All spot colors are global, so they update automatically if you change the definition; when the Swatches panel is in Thumbnail view, they have a small triangle in the lower right corner, as well as a small dot or "spot." In List view, they're also marked by the Spot Color icon.

Color groups and the Color Guide

The default document profiles that ship with Illustrator include several swatches and one or two color groups to start using in your document. To create and save your own groups of colors, select multiple colors from the Swatches or the Color Guide panels, or select the objects in your artwork that contain the colors you want and click the New Color Group icon in the Swatches panel.

The Color Guide panel helps you mix and match colors according to various color schemes. At the upper left of the Color Guide panel is the "base color" swatch. You can choose a base color by clicking on a color in the Color Guide, Color, or Swatches panel. To the right of the base color swatch, you can choose a harmony rule that will automatically select colors that go with your base color, based on scientific color theory. Or, in the Swatches panel, click on the Color Group icon in a color group to

The Swatches panel, shown in list view for color swatches only; the top two user-defined swatches are process colors; the middle two are spot colors; and the last two are global colors (at left with the document in CMYK mode; at right the same colors with the document in RGB mode)

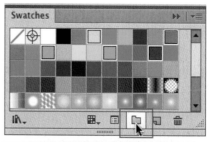

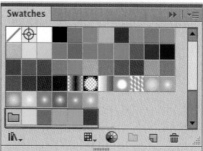

The New Color Group icon (top) makes it possible to organize your Swatches panel creating sets manually or from selected objects (shown selected at top and saved as a group at bottom); you also specify the name for the group

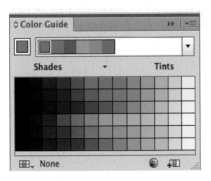

The Color Guide panel after changing the number of steps from the default 4 to 7, via Color Guide Options

Reset gradients to defaults

After you select an object that has an altered gradient angle (or highlight), new objects you draw will have the same settings. The fastest way to "re-zero" gradient settings such as angles is to press the "<" key to apply a solid Fill. Then click on your gradient swatch. For linear gradients, you can also type a zero in the Angle field. Or, you can use the Gradient panel to switch between Radial and Linear and then back again to reset a custom angle without removing or relocating color stops.

Extra big gradient panel

A special feature of the Gradient panel is that you can make it extra

tall and wide, and the Gradient slider itself will increase in size, making it much easier to design complex gradients.

load that group in the Color Guide panel. You can then preview variations of those colors by choosing to display them (using the Color Guide's panel menu) according to value, temperature, or saturation. Drag a selected swatch (or swatches) to the Swatches panel to save it, or click on the "Save color group to Swatch panel" icon. Clicking on the "New swatch group" icon in the Swatches panel will also save your current harmony.

To access the Harmony Rules menu, click on the pop-up menu to the far right of the base color. Once a new harmony rule is selected, its colors fill the strip beside the base color. Alter how many variations of that color group you see by choosing Color Guide Options from the Color Guide panel's menu. You can change the number of steps in each color's gradient (up to 20) and the amount of variation between steps. Also in the panel's menu you will find the choice to view the colors as shades and tints, warm and cool, or vivid and muted. The Color Guide panel is one that can be resized wider and taller to accommodate the size of the grid. If you want to use your current color group as a base for even more color variations, click the Edit Colors icon at the bottom of the panel to enter the Edit Colors/Recolor Artwork dialog (for more about this icon see the "Live Color" section later in this chapter).

GRADIENTS

Gradients create seamless transitions from one color into another, often creating the appearance of realistic modeling. Illustrator can create either Radial or Linear gradients. You can not only apply gradients to Fills, but now in many cases, you can also apply gradients to Strokes. There are many similarities and a few distinct differences between the ways gradients can be applied to Fills versus Strokes. First, here are some of the similarities:

For both Fills and Strokes, you can choose a gradient style from the Swatches or the Gradient panels, and via Swatch Libraries accessed with buttons in panels or from the Window menu. Click the New Swatch icon in the Swatches panel to save your current gradient or, if you've modified a gradient since it was last saved, you can save the current variation within the Gradient panel by clicking on the arrow next to the main gradient icon and click the Add To Swatches icon.

Within the Gradient panel, you can make a variety of adjustments, including adding color stops, changing the colors and opacities of stops, toggling between Radial and Linear, or reversing the direction of the gradient. To find out how the Gradient panel changes to accommodate the specifics of Gradient Fills versus Strokes, see below.

Gradient Fills and the Gradient Annotator:

In addition to Linear and Radial gradients, gradient fills also can become Elliptical gradient fills created from Radial gradients. If the Fill is selected in the Gradient, Tools, or Color panels, you can also apply the current or last-used gradient style to an object by clicking (or click-dragging) with the Gradient tool. You can start and/or end your gradient outside the object itself when dragging with the Gradient tool. This also places the Gradient Annotator onto your fill object. After applying a gradient to a selected object's Fill using the Swatches panel, or by clicking on the object with the Gradient tool, use the Gradient panel or the Gradient Annotator (View> Show Gradient Annotator) to edit the gradient. Using the Gradient tool you can make a variety of adjustments to one object; with multiple gradient-filled objects selected, you can click and drag across multiple objects filled with gradients and unify the objects.

Probably the biggest difference between gradient fills and strokes is that only gradient fills allow you to make adjustments to the gradient on the object itself, using the Gradient tool. When the Gradient tool is active *and* Show Gradient Annotator is enabled, the Gradient Annotator appears as a bar across the gradient on the Fill of a selected object. To modify a Fill gradient using the Gradient Annotator, add and/or move the stops along the lower edge of the Annotator. Adjust the blend between the color stops by sliding the diamond shapes along the top of the

Shortcut for last-used gradient

The shortcut key ">" applies the last-used gradient and its angle ("<"applies the last used solid fill).

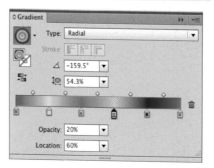

Gradient panel with Radial gradient selected

Adding color to gradients

- Drag a swatch from the Color or Swatches panel to the Gradient slider until you see a vertical line indicating where the new color stop will be added.

- Drag a solid color from the Fill or Stroke proxies in the Tools or Gradient panels.

- Hold down the Option/Alt key to drag a copy of a color stop.

- Option-drag/Alt-drag one stop over another to *swap* colors.

- For Fills, double-click the color stop on the Gradient Annotator or the slider bar in the Gradient panel, and select a color from the Swatches or Color panels.

- For Fills, click just beneath the Gradient Annotator bar, or on the slider where the stops are, to add a new stop; a small "+" sign appears next to your cursor when you are in the correct location for adding a new stop.

Panel pop-up after double-clicking a color stop to display either the Color or Swatches panel when using the Gradient Annotator

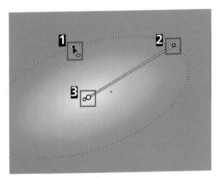

1) Dragging on the Radial Gradient circle to make it elliptical; 2) rotating or scaling the gradient (right); 3) moving the gradient start point

Annotator, and change the color by double-clicking on a stop to open a panel you can toggle between showing the Color panel and the Swatches panel. You can set transparency for the gradient here, as well. To rotate or scale your gradient, hover over the diamond end of the Annotator until your cursor becomes a scale or rotate icon. Reposition the start point of the gradient using the hollow circle at the other end. If your object has a Radial Fill, you can also drag on the solid anchor to interactively transform the circle into an elliptical shape.

Stroke Gradients

Stroke Gradients have some unique options that aren't available to Fill gradients. In the Gradient panel you can choose from three Align options: *within* the stroke, *along* the stroke, or *across* the stroke. You can control whether a gradient applied to a stroke using the *within* option is aligned to the Inside or Outside of the path using the Stroke panel (but you can't use these options with gradients applied *along* or *across* the stroke). You can apply a gradient to a Calligraphic or Bristle Brush Stroke, but not to scatter, pattern, or art brushes. With gradients applied to brush strokes, you'll be able to Reverse the direction, but you can't apply the gradient along or across the stroke. If you Expand or Outline a Stroke gradient (Object> Expand> Expand Appearance, or Objects> Path Outline Stroke), gradients applied *within* the Stroke become gradient-filled objects and can be edited as such, but Stroke gradients applied along or across the Stroke become gradient mesh objects.

GRADIENT MESH

A *gradient mesh object* is an object on which multiple colors can flow in different directions, with smooth transitions between the *mesh points*. You can transform a solid or gradient-filled object into mesh (you can't transform compound paths into mesh). Once transformed, the object will always be a mesh object, so be certain that you work with a copy of the original if it's difficult to re-create.

Transform solid filled objects into gradient mesh objects either by choosing Object> Create Gradient Mesh (so you can specify details on the mesh construction) or by clicking on the object with the Mesh tool, which manually places mesh lines. One way to get a head start in creating a mesh object is to transform a gradient-filled object into a mesh object: choose Object> Expand and enable the Gradient Mesh option.

Depending on where you click with the Mesh tool within a mesh object, you'll add points (or lines and points) to the mesh. Reshape the mesh with the Direct Selection tool, using the anchors and their handles as with any ordinary path. Select individual points, groups of points, or patches within the mesh using the Direct Selection tool, the Lasso tool, or the Mesh tool, in order to color or delete them. If the Mesh tool is selected, holding down the Option/Alt key and clicking on a mesh point deletes it. You can sample a color with the Eyedropper and either immediately have it apply to all selected areas of the mesh object, or, with the mesh object completely deselected, use the Option/Alt key to click with the Eyedropper tool on a mesh point or space between points. Adding color to a patch instead of a single point spreads the color to all surrounding points. When adding a new mesh point, the color currently selected in the Swatches panel will be applied to the new point. If you want the new mesh point to remain the color currently applied to the mesh object, hold down the Shift key while adding a new point.

To further modify the shape your gradient mesh takes, you can use any of the Distort tools, such as Warp or Pucker, to reshape it. You don't even have to select points first. Hover over the mesh to highlight it; the size of your distorting tool will determine how many mesh points and patches get distorted at the same time.

You can assign transparency to a gradient mesh object as you can to other vector objects. Simply select either the mesh points or patches you want and use either the Appearance panel (click on Opacity), or the Transparency panel, to reduce the Opacity below 100%.

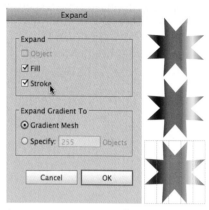

An easy way to create a gradient mesh is to begin with a linear gradient, then choose Object> Expand and enable the Gradient Mesh option under the Expand Gradient To section

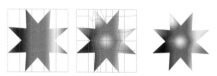

Once you've expanded a gradient-filled object to a mesh, you can edit the locations and colors of the mesh points, and add mesh points and lines

Ann Paidrick builds gradient mesh objects in the "Transparent Mesh" lesson later in this chapter

Get back your (mesh) shape!

To extract an editable path from a mesh, select the mesh object, choose Object> Path> Offset Path, enter 0, and click OK. If there are too many points in your new path, try using Object> Path> Simplify.

—Pierre Louveaux

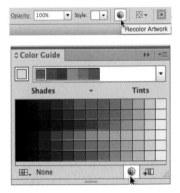

Enter the Edit Color/Recolor Artwork dialog from the Control panel (top) or from the Color Guide panel (bottom)

The Edit Color/Recolor Artwork dialog

Hint: Instead of applying a mesh to a complex path, try to first create the mesh from a simpler path outline, then mask the mesh with the more complex path. You also can stack simple objects with gradient mesh applied to them to construct a more complex object.

LIVE COLOR

Live Color is a phrase sometimes used by Adobe to describe the combination features introduced in CS3 that help you be creative with color. The heart of what Adobe calls Live Color is a dialog that can be entered a number of different ways, and is alternately, and somewhat confus-ingly, labeled either Edit Colors or Recolor Artwork.

If you have nothing selected, you enter a mode called Edit Colors. You can access this mode by clicking the Edit Colors icon at the bottom of the Color Guide panel. Once you're in the Edit Colors dialog, you'll be in Edit mode, which means that you can mix and store colors (see the following section for specific instructions on how to do this). You'll see a tab next to the word "Edit" titled "Assign," but it will be grayed out; since you don't have any objects selected, you can't access this tab. You can only assign colors to selected objects.

If, however, you have artwork selected, this dialog will now be titled "Recolor Artwork," and you will have access to the Assign tab of the dialog, as well as Edit mode. As long as your selection contains at least two colors, you'll see the Recolor Artwork icon in the Control panel. Another option is the icon at the bottom of the Color Guide panel mentioned above; note, though, that when artwork is selected this icon will now be called "Edit or Apply Colors." In the Swatches panel, with a color group selected, you can click the Edit or Apply Color Group icon. A final way into this dialog is Edit> Edit Colors> Recolor Artwork.

The Recoloring Artwork (and Editing Color) dialogs

After selecting the object(s) you want to recolor, click the Recolor Artwork button in the Control panel to open the

Recolor Artwork dialog; the colors from your selected art should still be all in order, and the selection edges will automatically be hidden. If you enter the Recolor Artwork dialog via Color Guide's Edit or Apply Colors icon, your image will initially appear with the color group in that panel assigned to your artwork. If that's not what you intended, click the "Get colors from selected art" icon to reload the original colors into your artwork. In fact, any time you want to quickly return to your original colors without canceling the dialog, simply click again on the "Get colors from selected art" icon.

Live Color shows a base color and active colors at the top, with a pop-up menu showing several of Adobe's Harmony Rules, just as the Color Guide panel does. You can drag colors within the Active Colors field to reorder them, and your selected object(s) will be recolored according to their new positions. To change the base color, simply select another color from among the active colors.

The Color Groups section lists any color groups you saved in your Swatches panel before you entered the Recolor Artwork/Edit Colors dialog, as well as any color groups you created during this work session by clicking on the New Color Groups icon. Rename a color group by double-clicking on its name and entering a new one in the pop-up dialog. Clicking on any color group loads those colors into your artwork. Deleting and creating new color groups in the Recolor Artwork dialog will also delete and add color groups in your Swatches panel, so don't click the Trash icon unless you're positive you want to delete that color group from your document entirely. If you create color groups you want to save during a work session, but don't want to apply the changes to your artwork, disable the Recolor Art checkbox and click OK. If you click Cancel, all the work you did creating (or deleting) new color groups will be deleted.

The two main tabs are Edit and Assign. The Assign tab (only available with an active selection) displays horizontal color bars, with each long bar representing one of the colors in the artwork currently selected. To their right

You can do a number of things in the upper portion of the Recolor Artwork dialog, including set the current color as the base color (on the left), choose from Harmony Rules (the arrow pop-up menu), and rename Color Groups (says "Artwork colors" above); from the upper right you can re-load the colors from your artwork

The center-right section of the Edit Colors/Recolor Artwork dialog has more powerful mini icons for "Save changes to color group," "New Color Group," and "Delete Color Group"

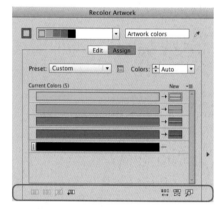

In Assign mode, these icons (circled) allow for merging, separating, excluding, and adding new color rows; you can also randomly change color order, saturation, and brightness, as well as find a particular color in your artwork

Special color sets

If your work requires that you use a very specific set of colors, such as team colors or specific "designer" hues for a season, you'll want to first create and save a Color Group (or groups) in the Swatches panel. Then, when you open Live Color, your Color Groups will be in the storage area, ready to recolor your artwork.

The power of Recolor Artwork

One of the many powerful capabilities of the Live Color toolset is the ability to globally change the colors of almost any kind of colored object in your Illustrator artwork. Colors in envelopes, meshes, symbols, brushes, patterns, raster effects (but not RGB/CMYK raster images), and in multiple fill and stroke objects can all be easily recolored with the Recolor Artwork dialog. —*Jean-Claude Tremblay*

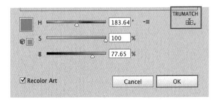

In Edit or Assign mode, clicking the miniature grid-like icon (the"Limits the color group to colors in a swatch library" icon highlighted here) will present a pop-up menu of swatch libraries

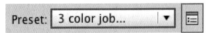

The Color Reduction Options icon (under the Assign tab in Recolor Artwork)

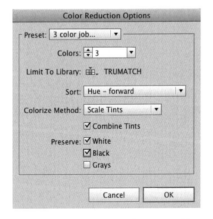

The Color Reduction Options icon opens this dialog

is an arrow pointing to a smaller color swatch that's initially the same color as the larger bar. This small swatch is where you can load or mix a replacement color. To protect a color from change, click on the arrow to turn it into a straight bar. You can drag and drop colors within this area; you can also access context-sensitive menus.

The Edit tab contains a color wheel with markers representing the colors in the selected artwork. Depending on whether the Lock icon is enabled or disabled, you can move the markers around on the color wheel individually (unlocked) or in unison (locked) to adjust the color in your art. You can also click the display icons to select a segmented wheel or a bar view. In addition to dragging markers on the color wheel, you can use the sliders and controls just below the color wheel to adjust the various aspects of color (hue, saturation, and value). You can work in the standard color modes, or you can choose Global Adjust to affect all colors at once. As you adjust individual colors with the sliders, notice that the color marker you selected will also move on the color wheel as you move a slider.

On either the Assign or Edit tabs, you can choose to limit colors to a swatch library such as a Pantone library using the "Limits the color group to colors in a swatch library" icon. On the Assign tab, you have a Preset list and a Color Reduction Options icon for restricting the colors that can be reassigned. When you restrict your colors to a swatch library, the color wheel or bar on the Edit tab displays only the library's colors, while Assign mode will replace all your original colors with those from the library that it thinks are the closest match.

The Presets on the Assign tab also help you limit the number of colors in your palette to 1, 2, or 3. This makes Live Color a huge timesaver when you need to reduce the number of colors used in a full-color project so it can be printed with spot colors, or even need to reduce a 3-color spot color job to 1 or 2. Use the Color Reduction Options to further determine how tints, shades, and neutrals are handled when colors get reassigned.

Ann Paidrick

After hours of intricately
creating gradient mesh-
based artwork, Ann
Paidrick can quickly and
easily change colors using
Live Color. Because you
can't recover colors once
you've changed them in
Live Color, each time she
wants to create a vari-
ant of her gold ribbon,
she starts by duplicating
the original artboard
(in the Artboards panel
she drags the gold rib-
bon artboard to the New
Artboard icon). Selecting
the new ribbon objects,
she clicks the Edit Colors
icon in the Control panel.
Clicking on the Edit
mode tab, she enables
the Lock icon, then drags
the Base Color circle in
the color wheel (the largest circle) until she finds
a color shift she likes, and
clicks OK. Saving this file,
she creates the next color
variation from another
copy of the original.

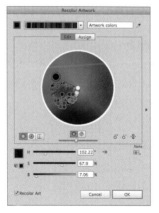

PAIDRICK

Custom Coloring

Creating Custom Colors & Color Groups

Overview: *Create an illustration; create custom swatches; create a custom color group from custom swatches; save a swatch library.*

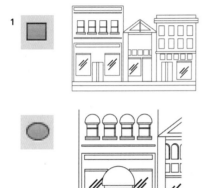

Creating an icon with the Rectangle tool, Ellipse tool, and Pencil tool

Filling icon paths with default swatches from the Swatches panel

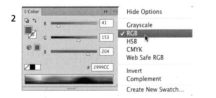

Selecting the correct color mode from the Color panel's pop-up menu

Ryan Putnam designs many illustrations he uses as icons in stock art and client projects. Creating custom swatches is an integral step in creating compelling and consistent icon illustrations. Illustrator comes with some great default color swatches, but they are not suited for most of Putnam's icon illustrations. Moreover, by creating a custom color group, Putnam can easily apply his custom swatches to other related illustrations.

1 Creating an icon illustration. To create the "Destination" icon, Putnam used the Rectangle tool, Ellipse tool, and Pencil tool. Putnam first created the buildings of the icon with varying sizes of rectangles with the Rectangle tool. He then used the Ellipse tool to create windows and awnings for the buildings. Next, he used the Pencil tool to draw the mountains. To distinguish the objects from each other, Putnam filled the building and mountain paths with default swatches from the Swatches panel by selecting each object and clicking the desired swatch.

2 Creating custom swatches. After Putnam roughed out the basic color schemes for his illustration, he then began to customize a more natural set of colors. First, he made sure the Color panel was set to the same color mode as his Document Color Mode. Since Putnam is creating his icon for a website and his Document Color Mode is RGB, from the Color panel pop-up menu he selected RGB. Putnam then selected an object and mixed the desired color with the sliders in the Color panel. Next, he opened the Swatches panel and clicked the New Swatch icon in the bottom of the panel. In the Swatch Options dialog he then named the swatch and clicked OK. Alternatively, you can choose Create New Swatch from the Color panel pop-up menu. Yet another option is to drag the mixed color directly to the Swatches panel, though by doing so, you won't get Swatch Options and the opportunity to name the swatch. Putnam then repeated these steps for every custom color he wanted to create.

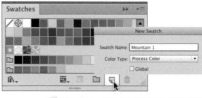

Mixing colors with the color sliders from the Color panel

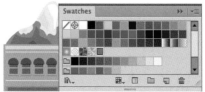

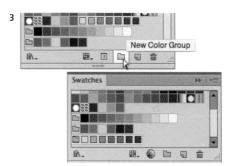

Saving custom swatches in the Swatches panel by clicking the New Swatch icon

3 **Creating a new color group.** After creating his custom swatches, Putnam wanted to organize his custom swatches so he could easily apply them to other related illustrations and icons. To do this, he created a custom color group. He selected the desired swatches in the Swatches panel by Shift-clicking to select contiguous swatches, or by holding ⌘/Ctrl and clicking for non-contiguous selections. Then he clicked the New Color Group icon, where he was given the option to name his color group. The new color group was then saved for Putnam and ready for use.

To use his custom color group in other documents, Putnam needed to save the color group as a custom swatch library. First, he selected all the swatches he wanted to delete from his custom color group and clicked the Delete Swatch icon in the Swatches panel. Putnam then clicked the Swatch Libraries menu icon at the lower left of the Swatches panel, chose Save Swatches, named it, and clicked OK. This saved Putnam's swatch library so it's accessible to Illustrator via the Swatch Libraries menu icon; by scrolling to the bottom under User Defined, he can select his defined library. (To find the location on your computer, search for the Swatches folder within the Adobe Illustrator CS6 Application Support folder.)

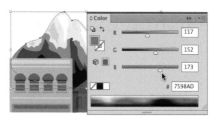

Saving custom swatches as a new color group in the Swatches panel

From the Swatch Libraries menu icon in the Swatches panel: choosing Save Swatches to save a custom color group; and accessing it later via a User Defined library

Scripting Colors

Tools for Adding and Editing Colors

Overview: *Use Premedia Systems'* **WOW!** *Artwork Colorizer script to automatically fill shapes with color; browse and download color themes with the Kuler panel; assign and edit a color group with the Recolor Artwork dialog.*

The Premedia Systems' script dialog

City shapes automatically filled with different colors by the Premedia Systems' script

Part of the Kuler web page showing the color theme Gordon created

Coloring adjacent areas is a common task in making maps—you click each area and fill it with a color. But when there are dozens of areas, special tools can help you perform this task quickly and effectively. For this map of Seattle Southside, Steven Gordon used Premedia Systems' (www.premediasystems.com) **WOW!** Artwork Colorizer script (included on **WOW! ONLINE**) and Illustrator's Kuler and Live Color panels to fill cities with distinctive colors.

1 Creating the map areas and using a script to fill them with different colors. Gordon started the map by importing GIS data using Avenza MAPublisher plug-ins. Once imported, the data produced a layer with 37 cities, each with a black stroke and no fill. You can fill areas with different colors automatically using Premedia Systems' **WOW!** Artwork Colorizer script (this script and its installation instructions, are on **WOW! ONLINE**; install the script before starting or restarting Illustrator). To fill the areas using the script, choose File> Scripts. From the script's dialog, leave the default option No Colors selected (new colors will be created from scratch) and click OK. The script will automatically fill your shapes with colors.

2 Creating a color group using Kuler. Gordon wanted to reduce the 37 unique colors created by the script to a handful of swatches that could be shared among the cities. He decided to tap into the vast collection of color groups (or "themes") from Adobe's online Kuler application. You can access Kuler by opening the Kuler panel (Window> Extensions> Kuler). If you don't find a satisfactory theme navigating the panel, go to http://kuler.adobe.com and create your own, as Gordon did. If you create a theme, give it a unique title, select Public, and click Save.

3 Importing a Kuler theme as a color group and editing its colors. With his color theme, "Seattle Southside," available on the Kuler website, Gordon added it to the Swatches panel using the Kuler panel. To do this, browse themes in the Kuler panel or find one (including one you've created) by typing its name in the Search field. With the theme selected, click the "Add selected theme to swatches" icon. Now your theme is available as a color group in the Swatches panel.

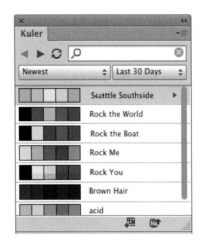

The Kuler panel with the color theme selected

Gordon applied the new color group by selecting all the cities and then double-clicking on the color group's folder icon in the Swatches panel to display the Recolor Artwork dialog. When the dialog displayed, it automatically recolored his selected artwork using the color group he double-clicked. Gordon wanted to fill the cities with the exact colors in his group and avoid using tints. You can limit colors by clicking the arrow on the right of any of the color rows to bring up the New Color pop-up menu and then choosing Exact.

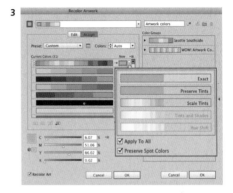

The Assign tab of the Recolor Artwork dialog with the New Color pop-up arrow icon and menu

As you work, you may wish to edit your colors. Gordon decided to lighten the colors in his group so they wouldn't interfere with the legibility of symbols and small type. To change the colors in your artwork, click on the Edit tab in the Recolor Artwork dialog. Lighten or darken colors by moving all of the circular color icons together (with harmony colors linked) or individually (with harmony colors unlinked) toward or away from the center. You can add another color to the group by clicking the Add Color tool. When you're done editing the colors, you can save the changes to your group or save them as a new color group. Finally, click OK to exit the Recolor Artwork dialog and return to your artwork.

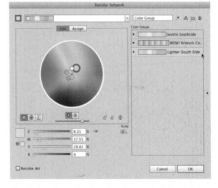

The Edit tab of the Recolor Artwork dialog with the edited color group saved as a new group and the new group is renamed (by double-clicking)

Kuler Colors

Using Kuler, Image Trace, & Live Color

Overview: *Trace a photograph with Image Trace; recolor artwork using a downloaded Kuler color theme; recolor color with Live Color; create and upload a color group; use a photograph to add detail; use artwork to mask a photograph; create a flare.*

1

The original photograph of the calendula

(Top) the Tracing Presents menu icon in the Control panel; (bottom) some of the Tracing Presets menu options

The traced artwork

MADISON BOTANICAL GARDENS

GORDON / CARTAGRAM, LLC

How can you enhance a photograph of a beautiful flower? Steven Gordon sought the answer with Illustrator's Image Trace and Live Color tools—and a trip to Adobe's Kuler website—in making this vibrant advertisement for a botanical garden.

1 Tracing a photograph, expanding the tracing, and moving artwork to new layers. Gordon began by placing a photograph of a calendula flower in Illustrator. Because he wanted to simplify the photograph, Gordon decided to posterize the image by tracing it. To do this, he chose Objects> Live Trace> Tracing Options. In the Tracing Options dialog, he chose the preset "6 Colors" from the Preset menu, and then modified the settings by changing Max Colors to 5. Knowing that he would need to select and manipulate some of the traced artwork later, he expanded the trace (Object> Live Trace> Expand) and ungrouped the artwork. Then he added two layers in the Layers panel, one for the green shapes and the other for the orange shapes. He selected and moved all of the green and orange shapes to their respective layers.

2 Browsing Kuler, downloading a color group, and recoloring the traced artwork. After reviewing the traced artwork, Gordon decided to make the traced green leaves and stems more vivid. For inspiration, he opened the Kuler panel (Window> Extensions> Kuler) and browsed the color themes until he found one with a variety of bright greens. Instead of recreating its colors using the Color panel, he downloaded the theme to the Swatches panel as a color group by clicking the Kuler panel's "Add selected theme to swatches" icon. Next he selected all of the green artwork and double-clicked on the color group he had just downloaded. In the Assign panel of the Recolor Artwork dialog, Gordon needed to assign three of the color group's five colors to the three greens that had been produced by Live Trace. With Recolor Art enabled he then clicked the "Randomly change color order" icon several times until the green shapes in the illustration looked the way he liked, then clicked OK.

To preserve the traced artwork's colors, Gordon selected all of the green and orange artwork and clicked the Swatch panel's New Color Group icon. After naming the group, he uploaded the group as a Kuler theme that others could access by clicking the Kuler panel's "Upload from Swatch panel to Kuler community" icon.

3 Adding detail, brightening the flower center, and creating and uploading a color group. With the traced artwork colored, Gordon wanted to bring some of the original photograph's detail back into the illustration. He created a layer above the traced artwork and placed a copy of the photograph. Selecting the photograph, he opened the Transparency panel and set opacity to 50% and the blending mode to Hard Light.

Because the focal point of the illustration was the flower's center, Gordon wanted to employ the photograph's full color and detail. He created a new layer and placed another copy of the original photograph on it. Then, from the layer with the traced green shapes, he clicked the Lasso tool and selected the green center shapes. He copied and pasted them in place and turned them into a compound path (Object> Compound Path> Make). After moving the compound path to the layer with the photograph, Gordon selected both and chose Object> Clipping Mask> Make. Finally, he brightened the center by drawing a flare with the Flare tool, opened the Transparency panel and changed the flare's blending mode to Soft Light. He finished by adding type to the illustration.

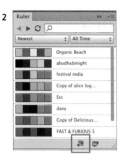

The Kuler panel with the "Add selected theme to swatches" icon highlighted

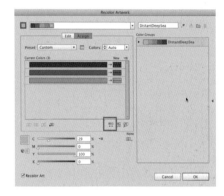

The Recolor Artwork dialog with the "Randomly change color order" icon highlighted

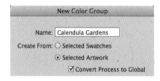

The New Color Group dialog (Swatches panel)

On the left, the flower petals after tracing; on the right, the flower petals overlaid with the photograph set to 50% opacity and Hard Light

At left, the traced flower objects; at right, the photograph masked by the compound path

Unified Gradients

Controlling Fills with the Gradient Annotator

Overview: *Fill objects with gradients; use the Gradient tool with the Gradient Annotator to adjust fill length and angle; unify fills across multiple objects with the Gradient tool and Gradient panel.*

JOLY

1

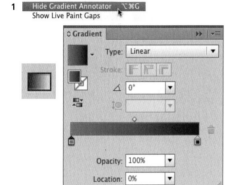

Working with the Gradient panel, Gradient tool, and Gradient Annotator

2

A single click with the Gradient tool on a selected object fills the object with either the default or last-used gradient swatch, and displays the Gradient Annotator, if selected in the View menu (be sure you don't click and drag when applying for the first time—you can click-drag to adjust the gradient later)

Using the Gradient Annotator to shorten the length of the gradient and to rotate the angle when the Rotate icon appeared

With the advent of the Gradient Annotator in conjunction with the Gradient tool, you can apply and customize gradients in most instances without needing to keep the Gradient panel open. In this illustration, Dave Joly only needed the Gradient panel to switch between Linear and Radial gradients, and to work with creating unified gradients. To control the colors, length, and angle of gradients for individual objects, Joly adjusted each gradient with the Gradient Annotator. He unified gradients across multiple objects using the Gradient tool and Gradient panel.

1 Applying gradients. To apply a gradient to a single object, such as the fish's body, Joly first made sure that the Gradient Annotator toggle was visible (if View> Show Gradient Annotator is available, choose it). Next he selected an object and the Gradient tool, and then clicked once on the object to fill it with either the document's default gradient (for the first object) or with the last gradient used in the document.

2 Editing single objects with the Gradient Annotator. Joly was able to edit a gradient almost exclusively using the Gradient Annotator. With the Annotator, he could modify the gradient length, angle, and colors on the object itself. He only needed to turn to the Gradient panel to choose a different existing gradient swatch, switch the current gradient between linear and radial gradient in Type, or reverse the gradient. Joly began his edits by moving his cursor just beyond the arrow endpoint of the Gradient Annotator. When his cursor turned into the Rotate icon, he dragged to interactively set the angle he wanted the gradient to take. With his cursor directly on top of the arrow end, he click-dragged to lengthen or shorten the gradient, and he dragged on the large circle at the other end to move the whole gradient to another position over the object. To adjust the colors, Joly double-clicked on a color stop along the Annotator, which gave him immediate access to proxies for both the Swatches and the Color panels, and a subset of the Gradient panel, as well. After choosing a suitable color, he dragged the stops on the Annotator to position the color blends more precisely, and on the gradient sliders to adjust their blend.

Changing the gradient colors by double-clicking on the Gradient Annotator color stops to pop up both the Color and Swatches panel proxies

After first selecting all objects and applying a gradient tool to them, but before unifying them

3 Unifying gradients across multiple objects. Unifying gradients across multiple objects is a bit trickier with the Gradient Annotator involved. Joly first created the gradient swatch he would need—for the tail fins, for example. Next he selected all the objects and clicked on the swatch in the Swatches panel to apply it. This automatically created a new Gradient Annotator for every object, but Joly wanted to unify the gradients under just *one* Annotator. Still using the Gradient tool with the Gradient Annotator visible, Joly dragged across all the objects. This now appeared to unify the multiple gradients under one Annotator, but it's then only possible to change the length or position of the unifying gradient. Instead, while adjusting one gradient that had been unified across multiple objects, Joly discovered the Gradient Annotator wasn't providing reliable feedback or controls. Therefore, when working with one unified gradient applied to multiple objects, instead of relying on the Gradient Annotator, he would ignore or hide the Annotator (Window> Hide Gradient Annotator). Joly simply used a combination of the Gradient tool (to make length and angle adjustments to the unified gradient) and the Gradient panel itself (for numeric precision, adjustments to color stops, and opacity).

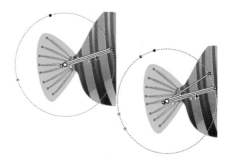

Unified gradients sometimes appear to retain the function of the Gradient Annotator, but if you attempt to edit angles or colors with the Gradient Annotator, you'll discover you aren't actually editing a single gradient

By using only the Gradient panel and/or the Gradient tool to edit unified gradients, you ensure that all changes will be made in unison

Gradient Paths

The Basics of Gradients on a Path

MCGARRY

Overview: *Create paths using strokes; apply linear gradients to each path; adjust gradient sliders and Stroke options.*

1

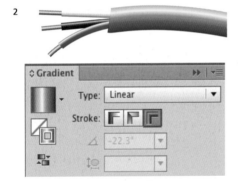

The separate parts of the power cord drawn using the Pen tool, increasing the stroke weight for each section: 7 pt for the wire, 12 pt for the insulation, and 40 pt for the jacket

2

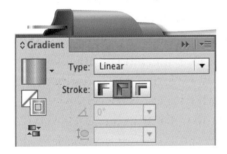

Applying a gradient to the copper wire from the Metals library using the third Stroke option to apply it across the stroke width

The plug prong using a gradient from the Metals library using the middle Stroke option to apply it along the stroke length

This power cord was created by San Diego-based illustrator Aaron McGarry, using gradients applied to strokes.

1 Creating the cord using strokes. McGarry drew each section of the power cord separately using the Pen tool, then he increased the stroke weight for each section: the exposed copper wires, the insulation, and the cord jacket. He also used the Ellipse tool to create the coiled section of the cord and duplicated the ellipse a few times.

2 Applying gradients to strokes. McGarry applied gradients to his paths using the Gradient panel chosen from Swatch Libraries> Gradients. The copper wire, for example, used a copper gradient from the Gradients> Metals library. In the Stroke area of the Gradient panel, he chose "Apply gradient across stroke" (the third option) and then adjusted it using the slider. He also used this option for the insulation and cord jacket. Since the live and neutral plug prongs were flat straight edges, he chose "Apply gradient along stroke" (the middle Stroke option) and moved the lightest stop on the slider to the left to indicate where the prong turns at the tip. He duplicated these prongs and used Paste in Place to put a copy on top. He then applied a Gradient> Fades swatch to darken the end of these prongs but still expose the brass beneath, creating a more natural transition than darkening alone. For the plug body end he drew the contour with the Pen tool and applied an orange gradient to the stroke and the fill; he adjusted the stroke gradient to indicate a soft edge transition.

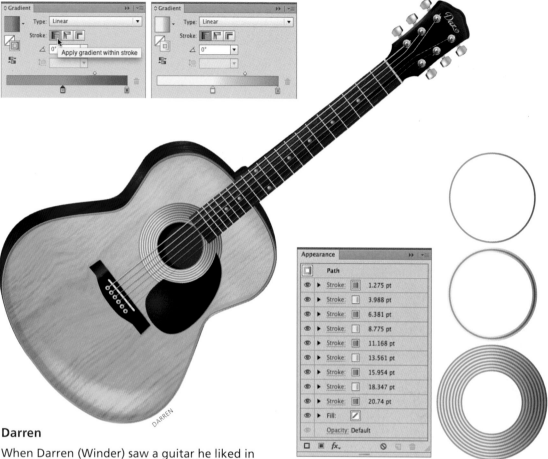

Darren

When Darren (Winder) saw a guitar he liked in a store window, he decided to reconstruct it in Illustrator with photorealistic detail. He began by constructing the basic shape and using Image Trace to add wood texture to the guitar, then created some wood-toned gradients. To mimic directional light and add an edge to the guitar progressing from dark to light, he created two paths outlining the body, then applied a gradient stroke to each path. To do this, Darren selected a path and targeted its Stroke attribute in the Appearance panel, clicked the Stroke color icon, and chose his gradient. With the path still selected, he opened the Gradient panel and chose the first Stroke option (Apply gradient within stroke). This stretched the gradient the length of the path. For the guitar's sound hole, he again used gradients applied within the stroke, this time using multiple strokes on a path. Using the Appearance panel, he clicked the New Stroke icon, which created a stroke below the first in the same style as the one selected (if no attribute is selected, strokes will be added above the others). Clicking on the Stroke swatch, he chose the lighter wood gradient and enlarged the stroke weight. He then continued to add alternating dark and light strokes, adjusting weights to create concentric dark and light circles from one path.

Bending Mesh

Converting Gradients to Mesh for Editing

Overview: *Draw objects and fill with linear gradients; expand gradient-filled objects into gradient meshes; use various tools to edit mesh points and colors.*

JACKMORE

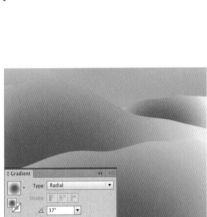

The hills shown filled with radial gradients—although there is some sense of light, it isn't possible to make the radial gradient follow the contours of the hills

The hills shown filled with linear gradients, which when converted to gradient meshes are easier to edit than radial gradients

For many images, gradients can be useful for showing the gradual change of light to shadow (if you need to learn more about creating and applying gradient fills, first see "Unified Gradients," earlier in this chapter). For her rolling hills, artist Lisa Jackmore expanded linear gradients into gradient mesh objects so she could better control the curves and contours of the color transitions.

1 Drawing objects and then filling them with linear gradients. Begin your illustration by creating closed objects with any of the drawing tools. After drawing each object, fill it with a linear gradient (although in some objects radial gradients might look better before you convert them to mesh objects, linear gradients create mesh objects that are much easier to edit). For each linear gradient, customize the colors, and adjust the angle and length of the gradient transition with the Gradient tool and Gradient Annotator until you can best approximate the desired lighting effect. Jackmore created three hill-shaped objects with the Pen tool, filled them with the same linear gradient, then customized each with the Gradient tool and Annotator.

2 Expanding linear gradients into gradient meshes. To create a more natural lighting of the hills, Jackmore converted the linear gradients into mesh objects so the color transitions could follow the contours of the hills. To accomplish this, select all the gradient-filled objects that you wish to convert and choose Object> Expand. In the Expand dialog, make sure Fill is enabled and specify Expand Gradient to Gradient Mesh. Then click OK. Illustrator converts each linear gradient into a rectangle rotated to the angle matching the linear gradient's angle; each mesh rectangle is masked by the original object (see the *Mastering Complexity* chapter for help with masks).

3 **Editing meshes.** You can use several tools to edit gradient mesh objects (use isolation mode, or lock/hide objects on specific layers as you work). The Mesh tool combines the functionality of the Direct Selection tool with the ability to add mesh lines. With the Mesh tool, click *exactly on* a mesh anchor point to select or move that point or its direction handles. Or, click *anywhere* within a mesh, except on an anchor point, to add a new mesh point and gridline. You can also use the Add Anchor Point tool (click and hold to choose it from the Pen tool pop-up) to add a point without a gridline. To delete a selected anchor point, press the Delete key; if that point is a mesh point, the gridlines will be deleted as well.

Select points within the mesh using either the Mesh tool or the Lasso tool, using the Direct Selection tool to move multiple selected points. Move individual anchor points and adjust direction handles with the Mesh tool in order to reshape your gradient mesh gridlines. In this way, the color and tonal transitions of the gradient will match the contour of the mesh object. Recolor selected areas of the mesh by selecting points, then choosing a new color.

If you hold Option/Alt while you click in the area *between* mesh points with the Eyedropper tool, you'll add the Fill color to the four nearest mesh points.

By using these tools and editing techniques, Jackmore was able to create hills with color and light variations that suggest the subtlety of natural light upon organic forms.

2

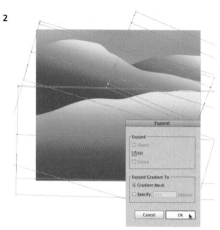

After expanding the gradients into gradient mesh objects

3

Using the Mesh tool to add a mesh line, then moving the mesh point with the Direct Selection tool

Using the Add Anchor Point tool, using the Lasso to select a point, moving selected point (or points) with the Direct Selection tool

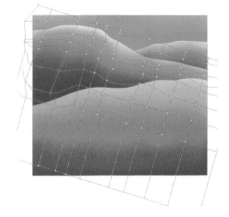

The middle hill, shown after making mesh adjustments

Transparent Mesh

Molding Transparent Mesh Layers

Advanced Technique

Overview: *Draw guides and create gradient mesh objects; contour rectangles; color gradient mesh points with color sampled from reference photo; apply transparency to individual mesh points to create realism.*

1

Making guides on top of the photograph in the template layer

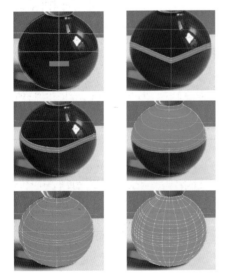

Developing the gradient mesh object from a rectangle, adjusting points with the Direct Selection tool, adding rows and columns with the Gradient Mesh tool (left to right, top to bottom)

PAIDRICK

Ann Paidrick transformed simple rectangular objects into complex, contoured gradient mesh objects to create an exact representation of an original photograph. By incorporating actual transparency into her mesh objects, she is able to reuse the finished vase in other settings (see the gallery following this lesson).

1 **Creating guides, drawing basic shapes, then creating gradient mesh objects.** Placing her JPG as a template into layers above, Paidrick drew a loose grid of paths and then turned them into guides (⌘-5/Ctrl-5) to help position her gradient mesh objects. Paidrick finds that adding a mesh to a rectangle, which she then reshapes, gives her more control over mesh points than if she added mesh to a path drawn with the Pen tool. Therefore, she always begins her gradient mesh objects by drawing one small rectangle with the Rectangle tool. To create the red globe

portion of the vase, she drew a rectangle, filled it with a bright color, chose Object> Create Gradient Mesh, and specified 1 row, 1 column. With the Direct Selection tool (A), she moved points to stretch the rectangle to the edges of the vase base, and eventually the top and bottom. With the Gradient mesh tool (U), she added more rows and columns. She continued to enlarge the mesh object and contour it into the desired shape by pressing U to add mesh points, then A to adjust the points. Paidrick added individual mesh points with the Add Anchor Point tool to further define the shape of the object. She Direct-Selected points and made adjustments to refine the contour of the object and its mesh to closely follow the shading of her reference photo.

2 **Coloring the mesh objects.** To color individual mesh points, Paidrick clicked on a mesh point with the Direct Selection tool (A), then switched to the Eyedropper tool (I) and filled that point with a color sampled from the photograph. She continued to color the mesh points by pressing ⌘/Ctrl to temporarily switch to the Direct Selection tool from the Eyedropper tool, picking up color from the photo, until a pixel in the photograph matched the color she wanted.

3 **Applying transparency to individual mesh points.** For effects such as reflections, she created additional mesh objects on layers above. She then selected individual points in the upper mesh objects and reduced the opacity, creating nearly invisible transitions between different mesh objects on layers above and below. She also reduced the opacity of individual mesh points to create smooth color transitions between more- and less-saturated colors (see bottom figure). To do this she first Direct-Selected a point, then reduced the Opacity in the Control, Transparency, or Appearance panels. She continued to choose mesh points and use various transparency settings throughout the illustration until she had matched the color of the reference photo as closely as possible.

2

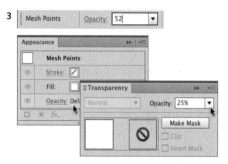

Coloring mesh points and sampling color from the reference photograph

3

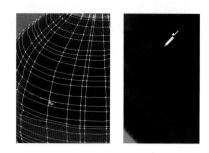
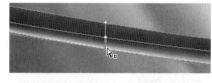

Decreasing the Opacity in Control, Appearance, and Transparency panels

Mesh point before (top) and after (bottom) the opacity is decreased

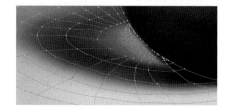

Paidrick applied transparency to mesh points along the edges of the individual rings of color to make smooth transitions between each change of color

PAIDRICK

Ann Paidrick

To explore combining a pattern swatch with mesh to simulate drapery folds, Ann Paidrick used Illustrator's Pattern Editing features to make a seamless, swirling design on a transparent background. She next created a gradient swatch, adding many stops in a range of values to mimic drapery. To add vibrancy to the gradient, she adjusted not only values but the hue and saturation of the main color. Paidrick filled a rectangle with the gradient and then, to ensure that the pattern would "disappear" into the darkest folds of the drapery, she colored the swirls of the transparent pattern the same color as the darkest color in the gradient. In order to distort the pattern to match the folds, she needed to create an expanded version of the pattern, trimmed to the dimension of the "curtain" gradient. To do this, she chose

Object> Expand, kept Fill enabled, and clicked OK. The expanded pattern consisted of both the portion clipped within the rectangle shape and of repeating pattern elements extending beyond the clipping mask. To work with only the pattern elements inside the rectangle, and with the expanded pattern selected, she chose Trim in the Pathfinder panel, deleting excess pattern objects. The pattern now trimmed to the correct dimensions, she chose Object> Envelope Distort> Make with Mesh, using 4 rows and roughly three times as many columns. Using the Direct Selection tool, she marquee-selected several rows at a time and dragged them until the pattern matched the "folds" in the gradient. She adjusted individual points to wiggle the mesh, until she succeeded in melding the pattern with the drapes.

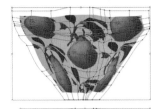

PAIDRICK

Ann Paidrick

Ann Paidrick enhanced her vase illustration from the previous lesson by adding the patterned pear wallpaper to the background. Paidrick locked all the layers of the finished vase and, on a new layer beneath these locked layers, placed a photograph of the wallpaper (saved as JPG) as the background.

With the Pen tool, she drew rough outlines where the distorted pears would be, and then turned these outlines into guides (⌘-5 /Ctrl-5). On a separate layer above the background wallpaper, she placed another photo of the wallpaper, this time one that she had cropped in Photoshop to fit between the top and bottom of the clear glass. In order to use an Illustrator envelope to distort the cropped part of the photo, she had to first embed the photo by selecting the Embed icon in the Control panel. Paidrick then chose Object> Envelope Distort> Make with Mesh (6 rows, 8 columns). She used the Direct Selection tool to adjust the envelope mesh object into the shape of the interior of the glass. To add more rows and columns, Paidrick clicked with the Gradient Mesh tool and added additional mesh points with the Add Anchor Point tool. She continued to adjust the mesh points, referring to her guides until she was satisfied with the distortion results. To make the envelope mesh object fit into the vase shape, on a new layer above, she drew a closed path with the Pen tool, selected the envelope mesh object, then chose Object> Clipping Mask> Make.

#123 Venture Across America

SOUTH CAROLINA
SUBMARINE MYSTERIES AT CHARLESTON

KING

DID YOU KNOW...

Using revolutionary technology ahead of its time, the H.L. Hunley inspired international submarine designs for decades. What caused her to mysteriously sink in 1864?
LEARN MORE ABOUT THE "HUNLEY" PROJECT AT...

uhaul.com

Steve King

U-Haul celebrates history and natural science with eye-catching images they call "Super-Graphics" displayed on their moving vans. Illustrator Steve King mixes intricate details with simplified shapes in this image of the *H.L. Hunley*, a Civil War submarine. King relied on the Gradient tool to create lighting effects and simulate the transparency of a see-through illustration. He employed a darkening orange-to-blue gradient fill on the submarine from the captain's lantern backward to the propeller. The Gradient tool gave King the economy of creating a few gradients that he reused as fills for

different objects. To illustrate the faces of four of the seated sailors, King drew shapes that he filled with the same gradient. He used the Gradient tool's Annotator to customize the length and angle of each sailor's gradient, which helped tie them together visually while keeping their shapes distinct.

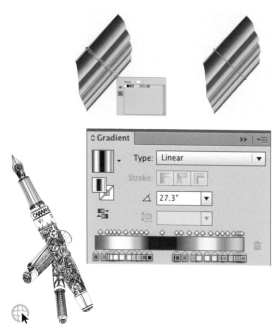

Caran d'Ache 1010 I LIMITED EDITION

MIYAMOTO

Yukio Miyamoto

Yukio Miyamoto created the numerous complex linear and radial gradients throughout this illustration with ease using the Gradient tool and the Gradient Annotator. Miyamoto drew each path with the Pen tool and filled it either with the default linear or radial gradient from the Swatches panel. He selected the Gradient tool to reveal the Gradient Annotator, which appeared on top of the object. Miyamoto double-clicked on the color stop of the Gradient Annotator to show the options. He clicked on the Swatches icon and chose a custom color from the Swatches panel that he had previously created to color the stop. Miyamoto clicked along the Gradient Annotator to add more color stops. He continued to add color stops and color them until he was satisfied with the results. Miyamoto click-dragged the color stops and moved them into the exact locations to

achieve the desired gradient effect. He grabbed the arrow endpoint and stretched the Gradient Annotator to change the length of the gradient. Miyamoto moved the endpoint side to side and adjusted the angle of the gradient. He made additional angular adjustments with the circular endpoint and clicked the center point, then moved it to various positions within the gradient-filled object. The entire illustration is made of gradient-filled objects with two very small exceptions; there is one blended object (the pen tip) and one mesh object (grip area, just beneath the tip). The Gradient Annotator enabled Miyamoto to have exceptional control of the gradient fills to achieve exacting realism.

Recolor a Pattern

Creating Variations on a Color Palette

Advanced Technique

Overview: *Edit a pattern swatch using Recolor Artwork; use the Assign tab to create variations on a single color group; save new pattern swatches and color groups.*

REINHART

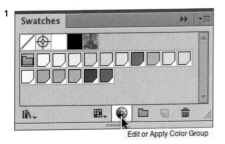

Using a selected color group to activate the icon for entering Recolor Artwork (alternately, click on the Recolor Artwork icon in the Control panel to open the dialog without affecting the original color assignment)

Reinhart's new colorway after creating a new color group with the same number of colors as the original, then applying and refining the color assignments in Recolor Artwork

Using Illustrator's Recolor Artwork (RA) you can start with any pattern, even a highly complex one created using a pre-determined color palette, and quickly experiment with different colorways by reordering the assignment of the same colors, or by generating, applying, and saving a new palette of colors. Sabine Reinhart creates color groups with the number of colors she needs, then lets Recolor Artwork help her develop a new colorway.

1 Entering Recolor Artwork while in Pattern Editing Mode (PEM). Find a pattern swatch to experiment with and duplicate it (drag the swatch to the New Swatch icon in the Swatches panel). If you didn't save your original colors as a color group and want easy access to the group, fill an object with the pattern, and while it's still selected, click on the New Color Group icon and enable Selected Artwork. Now, double-click on the pattern swatch to enter PEM, disable Dim Copies for easier evaluation, and Select All (⌘-A/Ctrl-A). To enter RA with your original colors intact, click on the Recolor Artwork icon in the Control panel. If instead you wish to enter RA with a color group already applied to your pattern, enter via the Swatches panel—click on the icon for a color group, then on the "Edit or Apply Color Group" icon at the bottom of the panel. (If the new color group doesn't contain as many colors as the original, RA reduces the number of colors, turning multiple color assignments into a single color.)

2 Creating a variation on the palette. Once in RA, to vary the color assignment for your pattern—but not allow RA to alter the actual hues, tints, or shades—click on the Color Reduction icon and choose Exact for the Recolor Method. Get inspiration for different colorways by clicking on the "Randomly change color order" icon at the bottom of the New column. Although your colors stay the same, they are applied to different objects in the pattern. There's no Undo in RA to recover a colorway, so when you see potential, consider saving your color group in RA, or click OK, then save a new pattern with Save a Copy in PEM (see below). To further modify the assignment of colors, drag one new color over another to swap them. You also can drag a color from the Current Colors column into the New column to restore an original assignment. Click the "Randomly changes saturation and brightness" icon (beneath the New column), to create even greater variation between your original colorway and a new scheme that is still based on your original color group.

3 Saving color groups and pattern swatches. Applying a saved color group will only give predictable results when applied to the original pattern (not the one you just created), so as you save a group in RA, be careful to include the name of the original pattern swatch in the color group's name. To save a pattern variation, click OK in RA, then click Save a Copy on the Pattern Isolation Mode bar. Name your pattern in the pop-up, and from this point forward, that swatch will retain both the palette and the color assignment. Remember you can still create a color group from a pattern swatch after exiting RA by following the instructions given in the first part of this lesson.

2

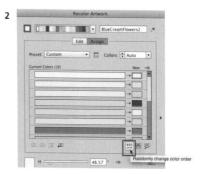

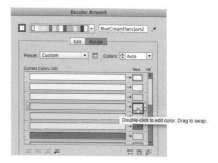

Using the Random button to reorder the color assignments for the pattern elements

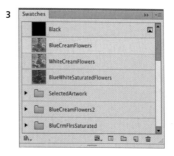

Dragging colors in the New column to swap their assignment

3

Naming color groups to keep them associated with their pattern swatch

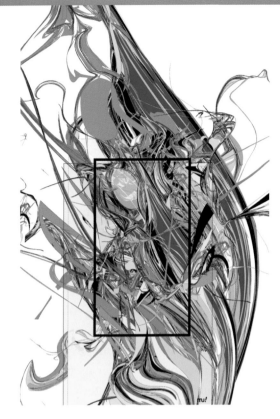

MURRA

Sebastian Murra (Mu!)

Sebastian Murra's highly abstract, organic, often edgy style seems tailor-made for smartphone cases. He used specs from the manufacturer CASE-MATE to begin with a correctly sized artboard for each device, although he only loosely observed the artboard size and orientation until the end. In fact, he made no attempt to restrain the art within the template, allowing it to flow freely beyond the boundaries. Murra began this design, "Saturday Morning Cartoons," by creating a palette inspired by the colors of fruity breakfast cereals for kids. He created several overlapping rectangles, each with a solid Fill and a very fine Stroke, and used Illustrator's Liquify tools, primarily Warp and Twirl, to push and pull the colored shapes into the swirling abstracts that are his signature style. He added

contrast and depth by transforming a few black rectangles along with the fruit-colored ones. He used blending modes, especially Hard Light and Hue, to further integrate the swirling tangle of objects. He often modified objects with the Direct Selection tool, and used Recolor Artwork to alter or introduce colors. Later he rotated everything to its final vertical orientation, then placed overlapping white rectangles on a layer above the artwork, which allowed him to experiment with different framing options until he found the right portion of the design that fit within the required size. For the final composition, he added a yellow-filled background layer and applied a yellow tint to all the lighter colors by adding another yellow-filled rectangle, set to Darken blending mode, on the top layer.

6

Reshaping Dimensions

Reshaping Dimensions

The three Envelope buttons in the Control panel, from left to right: Edit Envelope, Edit Contents, and Envelope Options

This chapter focuses on the Illustrator tools and functions that allow you to create objects that appear to move beyond two-dimensional space. With warps and envelopes you can easily use familiar vector tools to bend and bow objects (and text) in two-dimensional space, and with envelope meshes you can begin to create an illusion of depth as well. Using Illustrator's 3D effects you actually revolve, extrude, rotate, and map objects in three dimensions. Then, the Perspective Grid tool helps you to create art based on linear perspective using one, two, or three vanishing points. All of these demand a bit of a different mindset than flat Illustrator objects and the manipulating of the mesh. In their live states, 3D and the perspective grid work quite differently from other Illustrator objects. If you decide to expand the art, they become merely complex vector objects, letting you work upon them using any of Illustrator's editing tools.

WARPS AND ENVELOPES

Warps and envelopes may look similar at first, but there's an important difference between them. Warps are applied as live *effects*—meaning they can be applied to objects, groups, or layers. Warps have two advantages: They are easy to create by choosing from the predefined options in the Warp dialogs, and you can save them within a graphic style to apply them to other objects. Envelopes, on the other hand, are also live, but rather than effects, they're actual *objects* that contain artwork. You can edit or customize the envelope shape, and Illustrator will conform the contents of the envelope to the contour.

Warps

Applying a warp is actually quite simple. Target an object, group, or layer and choose Effect> Warp> Arc. (It doesn't matter which warp effect you choose, because you'll be presented with the Warp Options dialog, where you can choose from any of the 15 different warps.) While the warp effects are "canned" in the sense that you can't make adjustments to the effects directly, you can control how a warp appears by changing the Bend value, as well as the Horizontal and Vertical Distortion values.

Once you've applied a warp, you can edit it by opening the Appearance panel and clicking on the warp effect. Like all effects, a warp can be applied to just the fill or just the stroke—and if you edit the artwork, the warp updates as well. Since warps are effects, you can include them in a graphic style, which can then be applied to other artwork.

Envelopes

While warp effects do a nice job of distorting artwork (and allow you to save the effect as a graphic style), Illustrator envelopes provide a higher level of control.

There are three ways to apply envelopes. The simplest way is to create a path you want to use as your envelope. Make sure it's at the top of the stacking order—above the art you want to place inside the envelope. Then, with the artwork and your created path both selected, choose Object> Envelope Distort> Make with Top Object. Illustrator will create a special kind of object: an envelope. This object you created becomes an envelope container, which appears in the Layers panel as <Envelope>. You can edit the path of the envelope with any transformation or editing tools; the artwork inside will update to conform to the shape. To edit the contents of the envelope, click the Edit Contents button in the Control panel or choose Object> Envelope Distort> Edit Contents. If you then look at the Layers panel, you'll notice that the <Envelope> now has a disclosure triangle that reveals the contents of the envelope—the artwork you placed. You can edit the artwork directly or even drag other paths into the <Envelope> in the Layers panel. To again edit the envelope itself, choose Object> Envelope Distort> Edit Envelope.

There are two other types of envelopes, and they're closely related. Both types use meshes to provide even more distortion control. When using the first type, the

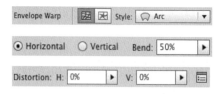

The tools that appear in the Control panel when an envelope warp is selected; you can change the shape of the warp using the pop-up menu

The controls that appear in the Control panel when an envelope mesh is selected; you can easily change the number of rows and columns, as well as restore the object to its original shape using the Reset Envelope Shape button

Michael Cressy turned the building on the left into the one on the right using the drawing tools, then modified with envelopes for each of the windows, the building, and the stacks using Object> Envelope Distort> Make with Mesh

Isolation mode for envelopes

An easy way to edit an envelope: Double-click it to enter isolation mode. —*Jean-Claude Tremblay*

Envelope distort options

To use envelopes to distort artwork containing pattern fills or linear gradients, choose Object> Envelope Distort> Envelope Options and enable the appropriate options. —*Mordy Golding*

Illustrator's 3D objects are only *truly* three-dimensional while you're working with them in a 3D effect dialog. As soon as you're done tweaking your object and you click OK to close the dialog, the object's three-dimensional qualities are "frozen"—almost as if Illustrator had taken a snapshot of the object—until the next time you edit it in a 3D dialog. On the page, it's technically a 2D rendering of a 3D object that can only be worked with in two-dimensional ways. But because the effect is live, you can work with the object in 3D again any time you want. Just select the object and then double-click the 3D effect listed in the Appearance panel.

Extruding an object using the Effect> 3D> Extrude & Bevel dialog—the two-dimensional object on the left was extruded to create the three-dimensional version on the right

AARON McGARRY

See the lesson explaining how Aaron McGarry created this photorealistic key and fob using Illustrator's 3D tools later in this chapter

envelope warp, you choose the overall envelope form from a pop-up list of options. When you use the *envelope mesh*, instead of starting from presets, you begin by choosing how many rows and columns your mesh will contain.

To create an envelope warp, select an object and choose Make with Warp (Object> Envelope Distort). This will open the Warp dialog. Once you choose a warp and click OK, Illustrator converts that warp to an envelope mesh. The Control panel will display the Envelope Warp controls, including a pop-up menu that lets you choose a different shape for the warp if you want to. You can edit the envelope warp's individual mesh points with the Direct Selection tool to distort not only the outer edges of the envelope shape but also the way art is distorted within the envelope itself. To provide even more control, use the Mesh tool to add, remove, and manipulate mesh points.

To create an envelope mesh, select your artwork and choose Object> Envelope Distort> Make with Mesh. After you've chosen how many mesh points you want, Illustrator will create the envelope mesh. The Envelope Mesh tools will appear in the Control panel, allowing you to easily change the number of rows and columns, and restore the envelope mesh to its original shape if necessary. You can also use the Direct Selection tool to edit the points and use the Mesh tool to add mesh points. (If you use other tools, however, you'll need to switch back to the Selection tool if you want the Envelope Mesh controls to reappear in the Control panel.)

3D EFFECTS

Illustrator offers you the power to transform any two-dimensional (2D) shape, including type, into a shape that looks three-dimensional (3D). As you're working in Illustrator's 3D effect dialogs, you can change your 3D shape's perspective, rotate it, and add lighting and surface attributes. And because you're working with a live effect, you can edit the source object at any time and observe the resultant change in the 3D shape immediately. You can also rotate a 2D shape in 3D space and change its perspective. Finally, Illustrator lets you map artwork previously saved as a symbol onto any of your 3D object's surfaces. Remember that Illustrator is primarily a 2D program—its 3D capabilities are very limited when compared to the plethora of available 3D programs.

To begin, think of Illustrator's horizontal ruler as the X axis and the vertical ruler as the Y axis. Now imagine a third dimension that extends back into space, perpendicular to the flat surface of your monitor. This is the Z axis. There are two ways to create a 3D shape using 3D effects. The first method is by extruding a 2D object back into space along the Z axis, and the second is by revolving a 2D object around its Y axis, up to 360°.

To apply a 3D effect to a selected object, choose one of the 3D effects from the *fx* icon in the Appearance panel (or via the Effects menu). (To simplify the instructions throughout this chapter, we'll be using the convention "choose Effect> 3D".) Once you apply a 3D effect to an object, it will show up in the Appearance panel. As with other appearance attributes, you can edit the effect, change the position of the effect in the panel's stacking order, and duplicate or delete the effect. You can also save 3D effects as reusable graphic styles so that you can apply the same effect to a batch of objects. Once the style has been applied, you can modify any of the style parameters by clicking the underlined effect name in the Appearance panel or double-clicking the *fx* icon to the right of the effect name. Editing the 2D path will update the 3D rendering. Following are a few of the key parameters for working in the different kinds of 3D:

- **To extrude a 2D object,** begin by creating a path; the path can be open or closed, and can contain a stroke, a fill, or both (if your shape contains a fill, it's best to begin with a solid color, not a gradient or pattern). With your path selected, choose Extrude & Bevel from the Effect> 3D submenu. In the lower portion of the dialog, enter a point size for depth for your object in the Extrude Depth field, or drag the slider. Adding a cap to your object makes the

Don't worry about the ° symbol

The degree symbol automatically inserts after entering a value into 3D dialog rotation text fields.

Customized bevels!

Each of the 3D Bevel paths are actually symbols, saved inside the "Bevels.ai" file. To add a custom bevel, open the Bevels.ai file, draw or paste a new path, drag the new paths to the Symbols panel, name the symbol, and resave the file. To find this hidden file: Control-click/right-click on the Adobe Illustrator application icon and choose "Show Package Contents," then Required> Resources; the Bevels.ai file is inside your language folder.
— *Jean-Claude Tremblay*

3D—three dialogs

There are three different 3D effects, and some features overlap. If all you need to do is change the perspective of an object, use Rotate. If you want to map a symbol to the object, use either Revolve or Extrude & Bevel (you can still rotate an object from these as well). —*Brenda Sutherland*

Not enough steps…

In the 3D dialog click the More Options button to adjust Blend steps; find a setting between the default (25) and the maximum (256) that's smooth enough, but not too slow to draw (and print).

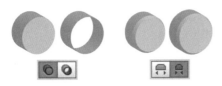

Left to right: Turn cap on for solid, Turn cap off for hollow, Bevel Extent In, Bevel Extent Out

AARON MCGARRY

Revolving an object using the Effect> 3D> Revolve dialog—the open path on the left was revolved to create the 3D wine cork on the right

AARON MCGARRY

An example of rotating an object in 3D space

ends appear solid; disabling the cap option makes your object appear hollow (see first two figures at left).

You can choose from ten different bevels to style the edges of your object; bevels can be added to the original using Bevel Extent Out, or carved out of the original using Bevel Extent In (second pair of figures at left).

- **To revolve an object around its Y (vertical) axis,** begin by creating a path. The path can be open or closed and stroked, filled, or both. With your path selected, choose Effect> 3D> Revolve to open 3D Revolve Options. Drag the slider to set the number of degrees or enter a value from 1 to 360 in the Angle text field. An object that's revolved 360° will appear solid. An object revolved less than 360° appears to have a wedge carved out of it. If you offset the rotation from the object's edge, a 3D shape will appear to be carved out in the center.

- **To rotate 2D or 3D objects in 3D space,** choose Effects> 3D> Rotate. The 3D Rotate Options dialog contains a cube representing the planes that your shape can be rotated through. Choose a preset angle of rotation from the Position menu, or enter values between –180 and 180 into the X, Y, and Z text fields. To manually rotate your object around one of its three axes, simply click *on the edge* of one of the faces of the white cube and drag. The edges of each plane are highlighted in a corresponding color that tells you through which of the object's three planes you're rotating it. The object's rotation is constrained within the plane of that particular axis. If you wish to rotate your object relative to all three axes at once, click directly on a surface of the cube and drag, or click in the black area behind the cube and drag. Values in all three text fields will change. And if you simply want to rotate your object, click and drag inside the circle, but outside the cube itself.

- **To change the perspective of an object,** enter a number between 0 and 160 in the Perspective field, or drag the slider pop-up. A smaller value simulates the look of a telephoto camera lens, while a larger value simulates a wide-angle camera lens.

Applying surface shading to 3D objects

Illustrator allows you to choose different shading (ranging from dull and unshaded matte surfaces to glossy and highlighted surfaces that look like plastic), as well as customized lighting conditions. The Surface shading option appears as part of both the 3D Extrude & Bevel and the 3D Revolve Options dialogs. Choosing Wireframe as your shading option will result in a transparent object, the contours of which are overlaid with a set of outlines representing the object's geometry. Choosing No Shading results in a flat-looking shape with no discernible surfaces. Choosing the Diffused Shading option results in your object having a soft light cast on its surfaces, while choosing the Plastic Shading option will make your object look as if it's molded out of shiny, reflective plastic. For mapped surfaces, enable "Shade Artwork" in the Map Art dialog.

If you choose either the Diffused Shading or Plastic Shading option, you can further refine the look of your object by adjusting the direction and intensity of the light source illuminating it. By clicking the More Options button, the dialog will enlarge and you'll be able to make changes to the Light Intensity, Ambient Light level, Highlight Intensity, Highlight Size, and number of Blend Steps. You can also choose a custom Shading Color to add a color cast to the shaded surfaces. If you choose to maintain a spot color assigned to your Extruded object during output by enabling the Preserve Spot Colors checkbox, be aware that this removes custom shading and limits your Shading Color to Black. If you choose Preserve Spot Colors, you should enable Overprint Preview (View menu) so you can see your shading and color accurately.

When expanded, the More Options dialog includes the light source sphere (shown at right). The small white dot within this sphere indicates the position of the light source, while the black box around it highlights this light source as currently selected. There is always one light source by default. Click and drag this dot within the sphere to reposition your light. With Preview enabled the lighting will automatically update on your 3D object.

LISA JACKMORE

Rotate objects in three dimensions by using the Effect> 3D> Rotate dialog (or the upper halves of the Revolve and the Extrude & Bevel dialogs); the symbol on the left was rotated in 3D space to create the figure on the right (any 2D object can be rotated in 3D space, without making the object itself 3D)

3D effect—pass it on

Although this book generally recommends working with the New Art Has Basic Appearance setting disabled, you might want to enable it when working with 3D effects. Otherwise, any new paths that you create subsequent to applying 3D effects to an object will also have the same appearance set, unless you first clear the appearance set from the panel or click on the default fill and stroke icon in the Tools panel. On the other hand, if you *want* your next object to have the same 3D effects as the one you just created, leave New Art Has Basic Appearance disabled.

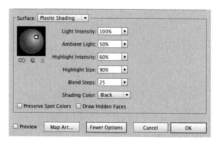

The expanded More Options dialog shows the position of your light source within the sphere; the three icons located below this sphere from left to right are "Move selected light to back of object," "New Light," and "Delete Light"

STAINLESS STEEL

AARON MCGARRY

At left are some images prepared for mapping to a 3D "washer" (shown reduced in size); middle figure shows the stroked compound path used to enter 3D Extrude & Bevel; at right is the 3D washer with art mapped to bevels and visible surfaces; at bottom the text art symbol used for mapping (shown at actual scale to the 3D object)

Mapping with gradients

Gradients saved as symbols are rasterized when they're mapped. Adjust the resolution for the rasterization in "Document Raster Effects Settings." Adjust this resolution via Effects> Document Raster Effects Settings.

Clicking on the "New Light" icon (below the sphere) adds more light sources. This also selects the new light source (indicated by the black "highlight" box around it). Adjust each selected source independently using the lighting controls (to the right of the sphere). The first icon below the sphere, the "Move selected light to back of object" feature, creates back lighting for an object. When your light source is behind an object, the source indicator inverts to a black dot within a white square. When using multiple light sources, this difference helps you see which light sources are behind or in front of an object. Select a light source and click this icon to toggle the light to the front or back of your object, depending on its current position. To delete a light source, first select it, then click the Trash icon beneath the sphere (you can delete all but one default light source).

Mapping art onto an object

To map artwork onto an object (as with the design on the washer to the left), first define the art that you wish to map onto a surface as a symbol; select the artwork you want to map, and drag it to the Symbols panel. You may also want to define a number of symbols. For instance, the texture and text on the outside of the washer (at left) is one symbol. The other objects were also each saved as symbols and added to surfaces in the Map Art dialog.

Map the symbols onto your 3D objects from the Extrude & Bevel or Revolve Options dialogs. In either of these 3D options boxes, you simply click on the Map Art button, then choose one of the available symbols from the menu. You can specify which of your object's surfaces the artwork will map onto by clicking on the left and right arrow keys. The selected surface will appear in the window; then you can either scale the art by dragging the handles on the bounding box or make the art expand to cover the entire surface by clicking the Scale to Fit button. Note that as you click through the different surfaces, the selected surface will be highlighted with a red outline in your document window. Your currently visible surfaces will appear in light gray in the Map Art dialog, and surfaces that are currently hidden will appear dark.

Note: *To see artwork mapped onto the side surfaces of your object, make sure the object has a stroke of None.*

THE PERSPECTIVE GRID

The perspective grid allows you to create art on a ground plane representing real world space as viewed by the human eye. Distances between edges converge as you approach the horizon, the terminal point of our vision. This tool is useful for creating scenes such as cityscapes where buildings or roads narrow in view as they recede from our vision, eventually vanishing on the horizon.

With this Perspective Grid toolset you can draw dynamically within the perspective environment itself so that shapes or objects automatically conform to the perspective grid as you create them, or you can attach existing flat vector art to the perspective grid by dragging selected art into the perspective grid using the Perspective Selection tool (see warning tip at right!). You can even position the grid on top of a reference photograph to add vector content. Symbols, text, and objects created with Illustrator's 3D effect are also supported within the perspective environment.

To begin working in perspective you must first define your perspective environment. Click on the Perspective Grid tool in the Tools panel to display the perspective grid on your Artboard, or click View> Perspective Grid> Show Grid. The default is Two Point Perspective consisting of two vanishing points. For one point perspective choose View> Perspective Grid> One Point Perspective> 1P Normal View, which has a single vanishing point. For three point perspective, choose Three Point Perspective> 3P Normal View, which has three vanishing points (if a perspective grid is customized and saved, it will appear in the respective submenu for 1P, 2P, or 3P Normal View as an additional choice).

When you select the Perspective Grid tool, your grid is displayed with grid plane control points on its extremities

The Plane Switching Widget shown left with the left side highlighted in blue indicates that the left plane (grid) is active; click on a side of the cube with one of the perspective tools (or press 1, 2, or 3 on your keyboard) to activate a different plane (second and third widget); click the area outside the cube within the widget (or press 4) to deactivate perspective mode, which allows you to draw normally (widget at far right).

Grid control points can be manually adjusted on the grid itself or more precisely using the Define Perspective Grid dialog box (View> Perspective Grid> Define Grid). Presets can then be saved for reuse. View> Perspective Grid> Show Rulers displays a ruler on the visible grid.

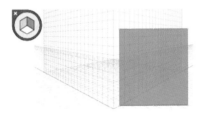

In this example, clicking within the Plane Switching Widget but outside the cube deactivated the perspective grid (note the cyan colored area surrounding the cube), so the rectangle was drawn in normal mode; to later apply perspective to the rectangle, select the Grid Selection tool, click on a Widget side to activate a plane, and drag the rectangle to the desired location.

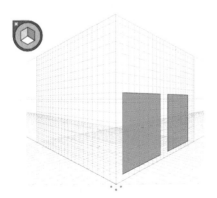

The above image shows a square drawn with the Rectangle tool. Notice the Plane Switching Widget indicates that the right plane is active, hence the illustrated shape in perspective relative to the right vanishing point (the cursor also includes a line and an arrow, which also indicates the active plane). The same square copied and moved with the Perspective Selection tool dynamically transforms it as it moves within the perspective plane.

(though some disappear when the Perspective Selection tool is used). These controls allow you to manually adjust parameters such as vanishing points, angles, repositioning of planes, grid height and width, etc. Scrolling the cursor over these controls yields an indicator below the pointer showing the directional choices available for that control.

To save a customized grid choose View> Perspective Grid> Save Grid As Preset. The new grid is saved under the respective perspective type; for example, a customized one-point perspective grid will be saved as an option to 1P Normal View when the View> Perspective Grid> Two Point Perspective fly-out menu is displayed. The Define Grid dialog (View> Perspective Grid> Define Grid) allows you to adjust the grid with greater numerical precision and save as a preset for further uses.

To begin working within your defined environment, first select an active plane to work in. The cube in the upper left-hand corner of the work area is the Plane Switching Widget. When you click on a cube side with the Perspective Grid tool (or any drawing or editing tool), the active plane is highlighted with a color. Orange, for example, is the default color for the right plane (see figures at left). The active plane means that anything drawn in perspective will conform to the perspective of that specific plane regardless of where it is drawn on the artboard (only one plane can be active at any time). The Perspective Grid tool cursor also indicates this with the shaded side of a cube below its pointer.

Once you choose an active plane, you can use any drawing or editing tool to draw in perspective mode. Select a tool such as the Rectangle tool and begin drawing on the grid. Use the Perspective Selection tool (hidden under the Perspective Grid tool in the Tools panel) to select and move art within an active plane (the cursor also has a line and an arrow, indicating the active plane). When you move objects within your plane using this tool, your objects appear to recede and advance within the perspective grid (using the normal Selection tool freezes an object's shape to the current viewpoint, so it won't continue to transform as you move it). You can also use the Perspective Selection tool to select existing vector objects and attach them to the perspective grid. To do so, activate a plane then select and drag the object to the perspective grid. When you use the Perspective Grid tool to select an object that's already associated with the grid, the associated side of the cube automatically becomes highlighted.

Clicking in the area outside the cube within the widget (or pressing 4) deactivates all perspective planes so you can draw in normal mode (no perspective applied)—see figures opposite. Once your object is created, use the Perspective Selection tool (or press 1, 2, or 3) to activate a plane by clicking on a Widget side, and then drag the object to position it in perspective. You can also marquee-select multiple objects with the Perspective Selection tool, then drag them (together) into the active plane.

If you wish to move an object perpendicular to its current location, hold down the 5 key (top row of numbers on keyboard only, not 5 on right numeric keypad) as you drag with the Perspective Selection tool; to duplicate an object and move it perpendicular to the original's position, hold Option-5/Alt-5 as you drag.

With the Perspective Grid tool, double-click on any of the grid plane controls (the three circles below where the planes intersect) to open a Vanishing Plane or Floor Plane dialog, which allows you to move a plane precisely, with or without the objects associated with that plane.

To work on an object in normal mode after applying perspective, from either the Object menu or the contextual menu, choose Perspective> Release with Perspective (remember, this function does not return an object to a normal state if created initially without perspective but just detaches it from the perspective plane). The object can now be modified normally. Once an object has been detached from a plane, however, you must use Object> Perspective> Attach to Active Plane to reattach it. If the object is not reattached this way, using the Perspective Selection tool will automatically add a new perspective to the object.

Double-click the Perspective Grid tool in the Tools panel to open the Perspective Grid Options dialog for Automatic Plane Positioning options

Warp & Distort

Bending Forms to Create Organic Variations

Overview: *Use Envelope Distort and Distort & Transform live effects to shape objects; use filled rectangles with blend modes to change the time of day.*

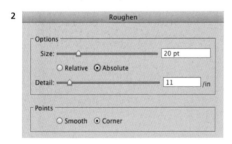

1

Using Warp Options to bend three rectangles into a curved and pointed arch

2

Using Roughen on a duplicate of the envelope layer to add texture to the tree trunks

When Michael Cressy needed to create scenes for an online video game, he turned to Illustrator's powerful Envelope Distort features and live effects to create a Halloween world where magic changes the shapes of things. By adding a few additional layers to colorize his images for different times of the day, his game scenes took on a consistent look with minimal fuss.

1 Using Envelope Distort to bend branches and trees.
To create the blighted trees, Cressy used the Rectangle tool to make three adjacent stripes with different fills (no stroke). He selected them and chose Object> Envelope Distort> Make with Warp. He set the Style to Arch with a Vertical Bend of 25%. He then used a Distortion amount of 99% in the Vertical dimension. These settings created a slightly curved set of stripes so distorted in the vertical dimension that they came to a point. With this horn as his base element, Cressy duplicated and scaled each horn (holding Option/Alt and dragging the bounding box) to be either branches or the main tree trunks. From the context-sensitive menu, he chose Transform> Reflect, and in the dialog chose Vertical to flip half of them. And since Cressy used Envelope Distort, his settings remained live and editable throughout the development of his image.

2 Texturing the tree bark. In order to have some of the tree trunks stand out from the rest, Cressy decided to add texture to them. Since the Roughen effect breaks up smooth outlines with some of the outlines falling inside the original form, Cressy retained the full shape by keeping the basic shape on one layer, then duplicating it to a layer above; this layer he modified by choosing Effect> Distort & Transform> Roughen. After enabling Absolute, Cressy played with the sliders until he found the right amount of the effect to appear like rough bark on his tree trunks—modest settings prevented the Roughen effect here from creating long, sharp needles. Having again chosen a live effect to alter his basic shapes, rather than attempting to draw each of them with the Pen tool, Cressy kept his options open for future editing and was able to work quickly and interactively with the effects.

3 Using Roughen for grass, then warping it to make a broomstick. To construct the grassy hill, Cressy drew a half-oval with the Pen tool, then applied Effect> Distort & Transform> Zig Zag. He next applied Roughen with a low setting, and added another instance of the Roughen effect, this time with a high setting for Details to create the tall, thin strands of grass. To create the bristles of the witch's broomstick, he used ⌘-F/Ctrl-F to paste a copy of the grassy hill in front, and applied an Envelope warp using the Shell Upper preset. He then edited the envelope with the Direct Selection tool and Free Transform until he had shaped the broom end.

4 Adding layers to coordinate scenes for different times of the day. Cressy maintained consistency from one scene to the next by adding tinting layers that could be turned on or off, each representing a different time of day. For midday, he added a layer with a light brown rectangle, then clicked <u>Opacity</u> in the Control panel to lower the Opacity to 50% and chose Screen for the Blending Mode. For early evening scenes, he used a white-to-dark brown radial gradient on a layer set to Multiply at reduced Opacity, and for night shots, he used a lavender-colored rectangle set to Multiply at 100% Opacity. He later reused these tinting layers with other scenes he created.

3

Creating the bristles of the broomstick from a duplicate of the grassy hill, then running Envelope Distort> Make with Warp, and choosing Shell Upper for the preset, then further transforming the envelope

4

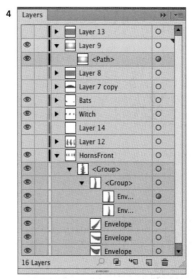

Using rectangles with different colors, blend modes, opacities, and gradients to tint the scenes

Dedree Drees

As part of her undersea illustration, "The Dory," artist and instructor Dedree Drees mimicked blades of seagrass by building an intricate blend that she then extruded as a 3D object. Drees started by drawing four overlapping, wavy lines using the Pencil tool and then giving each stroke a unique color. To begin blending, Drees selected all four lines and then double-clicked the Blend tool. In the Blend Options dialog she set Spacing> Specified Steps to 2, and then chose Object> Blend> Make. To make the lines of the blend look like flat seagrass blades, Drees extruded the blend by opening the Appearance panel, and from the *fx* icon choosing 3D> Extrude & Bevel. She experimented with different Extrude Depth values to make sure that the seagrass blades would not appear thick and dense. Drees brought this object into Photoshop where she positioned it among other elements. To finish, she selected individual blades of seagrasses, and created layer masks to make them transparent.

DREES

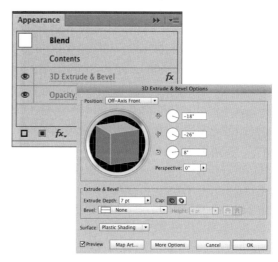

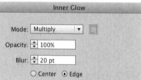

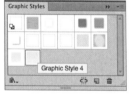

GLITSCHKA

Von R. Glitschka

For "Beautiful," Von R. Glitschka placed his model and Japanese text against one of his intricate patterns (see the *Mastering Complexity* chapter for more on how to create patterns). He then used Live Effects throughout to create the interaction between his objects and their environment. To lift the Kanji characters from the background, he used Outer Glow in Multiply mode, creating an even shadow around the calligraphy. But to separate his model from the background pattern, he maintained directional lighting. He filled an object that matched her shape with the same blue as the background, and moved it a bit to the right, added a 20 pixel Gaussian Blur, and set the layer to Multiply mode with a slightly reduced opacity. He used the Gaussian Blur effect frequently to create the shadows cast on her skin by her hair and to soften transitions when modeling the skin tones. He used the Inner Glow effect in Multiply mode to add a soft shadow within an object. Because he modeled her in a very detailed fashion, Glitschka streamlined some of his work by creating a few graphic styles to use when creating the fine shading and blending in her skin tones. Gradients—often using transparency—added to the live effects to create a soft, romantically styled illustration.

The Keys to 3D

The Basics of Realistic 3D Modeling

Overview: *Create 2D art to extrude as 3D; save graphics and images as symbols to use as maps; render and position 3D objects; map visible surfaces of the 3D object; adjust lighting; generate drop and cast shadows*

2D artwork before rendering as 3D objects

To create a realistic look for 3D surfaces, McGarry saved images and graphics as symbols to later map onto the 3D objects

Be thrifty with image maps

Size your map artwork appropriately (both in file size and dimensions) to avoid potential errors when rendering. You should also position your 3D objects first and then map only the visible surfaces.

Aaron McGarry, an illustrator working in the high-tech industry, often has to conceptualize the look and feel of a product before the physical product actually exists.

1 Creating the 2D art to be rendered in 3D. McGarry began his project by first creating the 2D art that he'd later extrude into 3D objects. Since the key blade and bow would require two different extrusion depths, he created each separately. He began creating the key blade in two parts; he drew one set of teeth, then double-clicked the Reflect tool, chose Horizontal in the dialog, and clicked Copy. After bringing both pieces together with a slight gap between, in the Pathfinder panel he clicked Unite. This joined the two parts of the key into one shape, yet allowed each of the surfaces to be separately mapped, with the gap creating a center line. In total, he created eight separate pieces: two for the key, three for the key ring links, and three for the fob, all of them with a gray fill and no stroke.

2 Saving artwork as symbols to be used as maps. To create a more realistic look, McGarry gathered and created artwork and saved each one as a symbol to later map onto the visible surfaces. He used Illustrator's vector tools to create the label for the bow of the key, the security buttons on the fob, part of the key blade, and key ring links, Illustrator and then saved each as a symbol (by dragging each separately to the Symbols panel). He also used File> Place to bring in two JPG photos of flat metal, one narrow strip for the fob edges—and a second larger piece for the fob front—and saved each of these photos as symbols.

3 Extruding and positioning the 3D objects. He selected one object at a time and chose Effects> 3D> Extrude & Bevel. For each piece he adjusted value in the Extrude Depth field until it looked right. For objects such as the bow of the key he applied a Rounded bevel selected from the Bevel menu. He changed the fill color of the key bow to blue, but he left the other objects gray, a color similar enough to the metallic maps that some surfaces wouldn't need image maps. Next, McGarry selected objects one at a time and re-entered the Extrude & Bevel dialog, where he rotated each object to the appropriate angle using the cube widget. With all the parts now positioned, he separately applied perspective first to the fob and then the key, this time by customizing the Perspective field in the Extrude & Bevel dialog.

Unlike conventional 3D software, Illustrator's 3D objects cannot pass through other objects occupying the same space; objects can only be moved in front or behind other objects. As a result, McGarry had to create the illusion of the interconnecting links in the image as separate pieces, arranging them in front or behind each other.

4 Mapping artwork to 3D surfaces and lighting. In order to map a saved symbol onto a selected extruded object, he re-entered the Extrude and Bevel Options dialog and clicked the Map Art button. Since the key blade originally consisted of two joined pieces, the map dialog treated each half of this top plane as a separate surface. This enabled him to map the right half of the blade with the metal symbol and the left half with a gradient symbol, creating the dark ridge down the center to give the illusion of a worn step on the blade's left side. McGarry then entered More Options in the Extrude and Bevel dialog and adjusted lighting for each part by moving the highlight on the sphere and reducing Ambient Light to darken the side shading. Lastly, to enhance the 3D illusion he manually added shadow effects (Effects> Stylize> Drop Shadow), and then drew paths to which he applied Effect> Blur> Gaussian Blur for the blade and key ring shadows.

3

Artwork extruded and rendered as 3D objects, then positioned before applying maps

4

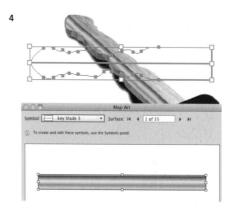

The Map dialog showing the selected surface outlined in red in the image, mapping a gradient map selected from the Symbol Library

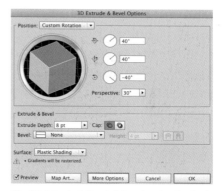

The 3D Extrude & Bevel dialog showing the final settings for the key blade; clicking the More Options button expands the dialog for lighting controls

3D shadow effects

Illustrator's 3D lighting doesn't cast shadows. Although in some situations Effects> Drop Shadows can be useful, in many cases you'll have to manually construct shadow objects with paths and blurs.

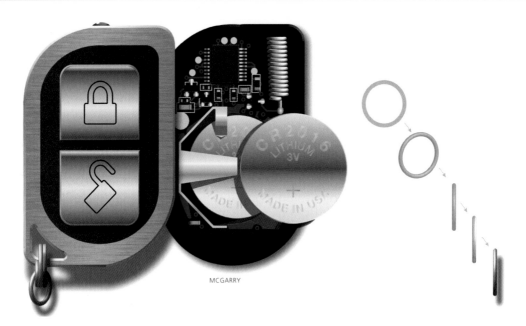

MCGARRY

Aaron McGarry

McGarry created this exploded view of a key fob using a variety of Illustrator features, including vector tools, symbols, and 3D, as well as texture and drop shadow effects. He created the PCB (printed circuit board) using basic paths and applied a variety of gradients and textures, saving some of the PCB components as symbols so he could easily duplicate them. For the batteries and buttons, he applied modified gradients from the Gradients> Metals library and placed icons on top of the buttons. For the batteries he added text on a curved path, slightly reducing the opacity of the text to blend it with the metal background. To easily apply edge bevels to the fob housing, buttons, and key ring section, McGarry separately applied Effect> 3D> Extrude & Bevel to each. While still in the Extrude & Bevel Options dialog, he also applied the image maps that he'd saved as symbols for the fob front and bevels. Clicking the Map Art

button, he navigated to the visible surfaces with the arrow keys, and for each he chose the image that he'd prepared. McGarry created the key ring using the Ellipse tool with a stroke, no fill; he extruded and applied a Rounded bevel; then rotated it in profile and applied maps and shadows (see detail above). He made three copies, shortening one to indicate the ring end. He rotated and moved the fourth ring (lowest) behind the others. Selecting each part of the fob separately, he adjusted lighting controls by clicking the More Options button in the Extrude & Bevel Options to expand the dialog. Finally, since the 3D lighting controls don't cast shadows, to create the illusion of different object depths he separately selected each part of the fob (front housing, buttons, key rings, and back), then applied and adjusted drop shadows using Effect> Stylize> Drop Shadow.

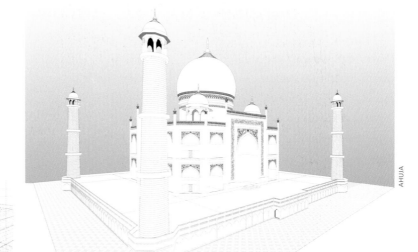

AHUJA

Anil Ahuja/Adobe Systems

Adobe Systems Product Specialist Anil Ahuja used a number of visual references to create this majestic Taj Mahal. To help him in the construction of the building in perspective, he created front- and plan-view sketches. He then referred to photos to set up the basic two-point perspective grid. As with a real structure, he built from the ground up using layers to organize his assembled pieces. The floor is a single design that he created normally (top left) and saved as a symbol. Then he dragged an instance of the symbol into the perspective grid using the Perspective Selection tool. Using a combination of Option-Shift/Alt-Shift, he dragged to create a duplicate, then used Transform Again (⌘-D/Ctrl-D) to repeat the floor pattern. The next object was the plinth (raised base) upon which the mausoleum sits (bottom left). Drawing a rectangle in perspective on the ground plane first, he then used the Automatic Plane Positioning feature when creating the sides. Though he created symmetrical objects such as squares and rectangles in perspective, he created the more intricate designs such as the curved archways of the iwan and pishtaqs normally and then placed them into perspective. The onion dome began as outlines on the plinth. He used the perpendicular movement feature to duplicate and precisely move an outlined ring straight up off the floor plane by using the Floor Plane dialog options (click Floor Plane control point to open). Once he had positioned the rings, he drew straight lines alongside the rings to complete the cylinder and drew a simple circle without perspective behind to create the dome shape. For more info about how he created this, see his ReadMe on **WOW! ONLINE**.

One Perspective

Simulating a One-Point Perspective View

Overview: *Create a one-point perspective grid; customize the grid by moving its control points; draw tile artwork and move it onto the grid using the Perspective Selection tool; duplicate the artwork to make a row; duplicate the rows to form a floor.*

The *"Perspective Grid Preset Options (New)"* dialog

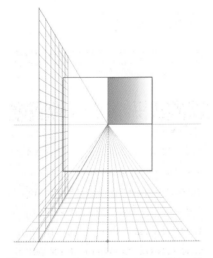

The new one-point grid created by modifying the [1P-Normal View] preset

Elaine Drew is an artist who is equally at home with traditional painting as with the latest digital drawing tools. For this Anubis image, Drew relied on Illustrator's Perspective Grid tool and presets to give the tiled floor and gradient walls the illusion of perspective.

1 Creating the one-point perspective grid. Drew designed the illustration to feature a one-point perspective view. She began by selecting the Rectangle tool and drawing the square that would form the rear wall of the room and serve as a guide for creating the perspective grid in the next step. She filled the square with a gradient.

To start the grid, from the Edit menu Drew selected Perspective Grid Presets, chose the [1P-Normal View] preset, and clicked the New icon. In the "Perspective Grid Preset Options (New)" dialog, she set Units to Inches, and changed Gridlines to every 0.5 inches and Horizon Height to 5 inches. Drew named the preset and clicked OK.

2 Adjusting the grid to fit the illustration design. To begin customizing the grid to fit her design, Drew chose

View> Perspective Grid> One Point Perspective and selected the preset she had created previously. Selecting the Perspective Grid tool (which made the grid editable), she dragged the left Ground Level control until it met the lower-left corner of the artboard. Then she dragged the Horizontal Level control down and the Vanishing Point control to the right. Finally, to extend the bottom grid plane to the rear wall, she dragged the Extent of Grid control upward so that the grid met the bottom of the wall (to accurately see the full extent of the grid, it may be necessary to zoom in).

3 Creating the floor tiles and moving them onto the grid. With the grid established, Drew was ready to create the two floor tiles. She decided to create the tiles and assemble them into rows outside of the grid before moving them into the grid to form the floor. She turned off the perspective grid by clicking inside the circle of the Plane Switching Widget with the Perspective Grid tool. (The circle's background turns blue.)

Next, Drew created one circular petal and one square tile to fit within the 0.5-inch grid size she specified in the previous step. To soften the look of the artwork, she applied the Effect> SVG Filters> AI_Alpha_1 filter. She duplicated the pair of tiles several times to create a row, then duplicated the row and offset it horizontally by one tile. She continued duplicating and offsetting the rows to complete the floor. To render the tiled floor in the perspective of her grid, she first made sure View> Perspective Grid> Snap to Grid was enabled, and then chose the Perspective Selection tool and clicked the Horizontal Grid plane portion of the Plane Switching Widget. Then she selected all of the tiles with the Perspective Selection tool and dragged them onto the grid.

Drew finished the room by creating the left wall. She drew a rectangle and filled it with a gradient. Then she selected the Perspective Selection tool, clicked on the Left Grid plane portion of the Plane Switching widget, and dragged the rectangle onto the grid.

2

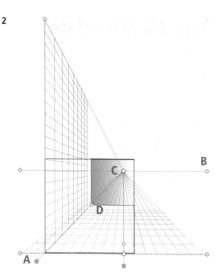

Perspective grid after all adjustments; **A** *is the left Ground Level control,* **B** *is the Horizontal Level control,* **C** *is the Vanishing Point control,* **D** *is the Extent of Grid control*

3

(Left) Turning off the perspective grid by clicking inside the circle of the Plane Switching Widget with the Perspective Grid or Perspective Selection tool; (right) selecting the Horizontal Grid plane

The original square tile and circular petal tile artwork created in Illustrator before being modified by the AI_Alpha_1 SVG filter

Out of controls?

While only four perspective grid controls were used here, 13 more await you. Find out about them by accessing Help> *Illustrator Help.* Click on Drawing and then Perspective. The About Perspective Grid section shows and describes all 17 grid controls.

Amplified Angles

Creating Details with Two-Point Perspective

Overview: *Set up a two-point perspective grid; use drawing and editing tools to create the basic drawing in perspective; add basic shapes in perspective; add more details to achieve the final result.*

1

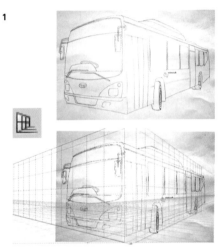

Using the Perspective Grid tool (at left) to set up and position the grid; the ground, right, and left plane controls visible on top of the sketch

2

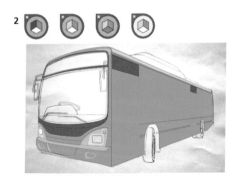

(Top) Using the Perspective Grid tool to click on a side in the widget to activate a plane (first 3 widgets from left) or outside the cube in the widget to deactivate all planes (far right widget); (bottom) creating the basic bus shapes in perspective using the Rectangle, Rounded Rectangle, and Ellipse tools

Anil Ahuja, a senior product specialist working for Adobe, created this bus for instructional materials that explain how to work with Illustrator's perspective tools.

1 **Setting up a perspective grid.** Ahuja sketched the bus from a photo reference, scanned it, and then placed it into Illustrator as a template layer. When you select the Perspective Grid tool, your artboard will, by default, display a two-point perspective grid. Ahuja then adjusted the grid to fit the scanned sketch by aligning the control points on the grid to match the sketch. Using the Perspective Grid tool, he then began by moving the ground level control point (the diamond on either extremity of the ground level), which allowed him to move all the planes together in any direction (this is indicated by the four-way arrow that appears next to the cursor when it is over this control point). Then he moved the left and right planes individually by using the tool to drag the right and left grid plane controls (the small circles beneath each visible grid). He then also adjusted the horizon (the diamond on either extremity of the horizon line) and vanishing points (circles on the horizon line where the planes converge).

2 **Drawing in perspective.** Clicking a widget side to activate the plane he wished to work in, Ahuja then drew the

basic shapes of the bus in perspective using tools such as the Rectangle, Rounded Rectangle, and Ellipse tools. After creating one side window, he held Option/Alt while dragging it to create the others. Duplicating objects this way automatically transformed them to their new perspective position as he dragged them.

3 Drawing complex elements. Ahuja created complex elements (such as the wheels) outside of the perspective grid, then attached them to the perspective grid by dragging them within the grid using the Perspective Selection tool. He converted the fills of some grid objects into gradients, and others into gradient mesh by clicking on them with the Gradient Mesh tool (meshes must be made by converting objects already in the grid; they can't be created first and then moved into a grid). He duplicated the outer rim of the tire to create the inner rim by holding Option/Alt (this makes the duplicate) and the 5 key (this makes the drag perpendicular to the original). To create the tire surface he used the curvature of the tire as a guide, used the Pen tool to draw a closed path within the space, and then filled it with a gradient.

Ahuja drew a few doors and windows using the Rounded Rectangle tool. After creating one door panel or side window, he duplicated it by holding Option-Shift/Alt-Shift while he dragged it to the desired location, using ⌘-D/Ctrl-D to transform again if needed. For each door or window he copied and used Paste in Front, converted this copy to a gradient mesh, and reduced the opacity of mesh points by clicking on <u>Opacity</u> in the Control panel.

4 The finishing touches. Ahuja created the most complex elements (like the logo and text) separately, then attached them to the perspective grid using the Perspective Selection tool. To create the bus shadow, Ahuja first selected the ground plane and drew a rectangle on the plane using the Rectangle tool choosing Effect> Blur> Gaussian Blur. He created the building side by drawing a series of filled and stroked rectangles in the perspective grid.

3

(Left) The wheels created outside the perspective grid; (middle) using the Perspective Grid tool to move the wheel into perspective and duplicating the outer rim (holding Option-5/Alt-5 while dragging); (right) after drawing a closed path to create the tire surface

(Left) Building one door panel by layering versions (shown alongside one another for clarity); (right) after creating one of each door panel and window type, duplicating them within the Perspective Grid tool to create the others

4

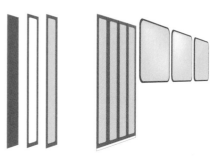

Creating the bus logo separately before attaching it to the perspective grid

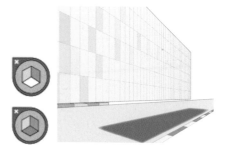

Selecting the right plane to draw the building side and the ground plane to create the bus shadow

Modifying a Photo

Inserting Photographs in Perspective

McGARRY

Overview: *Place a photograph and adjust the perspective grid to conform to the perspective of the image; add graphic elements in perspective; modify the photo to create a new product.*

1

(Top) The original product; (directly above) shown after drawing two pink lines on the left side, extending back until they intersect to form the left vanishing point, and relocating the horizon line to this point using the Perspective Grid tool

Aaron McGarry, an illustrator working for the electronics industry in California, was able to use a photo of an existing product and the perspective grid to conceptualize the next generation of the device.

1 **Working with an established perspective.** In order to add new elements to this photo, McGarry needed to find a way to fit a two-point grid to this uneven perspective. Using the Perspective Grid tool, he first grabbed the Ground Level control point and moved the entire grid so that the three-plane intersection point rested at the foremost point on the device. McGarry then needed to adjust the grid to the photo perspective. He began by identifying two parallel edges on the left side of the device. To use these edges as a guide, he used the Line tool to draw two lines along these edges, extending the lines into the background until they intersected (see heavy pink lines in image at left). This gave him the left vanishing point. He then used the Perspective Grid tool to grab the Horizon Line control point and move the horizon line up to meet the intersection point of the two guide lines.

Since the right plane of the device is essentially rounded with no straight edges to reference for guide lines, McGarry took the foremost straight edge on the top surface (heavy blue line in image) and extended a line back to intersect the horizon line, which gave him the right vanishing point. Since the horizon line was already in position only one guideline was needed for this side.

2 Creating the side buttons. McGarry began detailed items, like the icons and buttons, outside of the perspective grid. He sampled a light and dark color from the original buttons using the Eyedropper tool, then saved them as swatches. To make it appear that the button was recessed, he created a linear gradient using the sampled swatches, then adjusted the gradient stops so that the lighter color was pushed to a far edge. After rotating the icons 90° clockwise (you can't rotate objects within the perspective grid!), he activated the left plane, marquee-selected the buttons using the Perspective Selection tool, and then positioned them. After resizing the buttons using the bounding box, he completed the bottom ledge on the buttons by drawing a narrow rectangle in perspective mode, then added a gradient; since gradients do not transform when put into the grid, he adjusted the angle in the Gradient panel to match the plane angle. He held Option/Alt as he dragged this ledge to create the other.

3 Creating the LCD screen. Activating the floor plane, McGarry used the Rectangle tool to create a rectangle in perspective and filled it with a Sky gradient (from Swatch Libraries). Outside of the perspective grid, he next created the screen text and icon, rotated them, and then attached them to the perspective plane with the Perspective Selection tool. To create the illusion that the LCD screen was backlit, he layered an offset transparent copy of the LCD above the text. To do this he selected the LCD object, then used perpendicular movement by clicking on the Floor Plane control point to open the Floor Plane dialog. Entering a 2-pt value in the Location field, he selected Copy Selected Objects and clicked OK. With this duplicate now selected, he created a new layer and moved the duplicate to this layer by dragging the selection square (in the Layers panel). Using the bounding box, McGarry then brought the two foremost edges of the top LCD screen out to match the edges of the bottom one. Finally, he reduced the opacity of the top LCD in the Control panel, giving depth to the glass while also fading the text and icon.

2

(Left) Two buttons that needed to be relocated from the top of the device to the side to make room for the new LCD and LED; (right) after being rotated and color matched to the originals on the image

With the left plane activated, McGarry used the Perspective Selection tool to attach the buttons to the perspective grid

(Left) Before adding the light bottom ledge; (right) after adding the ledge by duplicating the first one (by holding Option/Alt while moving it with the Perspective Selection tool)

3

Floor Plane	
Location: 2 pt	OK
Object Options	Cancel
○ Do Not Move	
○ Move Selected Objects	
● Copy Selected Objects	

Selecting the LCD with the Perspective Selection tool and then clicking on the Floor Plane control point opens the Floor Plane dialog; moving a copy of the LCD up 2 points

Text and icon are on a separate layer between two LCD layers, with opacity of the top LCD reduced showing the text, icon, and bottom LCD below

Establishing Perspective

Aligning Grids & Planes to an Architectural Sketch

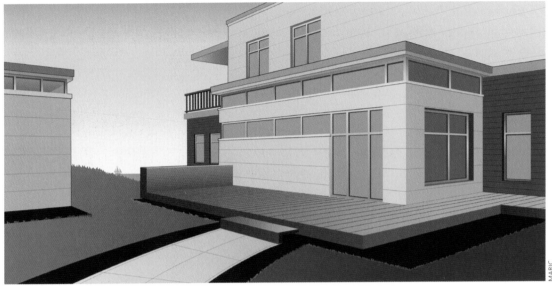

MARIC

Advanced Technique

Overview: *Import a sketch with a visible horizon line; set up and align a perspective grid; construct the rendering using the perspective grid.*

Horizon line shown in red

Detail of the original drawing on a template layer with a perspective grid placed accurately over the sketch

Creating architectural renderings in Illustrator got a whole lot easier with the addition of the Perspective Grid tool. For traditional illustrators like Pete Maric, who learned how to create architectural renderings by hand, this tool is similar to setting up vanishing points on a drafting board. Upon constructing the perspective grid, all lines and forms drawn snap to the grid for a faster workflow and provide perspective accuracy. The perspective grid can be repositioned for adjacent walls or turned off to create "out-of-perspective" elements.

1 Creating a reference image. Maric relied on a hand-drawn sketch as reference for the illustration, making certain that there is a strong visible horizon line to later help him establish the vanishing points. In Illustrator, using File> Place, he enabled the Template option to import the sketch into a locked template layer.

2 Constructing the perspective grid. Selecting the Perspective Grid tool in the Tools panel activated the default grid. Maric then began to align the grid to the sketch by moving the grid plane control handles until the grid matched the perspective of the sketch. Starting with the left (blue) plane, he click-dragged the control handle to align with the right front of the building. He aligned the right (orange) plane to the receding front wall and the bottom (green) plane to the porch. He then click-dragged each vanishing point control handle, moving them into position until both were aligned to the visible horizon line in his sketch.

3 Creating the architectural elements in perspective.
Leaving the perspective grid active and sketch template layer visible, Maric was able to easily focus on the current active drawing plane using the Plane Switching Widget. Maric primarily used the Rectangle tool to create the front entrance of the building and main architectural elements. He organized drawn elements (façade, windows, mullions) in the Layers panel in accordance with the way they appear in real life. So, windows would be lower on the layer stack, mullions would be in front of windows, and the façade would be on top of the layer stack. By selecting the right plane in the Plane Switching Widget, he created the receding front wall, windows, and mullions to align with this plane.

4 Moving the perspective grid to create additional architectural geometry and adding detail. Once one portion of the building was complete, he could reposition the perspective grid to create walls in other areas of the illustration. However, before moving the grid to adjacent walls, Maric saved customized grids for each plane of the structure by using View> Perspective Grid> Save Grid as Preset. Then he could realign the perspective grid by clicking and dragging the grid plane control handles so he could use the grid to construct different walls. To create repeating linear details within the walls, Maric needed to draw only one line, he then duplicated it in perspective by holding Option/Alt while dragging it.

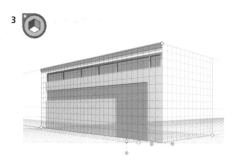

3

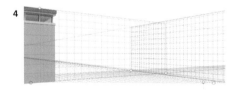

Creating architectural elements in perspective using the Perspective Grid tool and Plane Switching Widget

4

Aligning the perspective grid to adjacent walls and creating detail with the Line tool

DEL VECHIO

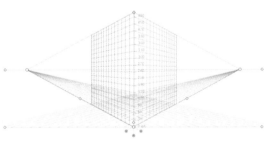

PHOTO BY JOHN MURPHY

Gustavo Del Vechio

Del Vechio placed a photo by John Murphy as a template reference for his Carrot Tree restaurant illustration. He chose the Perspective Grid tool (which enabled the visible grid), then used the tool to set the horizon line and adjust each plane to match the perspective of the photo template. To create each portion of the building in proper perspective, he first would use the Perspective Selection tool to enable one plane, then use a variety of Illustrator's vector tools to create most of the objects for that plane directly on the perspective grid. He repeated this process for each plane until he had built most of the restaurant on each of the three planes. In a few cases he created objects with the grid disabled, then—enabling the grid— used the Perspective Selection tool to select the objects and dragged and dropped them onto

a highlighted plane of the grid. To add variety and texture, he used custom bristle brushes to paint the sky and the foreground fade. To constrain his brush strokes to areas such as the lawn, he selected that object and enabled the Draw Inside mode (see "Draw Behind and Draw Inside" in the *Rethinking Construction* chapter for more about this). Finally, he resized the artboard using the Artboard tool to crop the image to his desired dimensions.

7

Mastering Complexity

Mastering Complexity

The organized whole is more than the sum of its parts. Combining tools and techniques in Illustrator can yield **WOW!** results. In this chapter we'll look at such synergy.

Please keep in mind that this chapter will be quite daunting, if not overwhelming, if you're not comfortable with what has been covered in previous chapters.

In this chapter you'll find a variety of techniques, including making patterns; working with opacity and transparency; creating multiple-object, shaped blends; working with different kinds of masks; and combining features to solve complex problems.

PATTERN MAKING

Prior to CS6, creating a pattern was laboriously manual. You had to draw all of the elements in a pattern tile within a bounding box. With the new Pattern Options panel, you can draw a pattern, adjust the size of the tile, create a repeat offset, and edit the elements, all while previewing multiple repeats with live updating of your edits.

Entering Pattern Editing Mode (PEM)

You can still create a pattern by simply dragging a pattern tile to the Swatches panel, but to explore the power of designing patterns in Illustrator you must enter Pattern Editing Mode (PEM). PEM is a special kind of isolation mode that fades back objects you're not working on and inserts a gray control bar (the PEM isolation bar) between your document and the title bar (if you're not familiar with isolation mode, see "Using Isolation Mode" in the chapter *Your Creative Workspace*). If you have specific artwork that you want to use in your pattern, select it before entering PEM. If you have nothing selected you'll begin with a blank tile 100 px by 100 px, or the equivalent size measured in whatever units you're currently using. There are two steps to being able to work in PEM: 1) you must open the Pattern Options panel, and 2) you must actually *enter* PEM. Following are a few ways to simultaneously open the Pattern Options panel and enter PEM:

- **Choose Object> Pattern> Make**—if you make patterns infrequently and you don't mind using menus.
- **Create a custom keyboard shortcut** (Edit menu) to quickly access the command if you make patterns often.
- **Double-click on an existing pattern swatch** in the Swatches panel. This places the swatch on the artboard in PEM and opens the Pattern Options panel.

Creating the pattern

While working in PEM you can always change the size of your pattern tile. To do this, either enter a new Width and Height for it in the Pattern Options panel, or use the Pattern Tile tool (located at the top of the Pattern Options panel) to interactively adjust the tile's dimensions.

Within a PEM session, you can create your pattern using virtually any of Illustrator's drawing tools. Use symbols and brushes, add gradients and effects, or modify paths with the Width tool, and Illustrator will happily allow you to make use of all these features *within* a PEM work session. However, because pattern swatches can't retain brushes, symbols, and other complex features, Illustrator will expand these objects when you save your pattern as a swatch, and you won't be able to take advantage of these features if you later try to re-edit the pattern. But unlike with older methods for creating pattern swatches, if you try to save a swatch in PEM, you'll see a warning dialog that Illustrator needs to expand some objects in order to create the pattern swatch.

Upon entering PEM, you'll be able to experiment with different layouts—in addition to a basic Grid layout, there are Brick and Hex layouts, both of which offer row and column offset options. Because editing a pattern with complex effects and appearances can slow down the redraw of your computer screen, you can control the number of tile repeats included in your preview from the Copies drop-down list. Directly below Copies you can choose to dim the repeats by a certain percentage, and

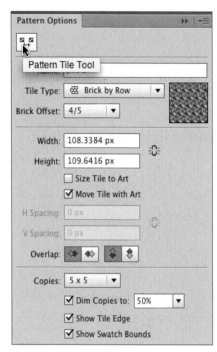

The Pattern Tile tool (not yet selected) for adjusting tiles, Swatch Bounds and offsets interactively

The PEM isolation bar

Vanishing artwork?

Objects and guides that were on the artboard before you entered PEM, remain on the artboard when you exit PEM. However, you can't select guides with objects to take with you into PEM. If you create artwork while in PEM, Illustrator clears the artboard of those objects when you exit, including any guides you added there. Objects that get saved to the Pattern Swatch itself (because it is partially or wholly within the Swatch Bounds) are accessible as discrete objects later on if you edit the swatch in PEM.

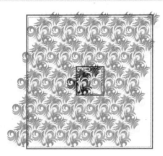

Using Brick or Hex offsets you may see differences between Swatch Bounds (the outside boundary) and Tile Bounds—shown in red for clarity

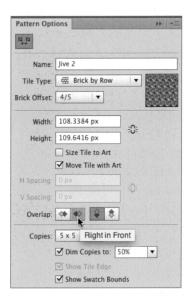

Changing the Overlap from Left In Front (left) to Right In Front (right), altering the appearance of the pattern

hide or show both the tile edge and the bounding box (called Swatch Bounds) of the full repeat. Your Swatch Bounds might be larger than your tile edge when you use an offset to create the pattern.

As you work on your pattern, you still have access to most Illustrator tools so you can edit paths and objects. Add and remove objects from the tile—even place objects straddling the tile edges. You'll be able to judge how your pattern will work while you edit and adjust the layout, offset, and tile repeats. The repeats effectively let you see the pattern as it wraps around to the other side. Objects can overlap, and you can interactively alter how they overlap using the graphical buttons in the Pattern Options panel—right over left, top over bottom, or vice versa.

Leaving Pattern Editing Mode (PEM)

Once you've designed your pattern tile, there are several ways to exit Pattern Editing Mode (to keep the panel in your workspace, see the Tip "Permanent Pattern panel" at the beginning of this introduction):

- Double-click with a Selection tool outside the artwork.
- Click on the Done button on the PEM isolation bar (similar to the isolation mode bar)
- Click on the Exit Pattern Editing Mode arrow beside the pattern's name on the PEM isolation bar.
- Press the Esc key.
- To simply exit Pattern Editing Mode *without* saving a swatch, click on Cancel on the PEM isolation bar.

Creating variations on a pattern

If you intend to enter PEM by double-clicking a current pattern swatch, it's best to get in the habit of editing a duplicate of the original first, then double-click the *duplicate* to begin editing. To do this, in the Swatches panel drag the pattern you want to duplicate over the New Swatch icon. When you then double-click on the duplicate, you'll be editing the duplicate.

While inside Pattern Editing Mode, Illustrator lets you edit only one pattern swatch at a time. However, if as you work you create something that you want to save as a variation, you can save a copy of the pattern swatch in its current state, then continue to work on your main pattern. To do this, click on Save A Copy on the PEM isolation bar and name the copy, which is then placed in your Swatches panel. You'll then be returned to PEM, and can resume editing your main pattern.

Editing pattern swatches without PEM

You can still edit your swatches conventionally outside of PEM; simply drag the pattern swatch onto the artboard and make whatever changes you like there. Edit the objects inside the main group, use Recolor Artwork, transform the scale of the pattern swatch, or add, remove, or reshape individual objects after selecting them with the Direct Selection tool. To make this tile back into a pattern, select the swatch with the Selection tool and drag it back into the Swatches panel. To replace a swatch, hold down the Option/Alt key as you drag a new swatch over an existing one.

TRANSPARENCY

Although the artboard may look white, Illustrator treats it as transparent. To visually distinguish the transparent areas from the non-transparent ones, choose View> Show Transparency Grid. Change the size and colors of the transparency grid in the File> Document Setup dialog. You can enable Simulate Colored Paper in the same dialog, if you'll be printing on a colored stock. Click on the top swatch next to Grid Size to open the color picker and select a "paper" color. Both Transparency Grid and paper color are non-printing attributes that are only visible in on-screen preview once you click OK to exit the dialog.

The term *transparency* refers to any blending mode other than Normal and to any opacity setting that is less than 100%. Opacity masks and effects such as Feather or Drop Shadow use these settings as well. As a result, when you apply opacity masks or certain effects, you're using Illustrator's transparency features.

VON R. GLITSCHKA

Using the Pattern Tile tool to interactively change the Brick offset by dragging on the diamond widget

Recoloring your patterns?

You've made a lovely pattern, but now you want to create color variations. Rather than just selecting individual objects within a pattern and assigning new colors, enter Recolor Artwork and apply custom color groups, or try to randomly rearrange color assignments! See the "Recolor a Pattern" lesson in the *Color Transitions* chapter for details on how to work with Recolor Artwork while in PEM.

Exporting to Photoshop

When you export Illustrator artwork in Photoshop (PSD) format, you may end up with many sublayers if the artwork uses objects such as brushes, symbols, and blends. To simplify the exported document, target the sublayer that contains the problematic objects, enable the Knockout Group checkbox in the Transparency panel, and then export again.

(Top) The conference logo by Ellen Papciak-Rose (for the "People's Health Movement") is made up of many different kinds of objects and text; (middle group above) a radial gradient on top of the illustration that will be turned into an opacity mask by selecting the objects and clicking the Make Mask button in the Transparency panel; (directly above) after clicking the Make Mask button, the top object (the radial gradient) made into an Opacity Mask, creating a spotlight effect, show with the Transparency and Layers panels

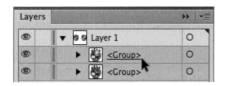

Objects being masked by an opacity mask are indicated by an underscore in the Layers panel

Opacity and blending modes

To reduce opacity, select or target an object, layer, or group in the Layers panel, then choose a blending mode or reduce the Opacity slider in the Transparency panel. You can also reveal Transparency panel controls for a selected object by clicking <u>Opacity</u> in the Appearance or Control panels. As it's called "Opacity" (and not "Transparency"), an object or group is completely opaque when Opacity is 100%, and invisible when Opacity is 0%.

Blending modes control how the colors of objects, groups, or layers interact with one another. Blending modes will yield different results in RGB and CMYK. As in Photoshop, the blending modes show no effect when they're over the *transparent* artboard. To see the effect of blending modes, you need to add a color-filled or white-filled element behind your transparent object or group.

OPACITY MASKS

With an opacity mask, you can use the dark and light areas of one object (the mask) to mark transparent areas of other objects. Black areas of the mask will create transparent areas in the artwork it masks; white areas of the mask leave corresponding areas of the artwork opaque and visible; and gray values create a range of transparency. (This works exactly like Photoshop *layer masks*.)

To create an opacity mask, position one object or group you want to use as the mask in front of the artwork you want to mask. Select both the artwork and the masking object. (To mask a layer, first target the layer in the Layers panel.) Finally, click on Make Mask in the Transparency panel. The topmost object or group automatically becomes the opacity mask.

You may want to start with an empty mask and draw into it—in effect, painting your objects into visibility. To create an empty mask, start by targeting a single object, group, or layer. Double-click on the empty right-hand thumbnail to add an empty opacity mask and enter mask editing mode. Since the default behavior of new opacity masks is clipping (with a black background), you'll need to turn off the "New Opacity Masks Are Clipping" option in the Transparency panel menu. If you don't do this, and your targeted artwork disappears when you first create the empty mask, simply disable the Clip checkbox in the Transparency panel.

Now use your drawing and editing tools to create your mask. (For instance, if you create an object filled with a gradient, you'll see your artwork through the dark areas of the gradient.) While the <Opacity Mask> thumbnail is selected, you won't be able to select or edit anything else in your document. You're in another type of isolation mode. To exit this mask-editing mode, you must click the artwork thumbnail on the right in the Transparency panel.

A few hints can help you with opacity masks. First, opacity masks are converted to grayscale, behind the scenes, when a mask is created (even though the opacity mask thumbnail still appears in color). The gray values between white and black simply determine how opaque or transparent the masked object is—light areas of the mask will be more opaque, and dark areas will be more transparent. In addition, if you select Invert Mask, you'll reverse the effect of dark and light values on the opacity—dark areas of the mask will be more opaque, and light areas will be more transparent. To identify which elements have been masked by an opacity mask, look for the dashed underline in the Layers panel.

The link icon in the Transparency panel indicates that the position of the opacity mask stays associated with the position of the object, group, or layer it is masking. Unlinking allows you to move the artwork without moving the mask. The content of the mask can be selected and edited just like any other object. You can transform or apply a blending mode and/or an opacity percentage to each individual object within the mask.

Precisely targeting and editing transparency

You can apply transparency to so many levels of a document that it can be a challenge to keep track of where you've applied it. For example, you can apply a blending

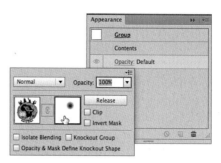

Display the Transparency panel by clicking the underlined word *Opacity* for a selected object in the Appearance or Control panel (or via Window> Transparency); here focused on the opacity mask for illustration on the opposite page

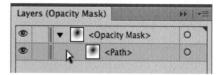

When you click the opacity mask thumbnail in the Transparency panel, the Layers panel displays only the objects within the opacity mask, and is indicated by the Layers panel tab name; try to keep the Layers, Transparency, and Appearance panels open when editing opacity masks

Editing opacity masks

- **Disable/Enable:** Shift-click the mask thumbnail to toggle the mask off (a red **X** will appear over the preview) and on.

- **Mask View:** Option-click/Alt-click the mask thumbnail to toggle the viewing and editing between the masking objects on the artboard, and the mask grayscale values.

- **Release (in the Transparency panel):** This releases the mask.

- **Working on artwork or opacity mask:** Click the appropriate icon to control what you are editing.

- **Link or unlink the opacity mask to artwork:** Click the space between the mask and artwork to toggle the link/unlink icon.

If you're having trouble seeing what you've just drawn, check the following:

- Are you still in mask-editing mode? When you have an opacity mask selected, the file title and Layers panel tab will display <Opacity Mask>.

- Are you in Draw Behind or Draw Inside mode? Check the Draw Mode icons at the bottom of the toolbar to make sure you're in Draw Normal mode.

The art of flattening

In Illustrator, transparency exists only within the program. In order to print or save in another format, Illustrator will "flatten" the objects where they overlap with transparency; in the case of printing, Illustrator flattens only temporarily, but if you save in formats such as EPS, or AI 9 or earlier, your image will be permanently flattened. When flattened, some objects may be split into many separate objects, while others may be rasterized. For more details, search adobe.com for "print production guide transparency" to access "Adobe Applications: A Print Production Guide."

mode to a path, then group it with several other objects and apply an opacity level to that group or to the layer that contains the group. To quickly and precisely locate and edit any transparent object, use the Layers, Appearance, and Transparency panels together. This is especially useful when you want to identify and edit the transparency of specific objects after using the Flattener Preview panel (covered in the next section) to see how current transparency settings will affect flattened output.

Remember that a gradient-filled circle in the Layers panel indicates that transparency is applied to an object, group, or layer, and an underlined name indicates that an opacity mask is applied. If the Appearance panel is open, it gives you access to the appearance details for the targeted object. Clicking the word <u>Opacity</u> in the Appearance panel (or the Control panel) displays detailed transparency settings for the targeted object. If you targeted an opacity mask, clicking the opacity mask thumbnail in the Transparency panel makes the Layers and Appearance panels provide information about the opacity mask.

BLENDS

Although gradients and mesh allow you to transition from one color to another, blends give you a way to "morph" one object's shape and/or color into another. You can create blends between multiple objects, and even blend gradients, symbols, compound paths such as letters, or even Point type objects. Because blends are *live*, you can edit the key objects' shape, color, size, location, or rotation, and the resulting *in-between* objects will automatically update. You can also distribute a blend along a custom path (see details later in this chapter).

The simplest way to create a blend is to double-click on the Blend tool to choose a setting for it, and then select the objects you wish to blend and choose Object> Blend> Make (⌘-Option-B/Ctrl-Alt-B). The setting you choose is persistent, so if you don't first double-click on the tool, your setting for it becomes the last-used setting. To later adjust settings on an existing blend: select the blend, then double-click the Blend tool (or choose Objects> Blend> Blend Options).

Another way to create blends between individual paths is to *point map* using the Blend tool. In the past, the Blend tool was used to achieve smooth transitions between blended objects. Now that it's been modified, however, it's probably best to use it for special morphing or twirling effects. To use the *point map* technique, begin by clicking on an anchor point of one object, and then on an anchor point of another object. Continue clicking on anchor points of any object you want to include in the blend. You can also click anywhere on the path of an object to achieve random blending effects.

To modify a key object before or after making a blend, Direct-Select the key object first, then use any editing tool (including the Pencil, Smooth, and Path Eraser tools) to make your changes.

Blend Options

To specify options as you blend, use the Blend tool (see the "point map" directions in the previous section) and press the Option/Alt key as you click the second point. In Blend Options you can change settings before making the blend. To adjust options on a completed blend, select it and double-click the Blend tool (or choose Object> Blend> Blend Options). Opening Blend Options without a blend selected sets the defaults for creating blends *in this work session*— these options reset each time you restart the program:

- **Specified Steps** specifies the number of steps between each pair of key objects (the limit is 1,000). Using fewer steps results in clearly distinguishable objects; a larger number of steps results in an almost airbrushed effect.
- **Specified Distance** places a specified distance between the objects of the blend.
- **Smooth Color** automatically calculates the ideal number of steps between key objects in a blend, in order to achieve the smoothest color transition. If objects are the same color, or are gradients or patterns, this option equally distributes the objects within the blend, based on their size.

Group-Select a key object and Option-drag/Alt-drag to insert a new key object (the blend will reflow). You can also insert new objects by double-clicking it to enter isolation mode, or by dragging them into the blend in the Layers panel.

Blend tool "W"

Aaron McGarry created this image of ripening tomatoes on a vine image using a variety of blends: the smooth color option for the vine, groups of objects blended into each other with Specified Steps, and a custom **S** curve "spine" (see Aaron McGarry's explanation on **WOW! ONLINE**)

What can you do with blends?

Besides editing objects you can:

- Reverse the direction of a blend, with Object> Blend> Reverse Front to Back. Or reverse the order of objects on a spine by choosing Object> Blend> Reverse Spine.
- Release blends (Object> Blend> Release) to remove blends, leaving key objects and spines. *Hint:* Select> Select All releases multiple blends simultaneously.
- Choose Object> Blend> Expand to turn a blend into a group of separate, editable objects.

- **Orientation** determines how the individual blend objects rotate as they follow the path's curves. Align to Page (the default, first icon) prevents objects from rotating as they're distributed along the path's curve (objects stay "upright" as they blend along the curve). Align to Path allows blend objects to rotate as they follow along the path.

Blends along a path

There are two ways to make blends follow a curved path. The first way is to use the Direct Selection tool to select the *spine* of a blend (the path automatically created by the blend) and then use the Add/Delete Anchor Point tools, or any of the following tools, to curve or edit the path: the Direct Selection, Lasso, Convert Anchor Point, Pencil, Smooth, or even the Path Eraser tool. As you edit the spine of the blend, Illustrator automatically redraws the blend objects to align to the edited spine.

Secondly, you can also replace the spine with a customized path. Select both the customized path and the blend, and choose Object> Blend> Replace Spine. This command moves the blend to its new spine.

You can also blend between pairs of grouped objects. If you're not getting the results you expect, try creating your first set of objects and grouping them (⌘-G/Ctrl-G). Now copy and paste a duplicate set (or Option/Alt and drag to create a copy of your group). Select the two sets of grouped objects and blend by choosing Specified Steps as the blend option. Once the objects are blended, you can rotate and scale them, and use the Direct Selection tool to edit the objects or the spine. (To experiment with a pair of grouped blends in this way, find the figures you see opposite on **WOW! ONLINE** as "AaronMcGarry-blends.ai.")

CLIPPING MASKS

All of the objects involved in a mask are organized in one of two ways depending on how you choose to make your mask. One method collects all selected objects into a group. The other method allows you to keep your layer structure, by placing layers within a master "container" layer (see the Layers panel illustrations, next page). With any kind of clipping mask, the topmost object of that group is the *clipping path*; this clips (hides) portions of the other objects in the group that extend beyond the clipping mask boundaries, leaving only the parts within these boundaries visible. Regardless of the attributes assigned to this top object, once you create the mask, it becomes an unfilled and unstroked clipping path (but keep reading to see how you can apply a stroke and fill to the new clipping path!). In the Layers panel, an active clipping mask will appear as an underlined <Clipping Path> and will remain underlined even if you rename it.

To make a clipping mask from an object, you must first create that object. Only a single path can be used as a clipping mask, which means that complex shapes or multiple paths must be combined into a single "compound path" before being used as a mask (using Object> Compound Path> Make). Make sure your path or compound path is above the objects to be clipped, then create the clipping mask using one of two options—use either the Make/Release Clipping Mask icon on the Layers panel, or the Object> Clipping Mask> Make command. Each has its inherent advantages and disadvantages. The Object menu command gathers all the objects into a new group as it masks, allowing you to have multiple masked objects within a layer. It also gives you the ability to freely move masked objects within a layer structure without breaking the mask. However, if you have a carefully planned layer structure, it will be lost when everything is grouped. In contrast, the Layers panel command maintains your layer structure as it masks, but you can't have separately masked objects within a layer without building sublayers or grouping them first. This makes it difficult to move masked objects as a unit.

After you've created a clipping mask, you can edit the masking object, and the objects within the mask, by selecting it using any selection tools, such as the Lasso or Direct Selection tools, then editing it with your typical path-editing tools, including live effects. When working

Draw Inside (fast masks)

See the *Rethinking Construction* chapter for details on the super quick way to make a clipping mask: using the Draw Inside mode.

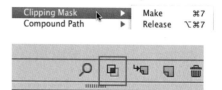

Choose Clipping Mask> Make from the Object menu (top), or use the Make/Release Clipping Mask icon on the Layers panel (bottom)

Pasting objects into a mask

To paste cut or copied objects into a clipping mask, make sure Paste Remembers Layers is off (in the Layers panel menu), then select an object within the mask and use Paste in Front or Back to place the copied object within the mask. You can also create or paste objects while in isolation mode.

Clipping Mask icon disabled

In the Layers panel, you must select the *container* (layer, sublayer, or group) that holds your intended clipping object before you can apply a clipping mask. Also, in order for the icon in the Layers panel to be enabled, the top item inside the highlighted container must be something that can be turned into a clipping path.

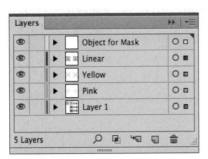

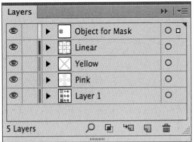

Choosing Object> Clipping Mask> Make puts all of the masked objects into a group with the clipping path at the top of the group

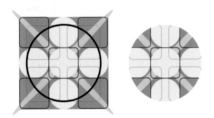

Before masking (left), the black-stroked circle is positioned as the topmost object in the stacking order, so it will become the clipping path when the clipping mask is created (right)

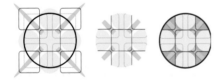

You can add a stroke and fill to a mask. The middle figure shows an unstroked mask; the right figure shows a dark blue stroke and a light blue fill added to the clipping mask

Selecting clipping masks

You can easily select all of your currently unlocked clipping masks at once by choosing Select> Object> Clipping Masks.

with masks created using the Object menu, clipped objects are now hidden when clipped by a mask; when the mask contents aren't selected, you won't accidentally select clipped objects outside of the masked path.

To move your clipped object (path and contents) simply select it with the Selection tool and move it. If you wish to select, move, or edit the clipping path or the contents independently, then you have a few options. If neither is selected, you can simply click on the clipping path or contents with the Direct Selection or Group Selection tool to edit or move that path or selection. If any portion of the mask or contents is already selected, you can click the Edit Clipping Path or Edit Contents buttons in the Control panel to focus on which portion will be selected and can be edited.

You also can edit your clipping group in isolation mode. To isolate the entire clipping <Group>, double-click on any portion of it with the Selection tool; this dims all other objects on your artboard. If you prefer, enter isolation mode via the Layers panel. Highlight the <Clipping Path> or any of the paths within the <Group> and choose Enter Isolation Mode from the Layers panel pop-up menu. You can now use the Edit Clipping Path or Edit Contents buttons, or use the Direct Selection and Group Selection tools.

Once in isolation mode you can freely edit or move the paths without affecting any other objects. If you are in isolation mode with one of the objects within the mask, you can even add additional objects within that grouping. To exit, double-click on the artboard (outside of the clipping group), press the Esc key, click on the gray isolation bar, or choose Exit Isolation Mode from the Layers panel pop-up menu.

Yet another way that you can determine which portion of your clipping group you wish to edit is by choosing Object> Clipping Mask> Edit Mask (or Object> Clipping Mask> Edit Content).

Once you have created a clipping group and mask, you can then add a stroke (it will appear as if it's in front of all masked objects) and/or a fill (it appears as if it's behind all masked objects). In addition, once the mask has been made, in the Layers panel you can even move the clipping path lower in the stacking order of the group or container (where it may no longer be the top path in the layer order) and still keep its masking effect.

Masking technique #1: The Object command

The simplest way to create masks for objects is using the Object menu command (⌘-7/Ctrl-7). Use this method when you want to confine the clipping mask to a specific object or group of objects that need to be easily duplicated or relocated, or when you have more than one clipping mask per layer. Since this method modifies your layer structure, don't use it if you need to maintain objects on specific layers.

As before, start by creating an object or compound object that will become your clipping mask. Make sure that it's the topmost object, then select it and *all* the objects you want to be masked (this topmost object will become the mask). Now, choose Object> Clipping Mask> Make. When you use this method, all the objects, including the new clipping path, will move to the layer that contains your topmost object and will be collected into a new <Group>. This will restrict the masking effect to only those objects within the group; you can easily use the Selection tool to select the entire clipping group. If you expand the <Group> in the Layers panel (by clicking the expansion triangle), you'll be able to move objects into or out of the clipping group, or move objects up or down within the group to change the stacking order. (Don't miss the Tip "Magical clipping path" at right.)

Masking technique #2: The Layers panel method

To mask unwanted areas of art within a *container* (meaning any group, sublayer, or layer), first create an object to use as your mask—make sure it's the topmost object in your container. Next, highlight that object's *container* and click the Make/Release Clipping Mask icon on the

At left the clipping mask (outlined in blue) above the floral illustration was created as 7 separate objects (6 petals and 1 center circle) and then united into a single compound path (using Object> Compound Path); at right after positioning this compound path on top of other objects, then using it as a clipping mask

In the Control panel: when a placed image is selected, the Mask button (left) appears; when an object using a mask is selected, the Edit Clipping Path and Edit Contents buttons (left and right respectively in the right-hand figure)

Figuring out if it's a mask

- <Clipping Path> in the Layers panel will be underlined if it's a mask (even if you've renamed it), and the background color for the icon will be gray.
- If Object> Clipping Mask> Release is enabled, it means a mask is affecting your selection.
- An *opacity mask* is underlined in the Layers panel.
- Select> Object> Clipping Masks can help you find masks within a document as long as they aren't inside linked files.

Collect in New Layer

To collect selected layers into one "master layer," Shift-click or ⌘-click/Ctrl-click multiple layers and choose Collect in New Layer from the Layers menu.

Layers panel. The result: The topmost object, *within* the highlighted container, becomes the clipping path, and all elements within that container extending beyond the clipping path are hidden (for details on how to use complex objects as a mask, see the section "Using type, compound paths, or shapes as a mask" below).

Once you've created a clipping mask, you can move objects up or down within the container (layer, sublayer, or group) to change the stacking order. But if you move items outside of the clipping mask container, they'll no longer be masked. Moving the clipping path itself outside of its container releases the mask completely.

Mask button

If you use File> Place to place an image, when the placed image is selected, you can instantly create a clipping path for the image by clicking the Mask button in the Control panel. However, masking is not immediately apparent because the clipping path has the same dimensions as the placed image's bounding box. Make sure the Edit Clipping Path button (in the Control panel) is enabled, then adjust the clipping path to shape the mask that is "cropping" your image.

Using type, compound paths, or shapes as a mask

You can use editable type as a mask to give the appearance that the type is filled with any image or group of objects. Select the type and the image or objects with which you want to fill the text. Make sure the type is on top, then choose Object> Clipping Mask> Make.

To use separate type characters as a single clipping mask, you have to first make them into a compound shape or compound path. You can make a compound shape from either outlined or live text. You can make a compound path only from outlined text (not live text). Once you've made a compound path or shape out of separate type elements, you can use it as a mask.

Psychotronic

Graphic Bloom

Single Cell

Grate Expectations

Funkus

Scorn Thistle

Alien Cells

Frillicious

Greener

GLITSCHKA

Von R. Glitschka

Shown above is just a small sample of unique patterns from Von R. Glitschka's book and DVD entitled, *Drip.Dot.Swirl. 94 incredible patterns for design and illustration* (How Publishing). Using similar techniques described on the opposite page (with some variation such as applying blending modes or effects to a layer), Glitschka created editable patterns in a wide range of styles. See www.vonsterbooks.com for details about the book.

Pattern Making

Navigating the Pattern Options Panel

Overview: *Create a pattern or edit an existing one; work in Pattern Editing Mode with the Pattern Options panel to adjust pattern repeats, varying spacing, offset, and overlap; create copies of patterns and experiment with offsets and settings to create and save pattern variations to the Swatches panel.*

1

Using the Pattern Options panel to access the Pattern Tile tool and experiment with settings

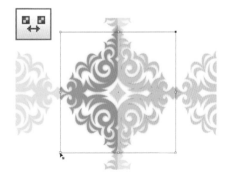

Using the Pattern Tile tool to change the gap between repeats with a Grid layout

Adobe commissioned Von Glitschka to produce a set of pattern swatches that would ship with Illustrator CS6. For each pattern he drew key elements for one tile, scanned and placed the sketch into Illustrator, and then hand-traced the elements as vector objects. Selecting the vector objects, he then used the Pattern Options panel to experiment with offset and spacing possibilities, getting instant feedback with each change. This lesson uses his "Diadem" pattern, which you can find in the Swatch Libraries menu under Patterns> Decorative> Vonster Patterns.

1 Creating the first pattern repeat. To follow along using Glitschka's Diadem pattern, first protect the original by copying it (drag the pattern in the Swatches panel to the New Swatch icon), then double-click on the copy to automatically open the Pattern Options panel and enter Pattern Editing Mode (PEM). To use your own artwork instead, select it and choose Object> Pattern> Make. In PEM, changes to settings immediately update, so when you adjust settings for Copies, be aware that with complex artwork, increased repeats can slow down screen redraw. When you open an existing pattern in PEM, PEM loads the Tile Type saved with the pattern. If you create a new pattern, then the default Tile Type will be Grid. You control the space between repeats by adjusting the size of the tile's bounding box, either with Size Tile to Art enabled and numeric input for H and V Spacing, or interactively

Chapter 7 *Mastering Complexity*

by using the Pattern Tile tool. With the Pattern Tile Tool selected, use the square anchors to enlarge or reduce the gap between repeats. To create an overlap, make the tile bounding box smaller and choose the desired Overlap features. As your pattern progresses, you might want to evaluate it by zooming out, temporarily disabling both Dim Copies and Show Tile Edge, and increasing the repeats. Undo/Redo is available while in PEM and can even back you out of PEM. At any time you can save the current version of the pattern as a swatch, but stay in PEM to create more variations, by clicking Save a Copy and naming it. Now you can continue editing and experimenting with the pattern. To save this version as the final one and exit PEM, click Done. If you click Cancel, no changes are saved to your original pattern in the Swatches panel.

2 **Experimenting with pattern offsets.** To experiment with pattern offsets, you can stay in PEM or start over with a new copy. Make sure that both Show Tile Edge and Show Swatch Bounds are enabled. Any artwork that is within, overlaps, or touches the Swatch Bounds will be included in the pattern. To make your tile resize to the exact size of your art, enable Size Tile to Art (if it's enabled, you may have to disable and then re-enable it).

Glitschka offset "Diadem" using the Hex by Row tile type, which naturally fits this design with little manipulation, but you can also use Brick by Row with a Brick Offset of 1/2 to tuck the repeats close together. Brick Offset controls the position of each repeat relative to the others. When the Pattern Tile Tool is active, you can adjust the Brick Offset in fixed intervals by dragging the diamond widget on the Tile Edge to the right or left.

With either Hex by Row or Brick by Row as your Tile Type, grab a square anchor on a corner or side, and drag inwards to bring the artwork closer together. Hold the Option/Alt key to resize two sides symmetrically, and add the Shift key to resize the entire tile proportionally. When you see something you like, Click Save a Copy and remain in PEM, or click Done to save the swatch and exit PEM.

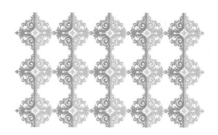

Viewing multiple repeats with both Dim Copies and Show Tile Edge disabled

The Pattern Isolation bar showing the pattern name, controls for saving the current state to the Swatches panel, and ways to exit PEM

Using Brick by Row to start an offset repeat of the pattern, adjusted with the Pattern Tile Tool to make the repeats fit with a slender gap between them

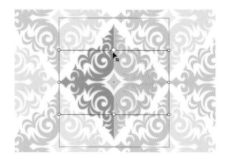

Resizing the Tile Edge by dragging on corner anchors, and dragging on the diamond widget to change the pattern repeat offset at fixed intervals from 1/4 up to 4/5 the distance of a full repeat

Layered Patterns

Building Depth and Complexity in PEM

Advanced Technique

Overview: *Design basic elements for your pattern and enter PEM; establish a height and width for your tile; choose a Tile Type; position the pattern elements and experiment with Swatch Bounds; vary the level of detail to enhance depth.*

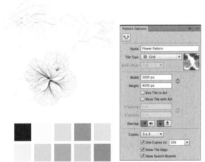

Planning ahead by drawing artwork, choosing a color palette, and setting the size of the Pattern Tile

Pattern elements shown in full color, with repeats dimmed to 50%, and the Swatch Bounds/Tile Edge outlined in red for clarity

Sabine Reinhart specializes in creating richly complex, layered patterns, constructed so all the elements involved enhance the illusion of depth. Illustrator's Pattern Editing Mode (PEM) makes it easier than ever to experiment with the placement of elements as Reinhart gradually builds up her pattern. Although her patterns are often large enough to slow most computers down to a crawl, the organic look she achieves rewards her patience.

1 Starting the pattern tile with its first elements. Reinhart had drawn her main elements, created a color group, and determined the size and tile type (Grid in this case) before she began her pattern. Selecting her artwork, she entered Pattern Editing Mode, (Object> Pattern> Make), and manually entered the Width and Height in the Patterns panel. Using the Move tool, she adjusted the position of each flower so that it overlapped the Swatch Bounds (which in the Grid tile type is the same as the Tile size, and shown at left outlined in red for clarity), leaving room for adding subordinate artwork both above and below the first objects.

2 Designing patterns using Swatch Bounds. As long as you are within PEM, you can freely use the entire canvas to design new elements and plan your pattern. Because the Swatch Bounds define the parameters of the actual pattern, however, your pattern will only be made up of any objects that are at least partially touching the edge or the interior of the Swatch bounds. Objects contained by the Swatch Bounds, overlapping it, or touching an edge somewhere will automatically appear in the opposite quadrants of the pattern repeat. For instance, when Reinhart placed a dark green flower outside—but still touching—the Swatch bounds, it was included in the pattern, and as long as she set Copies to more than 1 x 1, she could preview where the object was repeated within the pattern.

Be aware that if you're using Brick or Hex layout (instead of Grid), changing the offset or offset type (by row or column) can cause the Swatch Bounds to grow or shrink in size. Artwork that was previously outside Swatch Bounds might now fall within the pattern, and vice versa. In addition, when you create art in PEM, any objects that aren't included in the pattern swatch will be deleted; if you wish to keep any objects that are not included in the pattern, copy the objects to the Clipboard before exiting PEM, and paste them into a new file.

3 Adding new artwork. After getting the first flowers placed, Reinhart started adding more flowers, duplicating, transforming, and coloring them while inside PEM. She emphasized depth by overlapping some flowers in front and in back of others, by scaling, and by altering the artwork to show less detail as she moved it further to the back of the stack. She intermingled a few butterflies and, at the very bottom, added a light-colored rectangle with no stroke to conceal any gaps in the pattern and give it an airy, organic appearance. She named the pattern in the Patterns panel and clicked Done to save her pattern to the Swatches panel. Later, she would use Recolor Artwork to create variations (see her lesson in the *Color Transitions* chapter for details about how she did this).

2

Adding layers both above and below the initial artwork; elements transformed and recolored

3

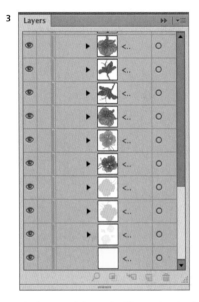

The bottom of the stack of layers showing how Reinhart created depth by incorporating more detail in upper layers, with diminishing detail as she moved further to the back of the stack

The final pattern showing the Swatch Bounds

REINHART

Sabine Reinhart

German designer Sabine Reinhart specializes in creating complex, organic patterns, and she often derives inspiration from cultures all over the world. Drawing upon her knowledge of traditional Indian decorative elements and indigenous flora, and adding her personal European touch to the designs, she created the patterns used on the cover of *The Adobe Illustrator CS6 WOW! Book* as part of a collection she called "Lost in Paradise." She used Illustrator's new Pattern Options panel and Pattern Editing Mode to help her visualize the flow of the elements as they were repeated. Peachpit designer

Mimi Heft later wove Reinhart's patterns into the cover design in InDesign, placing a version of one bird on top of the **O** in **WOW!** (For more about how Reinhart creates her patterns, see the "Layered Patterns" tutorial in this chapter and the "Recolor a Pattern" lesson in *Color Transitions*.) Reinhart named the leaf and peacock feather pattern (above right) "Kimaya," meaning "Divine," and the peacock and flower pattern (top left) "Jamini," meaning "Night." Through these patterns she celebrated the exuberance, rich heritage, and mystery found in India's ancient life and culture.

PAIDRICK

Ann Paidrick

When Ann Paidrick opened a package, she saw the crumpled paper used for shipping as an artistic gift of inspiration. She photographed a few pieces, then used Illustrator to trace each and create patterns using the traced objects. She chose the 16-color Preset in Image Trace to convert her scans to vector objects with strong abstract coloring. After some cleanup, she arranged two of the objects and entered Pattern Editing Mode. She experimented with the Tile Type and layout, and decided on Hex by Row for these versions. She used the Pattern Tile tool to interactively adjust the Tile Edge, squeezing and pulling on the hex shape, and adjusted the Overlap. Whenever she found a pleasing arrangement, she clicked on Save a Copy on the Isolation bar. Between Illustrator's Image Trace and Pattern Editor features, Paidrick was able to use found objects to quickly produce unique and complex vector patterns.

Roping in Paths

Using Masks and Pathfinders for Shapes

Advanced Technique

Overview: *Create and organize layers, place a scanned sketch, and draw shapes; draw paths for the rope, outline their strokes, feather their fills, and draw masks; make a compound path, duplicate it, and reshape it.*

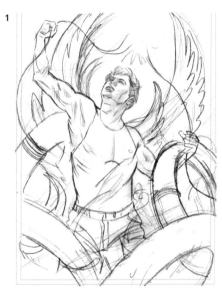

Hamann's scan of the pencil sketch he made from the photographs he took of himself

Hamann organizing his Layers panel

When *Angels on Earth* magazine needed an online illustration featuring a heroic angel saving a woman from drowning, illustrator Brad Hamann responded with layering, masks, and pathfinder tools in "Angel in the Rapids."

1 Scanning a sketch, organizing layers, and drawing shapes. Hamann began by drawing and scanning a pencil sketch and placing it in Illustrator on a template layer.

Hamann's design called for layering so that artwork like the tubes and rope appeared in front of or behind other artwork. He created layers in the Layers panel based on visual hierarchy. To outline the angel against the rest of the image, Hamann created a blue outline of the angel, then a white one. To do this he copied the head and body objects, then used Paste in Back, and then applied Pathfinder> Unite. Giving this new shape a blue stroke and fill, he copied it, used Paste in Back, and then gave this duplicate outline a white fill and a wider white stroke.

2 Making and masking the rope. Hamann created the rope in sections, drawing paths between objects for the tubes and hands. He smoothed the curvature of the ropes by adjusting direction lines with the Direct Selection tool. To give the selected rope paths a dark blue edge with a light fill, he first changed the paths to a 4-pt, dark blue stroke. Next Hamann chose Object> Path> Outline Stroke and changed the stroke to 1 pt and the fill to orange. Finally, to add a subtle highlight to the rope, Hamann chose Effect> Stylize> Inner Glow and in the dialog entered 24 for Opacity and 0.03 inches for Blur, and clicked OK.

Where each rope section was cut off by another object, Hamann masked the rope by the edge of the other objects' strokes. He decided that drawing the masks by hand would be precise enough for the resolution of a web graphic. To mask the rope where it joined the fist, for example, Hamann drew a shape with the Pen tool that loosely surrounded the rope except for where the rope was cut off by the fist. For that area, he drew the path of the masking shape by hand along the edge of the fist's blue stroke. Finally, he selected the masking shape and the rope and chose Object> Clipping Mask> Make.

3 Drawing the tube. For the tube draped over the angel's left arm, Hamann drew a yellow-filled path for the tube's outer edge and another path for the tube's center hole. He selected both objects and chose Object> Compound Path> Make. To form shadows, he copied the compound path and used Paste in Front, then filled this duplicate with a darker yellow. With the duplicate still selected, Hamann used the Scissors tool to make two cuts on the right side of the outer edge, then selected and deleted the outer left edge of the compound path. Next, he used the Pen tool to redraw the shadow path between the two open points. When he completed the path, he filled it with a darker yellow and then chose Effect> Stylize> Feather, changed the feather radius to 0.05, and clicked OK. Hamann finished by drawing highlight shapes and pasting another duplicate of the tube in front, changing its fill to None and stroke to dark blue.

2

On the left, the paths for two sections of rope; on the right, the paths after choosing Object> Path> Outline Stroke, filling them with orange, and then applying Inner Glow to the fills

The mask drawn as a green-stroked path

The Inner Glow dialog

3

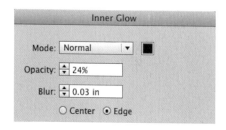

On the left, the drawn compound path; on the right, the compound path filled with yellow

On the left, a copy of the compound path pasted in front of the yellow tube; in the middle, the compound path cut on the right side; on the right, the finished shape filled with dark yellow

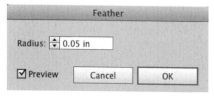

The Feather dialog

Adding Highlights

Using Transparency to Create Highlights

Advanced Technique

Overview: *Create highlights in objects for the interior of the cell using the Blend tool; stack them and lower opacity; create highlights with gradients for other objects and reduce opacity; create a bright lens flare.*

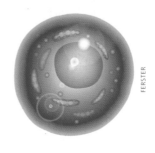

FERSTER

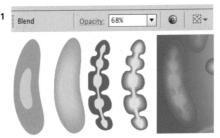

1

After creating an object by blending a light object with a darker, same-shaped object to represent a highlight, transparency further blends the "lit" object (mitochondrion) into its surroundings

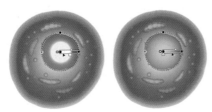

Adjusting the radial gradient adjusts the size and edge of the highlight, while transparency settings adjust the final blend into another object

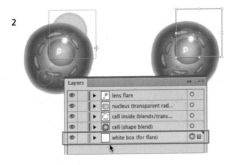

2

The Lens Flare tool needs a non-transparent background to reach maximum brightness

Adding transparency to blended or gradient-filled objects, or conversely, eliminating transparency beneath a lens flare, gives you a great deal of versatility when constructing believable highlights.

1 Using multiple techniques for blending colors in order to simulate natural highlighting. When Gary Ferster wanted to illustrate a living cell, he chose various methods for constructing blended highlights. For the mitochondrion (pinkish objects), he used the Blend tool to create two initial shapes, one very light, and one the "local" color. When blended smoothly, this method created soft highlights. He then stacked one blended object over the other and reduced the opacity in each, in order to make them appear to be part of the cell. For the small bubbles (lysosomes) and nucleus in the cell, however, Ferster used simple radial gradients with a very light center gradating to the local color of the object. By adjusting the gradient stops, he could make highlights bigger or smaller, with sharper or more feathered edges, and then adjust opacity to blend these objects into the cell.

2 Using the Lens Flare tool for maximum highlighting. Nothing suggests a powerful light source quite like a lens flare, but Ferster had observed that using the Lens Flare tool over a transparent background creates a dulled, gray flare. A simple solution was to draw a solid white rectangle, at least as big as the flare, behind all the objects. The part of the lens flare that extended beyond the cell became white, disappearing into the background entirely.

GUSMAN JOLY

Annie Gusman Joly

Transparency can be created with Blending Modes that interact with the layers beneath, forming new colors based on the type of Blending Mode used. Artist Annie Gusman Joly uses them here to create a complex pattern of shadows. In this tropical forest, light filters through the leaves and flowers to fall on the ground beneath the white bird's feet. To create the random and overlapping patterns, Joly first fills a large object on one layer with a solid blue. After drawing the path for the shadows on

the layer above, she fills it with blue and sets the Blending Mode to Multiply. If the shadow color is too dark, she reduces the layer Opacity to increase the shadow layer's transparency. She uses the same technique for the shadow beneath her three-toed sloth.

Moonlighting

Using Transparency for Glows & Highlights

Advanced Technique

Overview: *Create a Radial gradient with transparency for a circular object; use the Blend tool with a duplicate object to create a circular or oval blend with transparency; create a glow or highlight for a non-circular object.*

GUSMAN JOLY

1

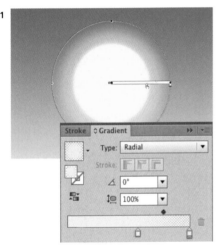

Using the Gradient tool with either the Gradient Annotator (top) or Gradient panel (bottom) to create a gradient with transparency

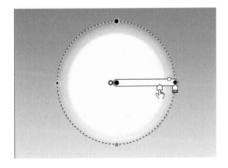

Drag the color stop for the inner object toward the transparent stop to make the object larger; drag the diamond to alter the size of the glow

Because the glowing moon is circular in Annie Gusman Joly's "Solo-Flight" illustration about growing up an identical twin, it could be created by using either a radial gradient or a shaped blend. The key to making a gradient or blend work against any background is to use transparency for the edge of the object that touches the background.

1 Creating a glow from a Radial gradient. With the object selected, click on it once with the Gradient tool to fill with the last-used or default gradient, and, if necessary, change the type in the Gradient panel to Radial. Either in the Gradient panel or with the aid of the Gradient Annotator, double-click on each color stop and choose the same color for them. Reduce the opacity for the stop that represents the outer edge to 0%; drag the opposite color stop inward to make the solid part of the object bigger and more solid, and adjust the Gradient slider between them (the diamond shape on the top of the gradient bar) to create a larger or smaller amount of feather (or "glow").

2 Creating a glow for a circular object from an object blend. With a pale yellow Fill color, choose a stroke of None, and draw a circle (Shift-drag with the Ellipse tool). With Smart Guides on (View menu), move your cursor over the circle until you see the word "center," hold down Option/Alt, and Shift-drag out a new, smaller circle. Set the Opacity of the larger circle to 0%. Select both circles and choose Object> Blend> Make (⌘-Option-B/Ctrl-Alt-B); then double-click the Blend tool in the toolbox to adjust the steps. For this example, somewhere between 20 and 30 steps makes a very glowing moon.

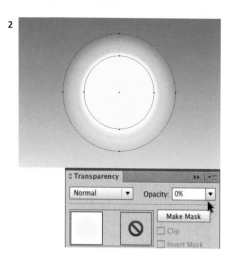

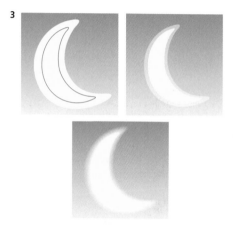

Creating a blend between two circles with one set to 0% Opacity

3 Shaping a glow with a blend made from non-circular objects. When you don't have a circle or oval path, only a blend can "shape" the glow evenly around the object. So that the glowing object can be placed over any background, we'll continue to create the glow with transparency. Create your first object—here, a crescent moon filled with pale yellow and no stroke. Many asymmetrical shapes don't scale easily relative to the original's boundaries, so with your object selected, choose Object> Path> Offset Path. Enable Preview and use a negative number for a smaller object. Select the larger object and, in the Transparency panel, set the Opacity to 0%. Now select both paths and choose Object> Blend> Make. If you haven't already created a blend with the Specified Steps or Specified Distance Spacing option in your current working session, Illustrator might use Smooth Color. Smooth Color doesn't create a glow, but rings the inner crescent moon with a lighter color. To get the glow, double-click on the Blend tool to open the dialog and choose Specified Steps for the Spacing option. Around 25 steps should create a decent glow. If necessary, adjust the offset, miter, and path edges until the blend is smooth and glowing.

This shaped-blend method can also be used for making any shape or size of highlight for any object. By creating the highlight as a separate object, you gain the advantage of being able to change the object's color later without having to reconstruct the object and the blend.

Creating the second object with Offset Path (top left) and using Object> Blend> Make; the default Smooth Color doesn't blend (top right), but switching to Specified Steps creates the glow

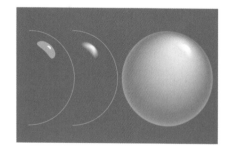

Creating a highlight using a shaped blend with one opaque and one transparent object

"CHINGON"

Copyright © 2012 Chris Nielsen

NIELSEN

Chris Nielsen

When Chris Nielsen came across this one-of-a-kind, custom chopper by Matt Hotch, he knew he had to illustrate it with his signature PhotoRealist technique. He knew his basic 8 MP digital point-and-shoot camera would capture enough detail, but with many other custom bikes parked in the same shop, getting the reference shot at all was a major undertaking. Once he brought it into Illustrator, he used the same methods described on the opposite page, relying on the Pen tool to draw progressively smaller details, and the Pathfinder panel with the Divide command to create the areas representing every nuance of the bike and its reflections. He worked on a section at a time, starting with less detailed areas, and bringing each to near completion before mov-

ing to the next area. Nielsen would often zoom to a comfortable 300% or so to work on fine details, but rarely more than that. In this manner, he always managed to keep an eye on the way the area he was working on was affecting the image as a whole. Color started with the photo itself, but Nielsen didn't rely upon the photo to produce the most accurate and pleasing tones. He used his artist's eye to adjust colors until the right hues and values were represented. Since Nielsen's work is so Photorealistic, he purposely leaves sections in an "outline view" appearance so the viewer will realize that it is still a drawing they're looking at and *not* a photograph. When completed, Nielsen's "Chingon" brought to life a rare, custom motorcycle for everyone to enjoy.

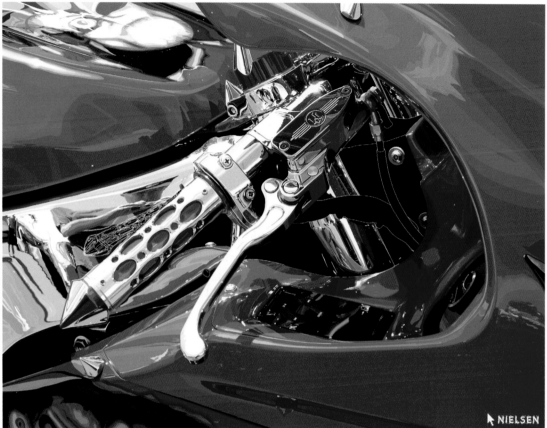

"Reflections In Red"

NIELSEN

Chris Nielsen

Chris Nielsen created another stunning image using the same drawing technique described on the opposite page. Nielsen likes to begin drawing an area of the photograph that contains a large object, such as a gas tank, or big pipe. Working over a template layer that contained his original photograph, he first drew the outline of a large object with the Pen tool. Then he drew paths for each area where the color value changed within that object. He selected the paths and clicked the Divide Pathfinder icon. He continued in this manner until there were enough shapes to define the object. This

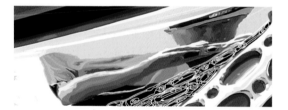

was a particularly challenging motorcycle to draw because there are only slight variations in one overall color. Nielsen filled each individual object with a custom color chosen from the Swatches panel. In all of his motorcycle illustrations, the reflection of Nielsen taking the photograph is visible—here it is shown in the magnified detail above.

Masking Images

Simple to Complex Clipping Masks

Advanced Technique

Overview: *Create a clipping mask; gather and order objects to clip; use the mask to clip objects; position masked objects; add finishing touches.*

1

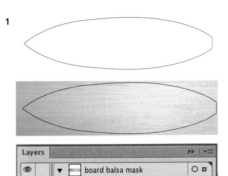

The surfboard path outline (top); with the balsa wood image placed and the path moved above it (middle); the stacking order of the two objects in the layers panel before making the clipping mask (directly above)

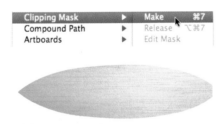

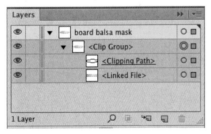

(Top and middle) Using Object> Clipping Mask> Make to turn the top path into a clipping path; (directly above) the Layers panel showing the surfboard <Clipping Path> masking the <Linked File> wood JPG

This custom surfboard design made of masks within masks was created by San Diego-based illustrator Aaron McGarry, who finds much of his work inspired by a life tailored to the beach communities and industries of southern California.

1 Inserting wood texture with a clipping mask. In a new document McGarry double-clicked the layer name to customize it. He used the Pen tool to draw the outline of a surfboard, which he would use as a clipping path for his new surfboard design. To add the wood texture for the board, McGarry used File> Place to place a JPG image of balsa wood into his document (making certain that the Template option was disabled). With his image selected, he used Object> Arrange> Send to Back to move the image to the back of the stacking order, making his surfboard outline the top-most object. Adjusting the alignment of the path and the wood, he then selected both objects and chose Object> Clipping Mask> Make (⌘-7/ Ctrl-7); this clipped the image into the path and thereby created the wooden surfboard.

2 Creating a complex (compound) clipping mask. With the surfboard itself prepared, and since his logo would be used for other purposes, McGarry created the logo in a separate document using the Pen tool, Pathfinder panel, and text. He would be "filling" this logo with a blue underwater image by using the logo itself as a clipping mask. His initial logo design consisted of two separate paths plus type, all styled initially with a black stroke and no fill so he could see his design as he worked. Only one path can be used as a clipping path for a mask, so if you have multiple elements (such as type and logo objects) you'll have to first combine the elements into a compound path or compound shape. McGarry had outlined his text so he could make some adjustments, so in order for all of the letters and the logo to behave as one mask, he needed to combine them into one compound path using Object> Compound Path> Make (⌘-7/Ctrl-7). Alternatively, if you're working with live type, you can combine logo design elements and type into a Compound Shape by choosing Make Compound Shape from the Pathfinder panel.

With this complex compound path prepared, McGarry placed his underwater JPG image. Using the Layers panel he positioned his logo path above his placed image. McGarry then selected both the logo and the image, then used ⌘-7/Ctrl-7 to make all of his logo objects into a clipping group. Then he renamed the layer "logo masked."

3 **Assembling the objects and finishing touches.** To add finishing details, McGarry created two more layers. On one layer ("speargun") he put additional type; into the "board edge" layer he moved a copy of board outline path (by holding Option/Alt while dragging the object proxy to the new layer); and then increased the stroke weight. He then created the light-to-dark edging around the board by applying a wood gradient to the stroke (from Swatch Libraries> Gradients) and in the Gradient panel. He enabled the first Stroke option (Apply gradient within stroke), and adjusted the angle in the field below to create the desired lighting effect. Finally, with the board edge outline still selected he chose the Draw Inside drawing mode to constrain his paint and used a charcoal art brush (Window> Brush Libraries> Artistic> Artistic_ChalkCharcoalPencil) to paint rough white streaks on the board surface (see the *Expressive Strokes* chapter for more about how to do this).

Finally, McGarry made sure that Paste Remembers Layers was enabled (from the Layers panel pop-up menu), and with both documents open, McGarry used drag and drop to move his logo into his surfboard document, automatically adding the layer names as well. He positioned his logo on top of the surfboard and resized it to fit.

2

Selecting all parts of the logo and using Object> Compound Path> Make to create a single compound object that behaves as one path

Selecting both compound logo and placed image before and after using Object> Clipping Mask> Make to create the mask

The Layers panel showing the objects <Clip Group> after applying the clipping mask, with the logo (<Compound Clipping Path>) above the underwater image (<Image>)

3

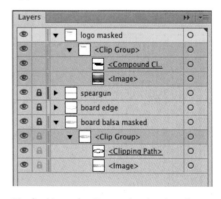

The surfboard outline after adding the white streaks and applying a wood gradient to the edging path

The final layers for the completed project showing the mask layers expanded

MCKIBILLO (AKA Josh McKible)

MCKIBILLO's NaniBird project (found at www.nanibird.com) is a collaborative website devoted to the art of papercraft. Here you'll find photos of his NaniBirds, as well as NaniBirds decorated with designs by others, along with a few non-Nani papercraft characters. MCKIBILLO spent a lot of time refining the original Nani-Bird silhouette, always mindful that, like a little sculpture, his papertoy, required consideration of all sides of the design. The blank NaniBird PDF template (on **WOW! ONLINE**) was created from a layered Illustrator file, with separate, simple, vector objects. To insert your art into the template, you can fill each object with a pattern, you could use Draw Inside mode to paint within a selected object (see the *Rethinking Construction* chapter for details about how to do this), or you can use each path as a separate clipping path, to mask any objects (or images) within. It's tricky to visualize, so print proofs and assemble to ensure artwork within is correctly oriented. The photo above shows a NaniBird surrounded by a flock of NaniPeeps (you can also download Peep templates from **WOW! ONLINE**). When your customized NaniBird template is complete, upload it (and photos of the papercraft results) to the NaniBird website to share.

MCKIBILLO

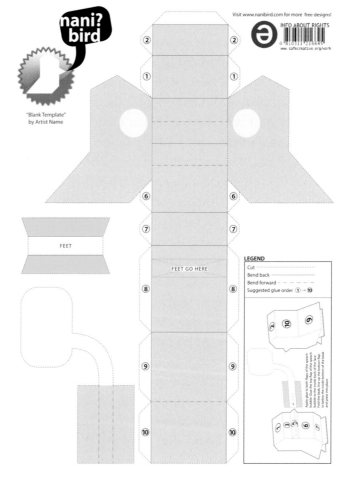

"Blank Template" by Artist Name

Visit www.nanibird.com for more free designs!

FEET

FEET GO HERE

LEGEND
Cut
Bend back
Bend forward
Suggested glue order ① → ⑩

GAUSE

Monika Gause

Monika Gause, the mastermind
behind the European Illustrator website Vektorgarten (www.vektorgar-
ten.de), made her papercraft zebra as
an homage to NaniBirds and similar
projects. After working out how to
physically construct her Paperzebra
(paper-colored animal in the photo,
above right), she then deconstructed
it and designed the flat template.
Gause draws into the template with
the Pencil tool, then she uses Live
Paint to add color to the blank spaces
formed between the lines (see the
Rethinking Construction chapter for
help working with Live Paint). Once
she figured out her first zebra, she
set about making a number of variations, some with a tongue sticking
out, others with a flat smiling row
of teeth. Gause also allows anyone
to use her templates, saying that her
goal is "to get a zebra into every
home on the planet."

Opacity Masking

Smooth Transitions & Intertwining Objects

Advanced Technique

Overview: *Create soft transitions using single-object opacity masks; interweave objects using complex multi-object opacity masks.*

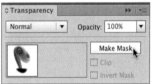

The head overlapping the hollow tendril (left); adding an oval with a Feather effect (middle); shift-selecting the head <Clip Group> and oval; clicking on the Make Mask button (right/below)

The finished critter and tendrils (including feathered ovals blending the tendrils into the pot)

Chris Leavens' fantastic realms are made plausible by the way objects interact with each other, creating depth and disguising vector edges. He often uses Opacity Masks to overlap objects believably, as well as to soften transitions between shadow and full light, or between transparent and opaque. Instead of cutting objects apart to create the illusion of objects intermingling, with opacity masks you can keep objects intact so you can continue to make adjustments. Whenever complex interactions or soft transitions are called for, Leavens finds it easier to construct and work with Opacity Masks than with Clipping Masks.

1 Masking with shadows for soft transitions. In order to create the illusion that a critter's head was inside the tendril's tube, Leavens attached a feathered oval for the area of the neck that would gradually disappear into the gradient that creates the hole in the tendril. To do this he drew a black oval on top of the neck and feathered it (Effect> Stylize> Feather). Because the head consisted of several objects contained within a <Clip Group>, to attach an opacity mask to the head, Leavens targeted the <Clip Group> in the Layers panel, held down Shift, and also selected the feathered oval. Opening the Transparency panel, he disabled "New opacity masks are clipping" from the panel menu so all new masks would be solid white (reveal all). Then he clicked the Make Mask button, turning the top object (the black feathered oval) into an opacity mask for the critter head clip group.

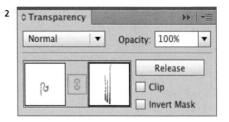

The default Transparency dialog with "New opacity masks are clipping" disabled in the panel menu in order to paste a concealing (black) object into the mask

2 Masking with multiple objects. Leavens began by drawing the snake and palms individually. All the objects were complex, and each was contained within a clip group, with a single clipping path defining its contour. To create the illusion that the snake was weaving through the trees, Leavens created an opacity mask for the snake by modifying a copy of the contour paths for the trees. Using the Make Mask button would only turn the top tree into a mask, so he needed to manually create the mask. To do this he selected all three clipping paths used to define the outline of the trees by holding Shift and clicking each clipping path with the Group Selection tool (or Shift-click each <Clipping Path> in the Layers panel) and copied them to the Clipboard. He selected the snake's <Clip Group> with the Selection tool (or targeted it in the Layers panel), opened the Transparency panel, then double-clicked on the empty mask thumbnail to enter Opacity Mask Mode for the snake's clip group (you'll see a thick line around the mask thumbnail, and <Opacity Mask> in the Layers panel). Leavens then used Paste in Front (⌘-F/Ctrl-F) to paste the copied trees in perfect registration; then clicked on a Black swatch to solidly fill the semi-transparent outlines. The snake now appeared completely behind the trees. Using the Eraser tool, he erased sections of the mask where he wanted the snake to appear in front of the tree. When the mask was finished, he clicked on the image thumbnail to exit Opacity Mask Mode.

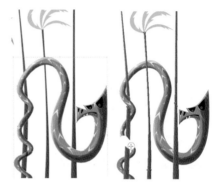

The snake and palms before masking (left); The snake with copies of the palms' clipping paths pasted into an Opacity Mask, and portions of the mask being erased (right)

After erasing the mask to reveal the snake slithering in front and behind the palm trunks, Leavens added the shadows cast by the palms to the snake's clip group

HUBIG

Dan Hubig

In this Illustration for *California Magazine*, Dan Hubig first combined blends, gradients, and transparency in Illustrator, and then enhanced his image in Photoshop with Blurs, Brushes, and Adjustment layers. Hubig used Transparency to render the cloak and torso only partially opaque, which kept his options open for expressing invisibility in Photoshop. He created his "cloak of invisibility" in Illustrator with a white Fill and Stroke and an opacity of only 19%, then duplicated it with a Stroke and no Fill to a new layer on top. By planning ahead, he would be able to reduce the cloak's visibility to zero, if he chose, but maintain that important outline. For one version, Hubig also made the man's torso completely invisible, but for the final version, he retained a hint of opacity. To learn more about how Hubig creates his illustrations, see the "Planning Ahead" lesson in the *Creatively Combining Apps* chapter.

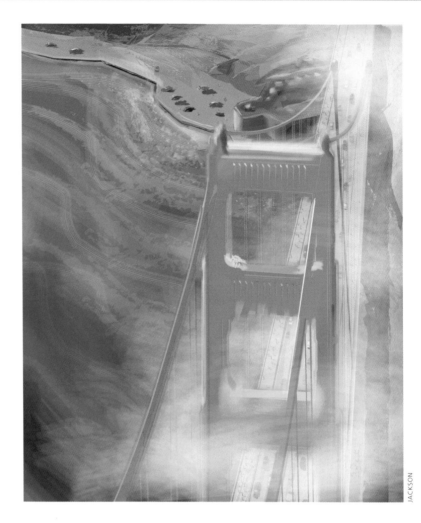

JACKSON

Lance Jackson

To create the cover illustration for *The Adobe Illustrator CS5 WOW! Book*, Lance Jackson generated atmosphere and depth with the Bristle Brush and constructed many of the details using the Blob Brush. He used various tools to block in the main components of his composition. He used the Pen tool to draw the basic cables and roadway for the Golden Gate Bridge, then modified the strokes with the Width tool. Next Jackson began brushing over the water and bridge with various brushes from the Bristle Brush library, especially Deerfoot, Cat's Tongue, Dome,

and Fan. To constrain the brushes to each main element, he often selected a base object and chose the Draw Inside mode. For added texture, he also used brushes from the Artistic and Grunge Brush Vector Pack libraries. Jackson drew a few cars and pedestrians using the Blob Brush, then duplicated and recolored several of them. Jackson toned down his palette, adding fog and more depth, by reducing the opacity of his brushstrokes, layering the strokes, and sometimes even changing the blending mode (by clicking <u>Opacity</u> in the Control panel).

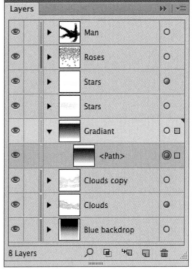

Jean Aubé

Jean Aubé created "Falling" as a personal response to lingering discussions with a friend about the emotional impact of the 9/11 disaster. He used many different techniques throughout, including Image Trace, scatter brush (to distribute the stars), gradients, and many instances of reducing opacity and changing blending modes. The hard edges of the man and roses falling from above keep these narrative elements in full focus, while the soft layers of clouds create a rich depth of field. To create these clouds Aubé first used Image Trace on scans of his pastel-drawn clouds. He then placed and offset layer upon layer of clouds, adjusting opacity and blending modes, and finally overlaying a gradient (purple to white) set to multiply mode.

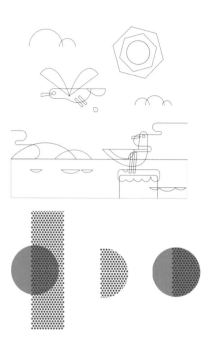

PEREZ

Richard Perez

To add warmth to his crisp vector objects, San Francisco-based illustrator Richard Perez often adds just a few touches of texture. Sometimes his textures are scans, while other times he creates textures out of repeating Illustrator objects. Depending on where and how he wants to add texture, he applies and constrains it using opacity masks or clipping masks. Perez often begins with a muted, restricted color palette and builds the basics of his image using mostly the Rectangle, Ellipse, and Polygon tools. He uses the Direct Selection tool to select points to delete or move, creating some open objects and elongating others, often constraining movement to 180°, 90°, and 45° axes. Though he sometimes combines objects using Pathfinder> Unite, often he keeps objects separate (such as the half-ovals that form the clouds), so he can make subtle adjustments to positioning.

With the main elements in place, he brings in the textural elements, which he collects and keeps in separate files for reuse. In the case of this lovely ode to the San Francisco Embarcadero waterfront, Perez brought in a field of repeating dots. Using a sequence of Option-dragging/Alt-dragging to duplicate, then ⌘-D/Ctrl-D to repeat the duplication, he transformed one dot into a line of dots, offsetting that line of dots into a pair, and then duplicating/repeating that pair into a field of dots. For the circle with dots (above left), he selected his masking object with the dot set beneath it and applied Object> Clipping Mask> Make. The masking object's fill disappeared, but by Direct Selecting (or targeting the <Clipping Path> in the Layers panel), he could reapply the fill. Keeping the dots related in color to the fill beneath helps to imply a halftone, overlay, or transparency.

TAN

Moses Tan

Moses Tan accurately rendered most of the details of this Kyoto Bus Station by carefully tracing over his own reference photograph using closed filled paths

drawn with the Pen tool. In a few cases, however, he used Illustrator's more powerful features such as blends, gradients, and clipping masks. To draw the central grill unit (detail directly above), Tan drew one vertical column, copied and shift-dragged it to the opposite side. With both objects selected he double-clicked the Blend tool to show Options, entered 50 for the Specified Steps, and set the orientation to Align to Page. Selecting the objects he choose Object> Blend> Make. Tan began the shadows beneath the passengers using linear gradients, then within the Appearance panel

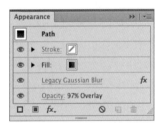

he selected the fill, clicked the *fx* icon, and chose Blur> Gaussian Blur. For other shadows he filled objects with gradients, then reduced the opacity and changed the blending mode (such as Overlay or Multiply).

Chris Nielsen

Chris Nielsen has trained his artistic eye to recognize subtle shifts of color within a photograph and translate them into a striking image using layers of filled paths. Nielsen first placed an original photograph in a bottom layer to trace upon. He worked on one small section at a time, such as the eye in the detail to the right. With the Pen tool he made paths (no fill, with a black stroke) and traced the areas of primary color he saw in the photograph. He chose the darkest value first (dark blue or black), then on another layer, he drew the objects with progressively lighter values (a lighter blue, red, gray, etc.). He continued building layers of paths until the area was completely covered. He moved throughout the image this way until the portrait was finished. When all of the paths were drawn he began to fill them with color. Nielsen chose the Eyedropper tool, pressed and held the ⌘/Ctrl key to switch to the Direct Selection tool, and selected an object to color. Then he toggled back to the Eyedropper tool by releasing the ⌘/ Ctrl key and sampled a color from the photograph. He toggled between the Direct Selection tool and the Eyedropper tool until the paths were filled. Most of the time, Nielsen liked the sampled colors, but if not, he would tweak the color using the slid-

NIELSEN

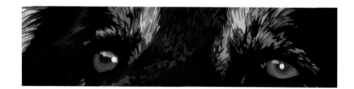

ers in the Color panel. Once all of the paths were filled with color, Nielsen hid the template layer. He saw small gaps of white in his drawing where the paths didn't quite meet or overlap. To fill these gaps, he made a large object that covered the area, filled it with a dark color, and moved it to the bottom-most layer.

BURKE

Pariah Burke

Pariah Burke used Illustrator to construct the cover illustration for his book, *ePublishing with InDesign*. Because he knew that projects often change as they progress, he also chose to construct his Illustrator file to be flexible for future editing. He divided the project into three parts: the book cover, the iPad, and the joining blank pages. He first constructed a highly realistic iPad that he later altered to a more generic tablet. He created a front view of the iPad, complete with a placed JPG image of an actual eBook page, clipped to fit precisely within the tablet's screen area. To distort the image and position it along with the bevel onto the iPad body, Burke selected the bevel and page objects and chose Object> Envelope Distort> Make with Mesh. He chose one row and one column, turning the mesh into a transform bounding box that he could continue to modify, and even un-transform (rare in Illustrator!). To edit or replace elements within the envelope, in the Layers panel he could move an object above "Envelope" to

remove the effect (moving all at once deletes the mesh), or drag elements into the Envelope group to apply (or reapply) the effect. Using Isolation mode made it even easier for him to focus on just the envelope objects. He made the book cover with equal attention to detail and again selected all the objects that would be placed onto the book's cover, distorting them using Envelope Mesh with the same method. To make the pages, Burke made individual, gradient-filled polygons, and added thin, white-filled shapes to represent the page edges. With the book-to-iPad constructed, he made a custom drop shadow by drawing two paths (one white and one dark gray), choosing Object> Blend> Make, and then applying a Multiply blending mode to the blend. Before the project was finished, he had to make several alterations to accommodate his publisher, a relatively easy task thanks to envelope mesh.

8

Creatively Combining Apps

Creatively Combining Apps

No Preview or Place option?

Disabling the PDF-compatible file option when you save in .ai will create a smaller file, but it will also create a file that you can only use from within that particular version of Illustrator or later. Most applications—including Adobe applications such as InDesign, Photoshop, Acrobat, and Adobe Reader—can't open or place the file with a preview. If you need to open, view, or place it outside of Illustrator, save a file with Create PDF Compatible File enabled; it's on by default.

Recovering missing linked files

If you don't have the original linked files for an .ai file, there is a way to get the images from the PDF side of the file—if the file was saved with Create PDF Compatible File enabled. Drag and drop the .ai file onto your Photoshop application icon, and choose Images in Photoshop's Import PDF dialog. You can then open any images from the PDF portion of the Illustrator file, save the images, and relink them in Illustrator.

Placing a file using the Link option

This chapter showcases some of the ways you can use Illustrator together with other programs. Moving artwork between Illustrator and other applications—such as Photoshop, Flash, After Effects, or Ideas—is often straightforward. But there are always rules and limits to moving files between programs, and the following pages address some ways to make your life easier when working with Illustrator and other programs.

LINKING VS. EMBEDDING IN ILLUSTRATOR

The major choice you'll need to make when placing art in Illustrator is whether to *link* or *embed* the file. When you link a file, you don't actually include the artwork in the Illustrator file. Instead a copy of the artwork acts as a placeholder, while the image remains in a separate file. Linking leaves the file editable in the original program, making it easy to update when the original is changed. Not only are .ai files with linked images smaller than those with embedded images, but linking permits you to link the same file several times in your document without increasing the file size for each instance. The Links panel keeps track of all the raster images used in your document, regardless of whether they were created within Illustrator, opened, or introduced via the Place command. Just remember that you have to include the separate, linked files if you move the .ai file to another computer.

When you embed artwork, you're actually including it in the file, which can sometimes be helpful even though the file size increases. Although it's trickier to update an embedded file in the original program, embedding is the answer if you need to be positive an image is included in the document. Consider embedding the image if you need to edit it in Illustrator or it's the only way to retain its transparency. Also, if there's a danger the linked file won't travel with the document when sending it to a client or press, you'll want to embed the file.

ILLUSTRATOR TO NON-ADOBE PROGRAMS

When moving artwork from Illustrator to non-Adobe programs, you must decide which objects in your artwork you want to remain as vectors, if possible, and which you can allow to become rasterized. What you'll be able to do with your Illustrator artwork in that other program depends both on how you prepare your Illustrator files as well as the strengths and limitations of the program into which you'll be moving your artwork. Parameters that you might be able to control include moving only selected objects or the entire file; bringing Illustrator files in as paths, styled vectors, or rasters; and bringing in images flat or with layers.

Copy and Paste/Drag and Drop

You may be able to preserve the vector format in programs outside the Creative Suite if they support PostScript drag and drop behavior. In order for this to work, enable AICB (Adobe Illustrator Clipboard) in Preferences> File Handling & Clipboard (disabled by default). When you copy/paste or drag and drop into a raster-based program without vector support, your artwork will be either automatically rasterized at the resolution set in that program or from Illustrator's Document Raster Effects Settings.

ILLUSTRATOR & ADOBE PHOTOSHOP

There are many options for moving artwork between Illustrator and Photoshop. In many cases you can control whether you want to maintain vector data, rasterize in part or whole, or whether to maintain layers, although those processes don't always work as you'd expect.

Illustrator to Photoshop: Smart Objects

Illustrator art brought in as a Smart Object can be scaled, rotated, duplicated, modified using Adjustment layers or Smart Filters, or even warped without loss of data. Smart Objects keep the original dimensions of your artwork, so further edits in Illustrator need to fit the original bounding box or the objects will be distorted in Photoshop.

PDF is often better than EPS

If the application you're working in can place or open native .ai, native PSD, or PDF 1.4 or later formats, it's better to use those than the old standard EPS, which cannot preserve layers, transparency, and other features.

So you think it's linked?

Flattening transparency (Object menu) of a linked image automatically embeds the image. Not only does this increase file size, but you can no longer update the link.

Getting it into Illustrator

From most programs, and on most platforms, you can Save As, or Print and Save As a PDF document. Illustrator will open any PDF document (if there are multiple pages, it will ask you which one you want). Your objects and text might be broken up, but everything should be in there.

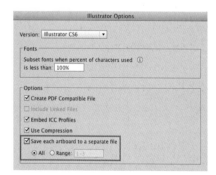

To save each artboard to its own file using Illustrator CS6 for Version, enable "Save each artboard to a separate file"

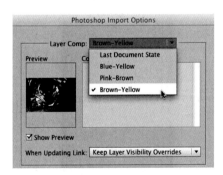
- **To create Photoshop Smart Objects from Illustrator data,** copy/paste to open the Paste dialog and choose Smart Object. Or create a Smart Object automatically by dragging and dropping or choosing File> Place.
- **To edit an Illustrator Smart Object,** double-click on its thumbnail in Photoshop's Layers panel to automatically launch Illustrator and open a working copy of your artwork. To update your Photoshop file, save your edits in Illustrator before returning to Photoshop.
- **To replace a Smart Object file with a different file on disk,** choose Layer> Smart Objects> Replace Content. This means you can use Smart Objects as placeholders for content you place in Photoshop later.

Illustrator to Photoshop: Pixels, Paths, and Layers
- **To create a pixel image, path, or Shape layer,** copy and paste an object, selecting from among these options in the Paste dialog that opens.
- **To preserve layers and keep text editable,** place the text on a top-level layer, not a sublayer, and choose Export to save the file in "Photoshop (psd)" format. The other vector objects are rasterized, but text stays editable. You can even use Illustrator's anti-aliasing options—None, Sharp, Crisp, Strong—which are comparable to and supported by Photoshop's text options.
- **To reliably export compound shapes to Photoshop,** place your compound shape on a top-level layer. To keep both the shape and any strokes you've added on separate layers so each is editable, remove strokes before exporting, or Photoshop might treat your shape and its stroke as a single object. Apply your strokes in Photoshop.

Photoshop to Illustrator
- **To keep text live,** in Photoshop save the file in PSD format. In Illustrator, choose File> Open (or File> Place with the Link checkbox disabled), and in the Photoshop Import Options dialog, enable Convert to Layers.
- **To link a file, rather than embed it,** choose File> Place and enable the Link (File> Open has no link options).

- **When linking a file,** you will be able to relink, or edit the original, and have the link update reflect your modifications, but you can't import layers from PSD or TIFF files.
- **When embedding a file,** you can import text layers and keep them live, with image layers flattened in a separate layer, but embedding won't allow you to edit the original PSD or TIFF file and have it update.
- **When importing Photoshop layers,** Illustrator doesn't understand Adjustment layers and will flatten all the nontext layers in a file if it encounters an Adjustment layer. If necessary, merge an Adjustment layer with the layer it's modifying before saving the PSD or TIFF file. When using Place or Open, enable the Convert to Layers option.
- **To preserve the appearance** of Density or Feather options applied to a layer mask, apply the mask to the layer in Photoshop before you import the file (Illustrator ignores Feather and Mask Density options found in CS6 Properties, or in the Masks panel in pre-CS6 versions).

ILLUSTRATOR & ADOBE INDESIGN

- **To edit Illustrator objects in InDesign when using copy/paste,** in InDesign's Preferences, disable Prefer PDF When Pasting. Then pasted objects can be ungrouped and edited. Paste objects containing complex appearances (such as brushes, effects, or gradients), either with preserved paths (objects lose any complex appearances), or with preserved appearances (complex appearances will be flattened and expanded). Control whether pasting preserves paths or appearances in the Copy As section of Preferences> File Handling & Clipboard.
- **To place Illustrator artwork (linking it rather than embedding),** save your file with the Create PDF Compatible File option enabled (it's on by default). InDesign, as well as other programs, can interpret and preview only the PDF portion of the file.
- **To control how an Illustrator file imports,** enable Show Import Options in the Place dialog. If you're placing an Illustrator file containing multiple artboards, InDesign allows you to select which artboard to import; the Layers

tab in the Import dialog lets you control visibility of top-level Illustrator layers.

ILLUSTRATOR, PDF, AND ADOBE ACROBAT

Acrobat's Portable Document Format (PDF) lets you transfer files between different operating systems and applications. By default, all Illustrator files created now are also PDF compatible files. And when you open an Illustrator document newer than the version of the program that you have, you're actually opening the PDF portion of the .ai file. When you choose File> Save As, keep the "Create PDF Compatible File" option enabled so Acrobat (and earlier versions of Illustrator) can open an .ai file.

- **To access the complete set of PDF options,** choose "Adobe PDF (pdf)" from the Save As format pop-up and click Save, which opens the Adobe PDF Options dialog; then choose from among the full range of PDF options, such as Optimize for Fast Web View.

- **To save layered Illustrator files as layered Acrobat files,** enable the "Create Acrobat Layers From Top-Level Layers" option in the Adobe PDF Options dialog.

WEB GRAPHICS

This section looks at some of the complexities of creating web graphics for modern displays. Adobe has worked to eliminate obstacles between Illustrator and web programs such as Flash, but some of its features can produce large files that result in long load times, or objects that don't scale to large and small displays.

Document profiles and templates, such as Flex Skins, were designed to optimize your design for the web from the start. If you choose the Web, Devices, or Flash Builder document profiles when creating a new document, most of the settings—including setting resolution, RGB color mode, pixels for ruler units, and enabling Align to Pixel Grid—are geared for screen display.

- **Use multiple artboards;** these are a great aid for sharing resources when you need to maintain a look or prep a number of files for quick export. Use Export to choose a format and output selected artboards. Save for Web keeps the assets, but only exports the active artboard.

- **To prevent colors from being altered when working for print and display,** work in CMYK (the more limited color space), and then convert a copy of your file to RGB.
- **To assist in creating bold graphics,** turn on Pixel Preview to see how the anti-aliasing is affecting each object.
- **To keep sharp-edged objects crisp and prevent unnecessary anti-aliasing** wherever Illustrator paths line up with the pixel grid, enable Align to Pixel Grid in the Transform panel (it will be enabled by default if you chose a Web or Flash Builder document profile).

From Illustrator to Flash

Because Flash and Illustrator objects are both vector-based, you can create just about any artwork intended for a Flash project inside Illustrator. If you own both programs, you can copy and paste or drag and drop between Illustrator and Flash. To get the best results in Flash, save your artwork in Illustrator (.ai) format and choose to import to the Flash Stage or Library. Note that if you save an .ai file and import it to Flash, you'll need to have top-level layers (not the sublayers automatically created by Illustrator's Release to Layers). Manually select all of the sublayers in Illustrator and drag them up to become top-level layers. Here are some strategies for maximizing the quality and usefulness of your Illustrator files in Flash:

- **Use Illustrator symbols for objects that you intend to place multiple times,** instead of using multiple copies of the original art. Symbols can reduce the size of files that you export from Illustrator for Flash.
- **To modify symbols while keeping the file size small,** select them and apply Effects from the *fx* menu of the Appearance panel. Flash imports only one instance of a symbol no matter how many different instances have effects applied (although the effects may not stay live). Don't use the Symbol Stainer, Screener, or Styler on your symbols; using these tools will result in a larger SWF file with many unique symbols.

Pixel Preview

While Illustrator's default preview is optimized for print, choosing View> Pixel Preview will allow you to see your art as it would appear when displayed on the web or on a digital screen. Pixel Preview will show the effects of anti-aliasing, which often will affect the visual appearance of your art.
—*Mordy Golding*

Pixel Preview off / Pixel Preview on

Illustrator to Fireworks

Although you can copy and paste artwork directly into Fireworks, to preserve multiple artboards, use File> Import in order to select a range of artboards to convert to pages in Fireworks, or use File Open to automatically convert *all* artboards to pages.

The Edge alternative

As an alternative to using Flash for web animation and interactivity, Adobe Edge is an application based on HTML code. Since iOS devices don't permit Flash, Adobe Edge provides the means to create files you can display on most devices and browsers, including the iPhone and iPad. If you're familiar with Flash, you'll find it easy to learn to use Adobe Edge.

Animate with Graphic Symbols

If you use Illustrator layers to create an animation that doesn't need to be tweened in Flash, try importing the layers as keyframes in a Graphic Symbol. The animation is complete as soon as you insert a frame on the Timeline for every keyframe (Illustrator layer).

9-slice scaling in Illustrator

Enable 9-slice scaling on symbols to allow you to protect outside areas of a symbol, such as its corners, from becoming distorted when transformed in Illustrator.

Symbols and guides

When aligning a symbol to an object or guide, be aware that its content, not just its bounding box, can snap to align with objects and guides. Choose this option from the Transform panel menu, and turn on Smart Guides to assist you.

Ideas—an Adobe Touch app

Ideas is an Illustrator-compatible vector app for iOS and Android devices that offers up to 10 layers plus one image layer, multiple undos, and drawing tools that create art similar to the Blob Brush. Use the Creative Cloud or send a copy by email for further development in Illustrator. See an example of Brian Yapp's Adobe Ideas art later in this chapter.

- **Flash preserves gradients with fewer than eight stops,** and retains transparency (called Alpha). Flash rasterizes mesh objects, and gradients with more than eight stops.
- **To create a Flash frame from each Illustrator layer,** export as a SWF file and choose Export Layers to SWF frames.
- **To control the way a symbol transforms,** set a registration point in Illustrator; it will be effective in both Illustrator and Flash. Use the registration point to precisely position and transform symbols relative to the artboard coordinates before exporting them to Flash. The registration point "anchors" the symbol to that point for transformations. When editing symbols in isolation mode, the registration point's x,y location is always 0,0, and can't be changed using the ruler.

CREATING ANIMATION WITH LAYERS

You can use Illustrator layers to design a sequence for an animation, or export it to another program for further manipulation. You can also place the parts of objects you want to animate on top-level layers, instead of a sequence. For best results, export in .ai format when possible.

- **To create layers so each object (or layer) can be manipulated/animated separately** in another program, such as After Effects, choose Release to Layers (Sequence).
- **To create the animation in Illustrator before exporting it** (similar to onion-skinning), choose the Build option; the bottom layer's object gets placed on every layer, with the next object placed on every layer except the first layer, and so on, until all the objects are placed on the top layer and the animation sequence is complete.
- **To create a composition to import into After Effects,** use the Video & Film Document Profile. This creates two artboards—one large artboard that serves as a "scratch" area on which you can place objects for later use in After Effects, and one sized for your chosen video format. To retain each artboard and the layers, create a multi-layered file and save with Create PDF Compatible File enabled.

ROBERTS

Andrew Roberts
Illustrator & Flash

Andrew Roberts, Illustrator and designer, was commissioned to creates flipbooks for institutions such as The Royal Shakespeare Company and The Metropolitan Opera, so when it came to creating a banner for his website, he decided to bring a similar sensibility to an animation to run along the top. In Illustrator, Roberts created an extremely detailed background (almost 30MB) based on his hometown cycling route called the Backs; this is the spot in Cambridge (UK) where you'll find both Clare College and Kings College (famous for its 500-year old Chapel). On a separate layer above he created the foreground elements, and then in yet another layer, Roberts created groups of elements that form his academic cycler. Each of the cycler's groups represents a detail for the animator to articulate (the hat, the arm, legs, petals). Then, with detailed instructions as to what he wished the cycler to do (bicycler rides enters from off-frame on the right, rides across and to left and tosses his hat along the way), he passed off the files to Feel Design folks, who imported the elements into Flash where they created movie clip symbols and animated it on a timeline; the final animation contains more than 200 frames. The cyclist was the most complex part, with each part of the leg and bike as a separate symbol. Once complete and approved by Roberts, Feel Design exported the final animation as a .swf and embedded the file in Roberts HTML page as part of the header of andyrobertsdesign.com/illustration (if your device supports Flash).

Twist and Slice

Making Web Page Elements in Illustrator

Illustrator & Web

Overview: *Set up a document for web page design; use layers to structure artwork; create slices with the Slice tool or by using guides or artwork; save slices as image files.*

ROORDA

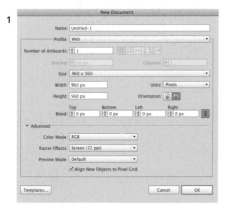

The New Document dialog

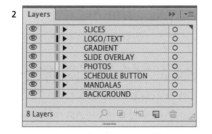

The Layers panel with different web page elements on their own layers

Take the artboard to the limits

To limit the objects that will be saved as web images to those within the current artboard, be sure to enable Object> Slice> Clip to Artboard.

If you're comfortable designing and drawing in Illustrator, why not start your webpage in Illustrator? Jolynne Roorda used Illustrator to design and preview web pages, create comps for client approval, and slice and optimize artwork for use in this website for Yoga on High.

1 Setting up your document. To start designing your webpage, create a new document using File> New. From the New Document dialog's Profile menu, select Web, and then choose one of the default sizes from the Size menu or enter your own custom size. Be sure to keep Align New Objects to Pixel Grid enabled to assure that the horizontal and vertical edges of objects you draw remain sharp when you slice and save as images later.

Because your artwork will be saved in a raster format like GIF, PNG, or JPG, consider turning on pixel preview (View> Pixel Preview). With pixel preview you can see the pixel grid (zoom in 600% or more) and the anti-aliasing of your artwork as if it were rasterized, so you can adjust it if necessary.

2 Structuring pages with layers and adding artwork. Let the Layers panel help you organize the artwork comprising your webpage. Roorda began by drawing the artwork, placing images, and creating text on a single layer. Then she added layers in the Layers panel, selected the artwork she planned to slice, and moved it to these new layers (for layers help, see the chapter *Your Creative Workspace*). This separated the artwork so overlapping text and graphics would not appear for elements like backgrounds when she saved slices as images later. Finally, she added a layer at the top of the Layers panel for the slices she would draw next.

Roorda selected the slices layer in the Layers panel and began creating slices. To draw slices, select the Slice tool and click and drag to draw rectangles that match areas of your webpage design such as the banner, navigation bar, and content areas. To manually change a slice, click the Slice Selection tool, then click an edge or corner point of the slice and move it. Because slices are objects like other artwork you draw, you can change their dimensions in the Control or Transform panel to make them fit precise sizes you plan for the HTML or CSS elements you'll create later in Adobe Dreamweaver or other web software.

Instead of drawing slices with the Slice tool, you can also create guides or draw objects that define the areas of the artboard containing artwork you want to slice. To create slices from guides, choose Object> Slice> Create from Guides. To create them from objects, choose Object> Slice> Create from Selection. The resulting slices, like those Roorda created with the Slice tool, can be moved, deleted, or resized if necessary.

3 **Saving an image and slices.** To save your artwork as images that you can use in your web software, choose File> Save for Web and in the dialog, click the Export menu. If you want to save all slices (including slices that fill empty space on the artboard), choose All Slices. If you only want to save some of the slices, choose Selected Slices. With Selected Slices you can specify different image formats (such as JPG or GIF) and color tables for different slices. To do this, click the Slice Select Tool icon and click on a slice, Shift-click or marquee select several slices, or drag over the slices, choose the Preset to make any other adjustments you need, and click Save to save the slices as images. Repeat as often as you need to save all of your slices.

2

Slices created by manually drawing the first slice (labeled as "1")

The numbered slices created after manually drawing the slices using the Slice tool

3

The Save for Web dialog showing the slices

Put slicing on automatic

Do you want the boundaries of slices to precisely fit the boundaries of your artwork? Simply select one or more objects, choose Object> Slice> Make, and Illustrator will generate slices for all selected objects and for the empty spaces on the artboard. These slices are dynamic; you can add, delete, or change artwork and the slices adjust automatically.

STIKALICIOUS™

Stikalicious™ Artists

Illustrator & iPad App Development

Mark 'Atomos' Pilon, Podgy Panda, Frazer, Dacosta!, Charuca, Tokyo-go-go, Jared Nickerson, Steve Talkowski; Killamari, kaNO, MAD, Abe Lincoln Jr., Gabriel Mourelle, Shawnimals, EdWarner, Junichi Tsuneoka

(top to bottom; left column then right) Using Illustrator, artists from all over the world create the Stikalicious™ characters that Dacosta! of Chocolate Soop® then prepares for his wallpaper app for the iPad, (see their lesson in the *Your Creative Workspace* chapter for more). Users purchase character sets, then drag a background and characters into the screen area. Overlay controls allow you to move, scale, rotate, and change the characters stacking order. Wallpaper designs are automatically saved to your workspace (WIP), where you can edit, copy, delete, or even share a design.

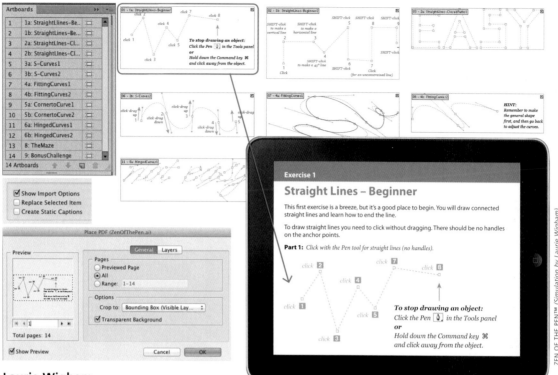

ZEN OF THE PEN™ (Simulation by Laurie Wigham)

Laurie Wigham

Illustrator, ePub, & iBooks Author

When Laurie Wigham was working with Sharon Steuer on editing and redesigning *The Zen of The Pen*™ (info@zenofthepen.net) as both an ePub and for Apple's iBooks Author (iBA), she realized that collecting all the Illustrator files into one document would streamline the workflow. The key to doing this was putting each figure and its caption on its own artboard so it could be placed separately into InDesign for export to ePub. In InDesign's Place dialog she enabled Show Import Options so she could then choose to import all artboards. To use the same images in iBA, Wigham went back to Illustrator and selected File> Export. In the dialog she enabled the Use Artboards option, chose JPG format, and clicked Export to save each artboard as a separate JPG file. Because

she had scaled the files in Illustrator to actual size and cropped the artboard to fit the images, she was able to drag the JPG files into position in iBA without doing any extra work. However, after viewing the test document on her iPad, Wigham realized that the captions were hard to read. She went back to Illustrator to adjust the size and weight, using the Character Styles panel to change all the files with a few keystrokes. Back in InDesign she was able to automatically update the placed images, but she had to go through one more step for iBA. After exporting the revised artboards as JPG files, she had to individually replace the files in iBA. (Figures above, counter-clockwise from top: Artboards panel and artboards in Illustrator, InDesign Place dialog with import options, iBA file preview.)

Von Glitschka

Illustrator & DrawScribe/VectorScribe

For its part in the 2011 London International Technology Show, Astute Graphics commissioned Von Glitschka to create a poster with a British theme that demonstrated their latest Illustrator plug-in set, DrawScribe. Glitschka researched heraldry, then combined a rampant lion with the recently-popularized 1939 WW II "Keep Calm and Carry On" posters, and came up with this poster concept. Glitschka made the initial sketch on paper, then scanned and opened it in Illustrator. To begin manually tracing over it, he selected the InkScribe tool contained within DrawScribe. InkScribe consists of a tool (added to the Tools) and a panel with a new set of functions (accessed from the Window menu), so using it is completely seamless with using any other Illustrator features. The InkScribe tool replaces not only the Pen tool but also its editing tools (Add, Convert, Direct Selec-

tion, etc.). The InkScribe tool requires minimal use of modifier keys to perform most functions, and also includes a customizable Annotations overlay (see middle, above), making for a very efficient workflow. Glitschka used the InkScribe tool to both draw and edit his paths. The user-customizable functions and onscreen annotations made it easier for him to precisely adjust Bézier handles, change anchor point type, and minimize the number of anchor points as he drew, making clean-up and editing much easier. He occasionally also used Illustrator's geometric shapes and Pathfinder operations, such as when he created the lion's claws, and used Astute Graphics' Dynamic Corners plug-in, part of Astute's VectorScribe set, to round off some of the very sharp corners, adding a more organic flow to the vector art.

Brian Yap

Illustrator & Adobe Ideas

Working with Ideas, a new Adobe Touch app for Android and iOS devices, Brian Yap sketched most of this illustration on his iPad. He began with a photo reference layer of the shoes, drawing the linework with a NomadBrush Compose stylus on the layer above that. He next added other layers to develop the colors for the piece. To further enhance the image in Illustrator, he emailed the file to himself (he could have used the Creative Cloud to sync with his computer instead). Ideas produced an Illustrator-compatible PDF, which Yap then opened in Illustrator. Every stroke he made in Ideas became a filled object with no stroke (similar to the Blob Brush, but without the ability to merge strokes). To simplify and merge similar paths, he selected all strokes of the same appearance, clicked Pathfinder> Unite, and then used Object> Path> Simplify and the Smooth tool to clean up paths and get rid of excess vector points. To finalize

the image for silkscreen printing, Yap also took advantage of Illustrator's robust color editing and transparency tools, adding gradient fills, applying blending modes, and adjusting transparency. Because Ideas runs on his lightweight, portable iPad, Yap can begin conceptualizing images wherever inspiration strikes, and then later use Illustrator's advanced tools to bring his initial Ideas concept to fruition.

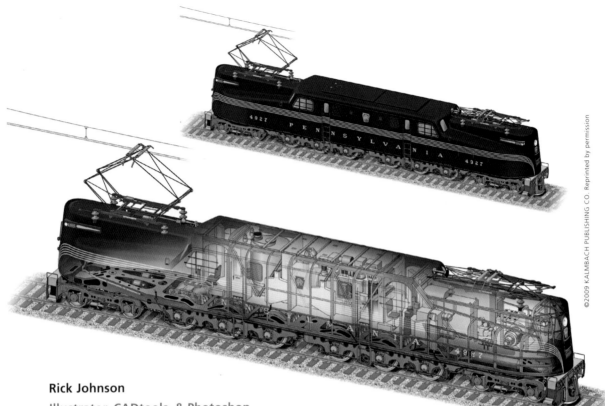

Rick Johnson
Illustrator, CADtools, & Photoshop

Rick Johnson illustrated this GG1 electric loco-motive, most of which were built in the late 1930s for the Pennsylvania Railroad by General Electric, for *Classic Trains* magazine using blue-prints, photographs, and field notes. One might be tempted to draw this using Illustrator's per-spective tools, but Johnson needed this draw-ing to be as technically accurate as possible. He began by drawing everything precisely to scale in "flat" orthographic top, front, and side views, in Illustrator using HotDoor's CADtools plug-in (download the latest demo versions from www.hotdoor.com/cadtools). Then, also using CADtools, Johnson projected those sur-faces to their respective trimetric angles. With the help of custom-angle Smart Guides (set to 39°, –12°, 90° in Preferences> Smart Guides),

he aligned the pieces to their appropriate X, Y, and Z axis. He divided the art into 76 layers based on logical groups (e.g., tracks and power trucks, underframe, interior components, skel-eton, and shell). He then exported the art to a layered Photoshop (psd) file, and in Photoshop he adjusted the coloring, contouring, and shad-ing. He used layer masks to reveal the most (and most interesting) interior detail while still showing the outside form of this classic locomo-tive, which meant sometimes ghosting several layers at once. Since he had already drawn the entire locomotive from the inside out, the ClassicTrains.com Web site was able to repur-pose the art, so visitors could disassemble the locomotive, peeling away a layer at a time.

MCGARRY

Aaron McGarry

Illustrator & Photoshop

To create this urban portrait, Aaron McGarry used the combined strengths of Illustrator and Photoshop. He began in Illustrator by placing original photos as template layers, and hand-tracing over them into another layer using the Pen, Rectangle, Ellipse, and Type tools. To simulate metal on the various components, he filled the objects with gradients from the Metals library (Window> Swatch Libraries> Gradients> Metals). Since each of the main objects represented a different depth, he next selected each main grouping of objects and applied separate drop shadows (Effect> Stylize> Drop Shadow). With the objects complete and assembled on various layers, he hid the template layer (see inset). Placing a photograph of a wall as a background layer (below the objects), McGarry then exported the file to Photoshop, preserving the layers. In Photoshop he created the illusion of a glass cover on the meter by placing a photo of the sky. Then, using the Warp command (Edit> Transform> Warp), he warped the photo to the roundness of the meter face. He next added a layer mask to the photo layer and used a gradient (Black, White) to fade the lower part of the photo, blending it in with the background image and adjusting the opacity to simulate the reflective, transparent quality of curved glass. For the finishing touches he used a variety of Photoshop's Brush tools, as well as the Eraser and Smudge tool (all with varying opacity), to paint the rust, stains, and grime, thereby creating a grittier look.

Ready to Export

Exporting Options for Layers to Photoshop

Illustrator & Photoshop

Overview: *Organize objects on layers that Photoshop can understand; use Export to Photoshop (psd) or Copy/ Paste as Smart Object for editing layers in Photoshop; add texture or run other filters as Smart Filters.*

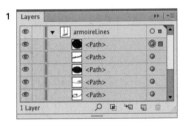

Each brush object is listed in the Layers panel as a <Path> with a filled target icon (see the chapter Your Creative Workspace for help with targeting)

Upon Export to Photoshop, each object stroked with a brush in Illustrator becomes a layer within a Layer Group in Photoshop

If Knockout Group is enabled in Illustrator's Transparency panel (see the Mastering Complexity chapter intro for more about the Transparency panel), sublayers become one layer in Photoshop

ATTEBERRY

When Kevan Atteberry wants to add finishing touches to his illustrations in Photoshop, he has several options for preparing and exporting his artwork from Illustrator. Shown above is a detail from his "Frankie Stein" series, where Atteberry uses Illustrator's ability to write Photoshop layers when exporting to the PSD format, as well as Photoshop's ability to paste selected and copied objects directly as Smart Objects. Exporting layers as PSD layers is the quickest method for adding texture or other raster effects in Photoshop. To use Transform on the object (scale, rotate, etc.), Atteberry copies and pastes it from Illustrator as a Smart Object, which preserves the underlying vector for Photoshop to work with. (For the full illustration, see the "Frankie Stein" gallery following this.)

1 Organizing and rasterizing the layers in Illustrator for export as Photoshop PSD. When Illustrator writes layers for a Photoshop file, it attempts to maintain the layer structure, including all the sublayers. But some types of objects, such as those created with brushes, blends, symbols, or envelopes, generate an unmanageable number of extra sublayers. Two important steps in Illustrator can prevent this from becoming a nuisance in Photoshop. First, Atteberry collects all paths that make up a given object into a named layer. This might be a sublayer of a layer that contains more of a subject, such as the "MUM-layers" containing a "mumsDress" layer. This is just like organizing your hard drive in miniature, making it easy to quickly identify what objects the layers contain. Next, he targets the sublayers, opens the Transparency panel and enables Knockout Group (you may need to expand panel options). To extend our example, "mumsDress" now becomes a single, rasterized layer in Photoshop, but is still separate from "mumsHair," and both are contained in a Layer Group called "MUMlayers." Photoshop now can preserve Illustrator's file structure and layer names, without creating too many nested groups.

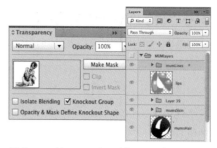

Well-named layers and enabling Knockout Group keeps layers manageable in Photoshop

2 **Using Smart Objects and Smart Filters.** Although any layer or Layer Group can be converted to a Smart Object inside Photoshop, Atteberry copies and pastes Smart Objects directly from Illustrator when he wants to Transform or Warp them. After importing and merging layers as described above, he goes back to Illustrator, selects and copies an object—such as Mum's hand—that he wants to fine-tune in the final version in Photoshop. With the object copied to the clipboard, he returns to Photoshop and chooses Paste. A dialog pops up with options, and he chooses Smart Object. Once the Smart Object is in the right position both in the image and in the stack of layers, he hits Return/Enter to accept it. He then can delete the rasterized layer he had exported earlier, if it doesn't contain other paths. The new layer will always link to the vector file for transforming (so the art won't degrade the way pixel-based artwork would) and for editing in Illustrator.

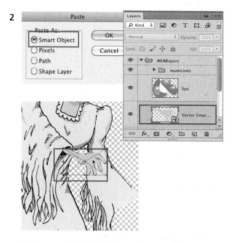

Pasting an object into Photoshop as a Smart Object in order to Transform the object without pixel degradation (blurring)

If he doesn't need to transform an object, but wants to add texture inside Photoshop using a filter, instead of copying and pasting from Illustrator again, Atteberry converts the layer to a Smart Object from within Photoshop. Now he can run a Smart Filter on the Smart Object layer (in our example, mumsDress). This allows him to reopen the filter dialog at any time, change settings, delete or add filters, etc., all without altering the original object.

The dress before adding texture in Photoshop—and after, running Texturizer as a Smart Filter

After choosing Filter> Convert for Smart Filters, a Smart Object layer protects the original pixels and any filter becomes editable

ATTEBERRY

Kevan Atteberry

Illustrator & Photoshop

For his "Frankie Stein" series of illustrated children's books, Atteberry uses Illustrator to create the basic illustration, and then moves into Photoshop to add textures and special effects. He carefully constructs his layers in Illustrator to make sure that he can work freely and easily in Photoshop, taking advantage of Photoshop's unique way of creating original artwork. In this illustration (spread over two pages), he prepared his Illustrator layers to use filters, Layer Styles, and Photoshop's soft, feathered brushes. He did this by ensuring the elements that would receive the same treatment in Photoshop were kept on different layers from other elements. See the "Ready to Export" lesson earlier in this chapter for more about layer organization.

ATTEBERRY

Kevan Atteberry
Illustrator & Photoshop

Once Atteberry has imported his descriptively-named Illustrator layers to become rasterized Photoshop layers, he depends upon Photoshop's ability to add texture with filters and images, blending it seamlessly into the objects he drew in Illustrator. He makes extensive use of Photoshop's natural soft, feathery brushes to add shadows and highlights to his characters and their environment. He even paints entirely new characters, such as the ghost (opposite page), using soft brushes and building it up gradually with multiple layers set to varying opacities, giving it its ethereal, ghostly quality. Adjustment layers are added to tweak color. The final results of his multi-layered approach achieve his unique blend of the real and the imaginary.

Ready for Flash

Creating an Animation from Layers

Illustrator & Flash

Overview: *Draw the subject in different positions, using blends to create intermediate positions on duplicates; group and move each complete instance to its own layer; import layers as keyframes into Flash, creating a graphic symbol for the sequence.*

GRACE

1

Starting with a sketch of the main movements of a running dog

Redrawing the dogs, refining their forms

After blending and before expanding the blend to add a new limb to the dog in the middle

2

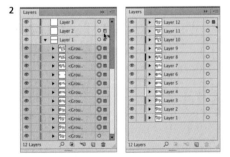

Moving each group (dog) to its own layer, above left, so the groups can be aligned and the layers imported as keyframes in Flash

To create an animation of a running dog, Laurie Grace used Eadweard Muybridge's early photographic sequences of animal locomotion for inspiration. In an RGB document, she created several instances of a dog in different positions using blends, and used Illustrator layers to import the animation into Flash, keeping their top-level layers intact. By creating a graphic symbol in Flash from the .ai file, she tied it to the Timeline and could convert each layer to a keyframe in the Flash animation.

1 Drawing the dogs. Grace used the Blob Brush to loosely sketch a few instances of the dog in running positions. She used the layer as a template and redrew the dogs on a new layer with the Pen tool. She added an intermediate duplicate between each original for a smoother animation, and then deleted one leg or other part she wanted to reposition from the duplicate dog in the middle. She selected that part on each of the originals and created a one-step blend between them, then chose Object> Blend> Expand. The blended object gave her a good idea of the intermediate positions required, even if she had to redraw some of the parts on the duplicate dog in the middle. Once she had all the dogs drawn, she filled them with color and used a 2-point oval brushstroke to outline them.

2 Grouping and placing on layers for Flash. The next steps required that Grace select and group the paths for each dog. She would need each dog to be a separate group in order to align them all later. She then added 11 more layers (one for each dog), selected all the dogs, and de-selected the first dog by Shift-clicking on it. She dragged the small colored square in the Layers panel to the layer above (moving all except the first dog to the second layer), and repeated the Shift-click to deselect one dog at a time, moving the rest to the layer above, until all 12 groups were distributed among the 12 layers. With all the dogs selected, she clicked on Horizontal Align Center and Vertical Align Bottom in the Control panel. She moved the aligned dogs to the center of her artboards, and saved the file in Illustrator (.ai) format.

3 **Creating the animation in Flash.** Grace created a new document in Flash, and chose Insert> New Symbol to create an empty graphic symbol named dog_running (Flash would automatically convert the .ai file to the symbol on import). Graphic symbols sync with the main Timeline, and don't have interactive controls, but they do keep file size down. With the empty graphic symbol still open, she chose File> Import> Import to Stage and chose her .ai file. She kept all the layers selected in the Flash Import dialog, and chose Convert Layers to Keyframes. When she clicked OK, Flash automatically placed the first keyframe of the running dog graphic symbol on the stage, still in the edit symbol isolation mode. She could see that all 12 keyframes were there, but in order to configure the animation on the Timeline, she needed to click back on "Scene." She next dragged the symbol into the Scene, showing only the first keyframe within frame one. To create the right number of Timeline frames (12) to display each keyframe, she Control-clicked/Right-clicked on the twelfth frame in the Timeline and chose Insert Frame. Grace then slowed down the frame rate (fps) at the bottom of the Timeline (from 24 to 12). She tested the animation inside Flash by pressing the Enter/Return key and choosing Control> Loop Playback. Finally, she used Export to create a Flash movie in SWF format (see the animation at: http://lauriegrace.com/wowdogs.htm).

3

Adding an empty Graphic symbol to Flash's library, so that the .ai file could be added as a symbol to the Library when imported to the Stage

Keeping enabled the layers of the .ai file to import (or disabling some if desired), and choosing how to convert them (to Flash layers, keyframes, or flattened to a single Flash layer)

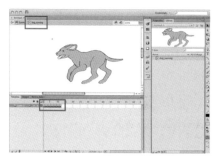

The layered .ai file opens on the stage in isolation mode with the Graphic symbol in the library, ready to be edited—all 12 Illustrator top-level layers convert to keyframes

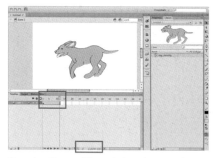

Dragging the graphic symbol to the stage, inserting frames, and changing the frame rate

Symbol Animation

Turning Objects into Flash-ready Symbols

Illustrator & Flash

Overview: *Draw characters using discrete objects for each part which the animation will be constructed from; save objects as symbols; import the saved .ai file to a Flash library.*

1

The assembled snowbunny and carrot that would be animated in Flash

The working parts on the artboard that are later assembled in Flash as an animation

When designing a Flash animation, Kevan Atteberry uses Illustrator's advanced vector capabilities for preparing a "morgue" of parts, and converts those parts to symbols for easy import into Flash. There Atteberry assembles his scene and his characters, creating the final animation for SWF output. He created an animation to send to friends as his Christmas greeting e-card using a snowbunny who finds a Christmas carrot.

1 Creating characters and splitting artwork into parts for animating. In order for his snowbunny and candy carrot to have "moving" parts, Atteberry drew each part that might be animated with custom artbrushes. By starting off with parts even before planning the animation, he ensured that he would have the maximum "play" to all their features when it came time to create with motion. The snowbunny and carrot were designed with unarticulated separate parts. He planned to use Flash's transforming tools to generate motion "tweens." However, had he needed a leg to bend in the middle, for instance, he could have drawn a path stroked with his artbrush in a start and ending position, and used an object blend in steps to generate in-between positions. (See the *Mastering Complexity* chapter for details on creating object blends.)

2 Converting the separate parts to symbols. Having placed his objects on named layers, the next step to an animation was for Atteberry to select each part that he planned to animate in Flash, or parts of the scene he simply felt more comfortable drawing in Illustrator, and turn it into a Flash-compatible symbol. Since the panels are "spring-loaded," he was able to simply hover over the icon with the object he was dragging until the panel popped open to receive it, which automatically opened the Symbols Options dialog. There he could give each symbol a descriptive name and designate it as either a Movie Clip or a Graphic. He could also have used the keyboard shortcut F8, or, if he'd wanted to keep that panel open during this process, he could click on the New Symbol icon in the Symbols panel (Option-click/Alt-click to skip the dialog). He kept the Movie Clip designation because Atteberry planned to animate most, if not all, of the symbols he imported. If he only wanted a symbol that would remain static in the scene, he could have chosen Graphic instead, but it wasn't really necessary to change the default for one or two symbols, since Flash lets you change the designation for a symbol at any time. Enable Guides for 9-slice scaling when Movie Clip is chosen and you want to create an interface element, such as a button, later on. Atteberry left that disabled. And finally, he could choose to save his symbols with a Flash registration point. This is the "transform" point that anchors an object being rotated or scaled, for instance, in the animation. This registration point, too, can be modified in Flash later on.

3 Importing Illustrator symbols to a Flash library. Once Atteberry had saved the Illustrator file, he opened Flash, began a new document, and chose File> Import> Import to Library. He browsed to his Illustrator file, and when the Import (file) to Library dialog opened, he checked that all the layers for the objects were enabled, he enabled "Import unused symbols" (just in case an object was left off the artboard), and accepted Flash's suggestion for handling an object that was not compatible with Flash. From this point on Atteberry was set to construct his scene and animate his characters using his Illustrator symbols.

2
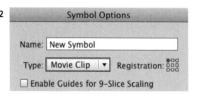

Checking out all the options for exporting symbols that are ready to go inside Flash

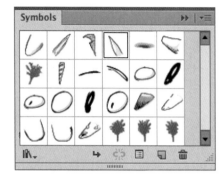

Everything that needs to be animated in Flash becomes a symbol

3

The Import to Library dialog in Flash

The Flash Library containing all the file's assets; here, previewing a symbol

Laurie Wigham
Illustrator & Flash

Using Illustrator, Laurie Wigham created the art for the Flash animation, "The Last Draw," a web-based application designed to help people stop smoking (produced by Health Promotion Services, Inc., funded by the National Heart, Lung, and Blood Institute). To make the lines simple and expressive, Wigham drew the characters and other objects with the Pen tool. To create a relaxed and casual look, she drew open-ended unfilled paths, using a thick black stroke with a rounded end cap and corners (Window> Stroke). Beneath the outlines she created unstroked solid-colored objects, deliberately misaligned with the strokes to produce a loose, cut-paper look. Wigham created a collection of drawings that would provide a library of symbols for the animator to later assemble in Flash. She drew each character with different positions and facial expressions, and included a collection of separate body parts and props that could move independently. She assembled all the drawings needed for each tutorial unit in a single file, positioned on a "stage," framed by the navigation and play controls of the website and browser. Each master layer in the file contained all the elements for a key frame within the animation, as well as motion paths and detailed instructions for the animator.

WIGHAM / Health Promotion Services, Inc.

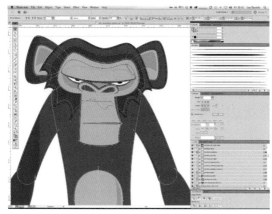

LeeDanielsART

Illustrator & After Effects

Lee Daniels is a UK-based artist and animator who moves fluidly between Illustrator, Photoshop, and After Effects (AE). Daniels's memorable animated shorts add cinematic production values to his classic vector art characters. Although his animations end up in AE, they all begin with his meticulous organization in Illustrator. It's in Illustrator that he creates every possible animated component of each character, separated into vector object groups and organized within a clear and well-labeled layer structure in Illustrator. Once everything is clearly organized, Daniels can move into AE to pull in layers and choose specific objects (such as "monkey eyebrows") to move into position in the AE timeline. As long as his Illustrator files

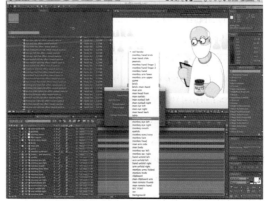

are logical and orderly, once he's in AE he can find what he needs to keep production flowing (the two screenshots directly above). You can see this and many others Daniels animations at www.LeeDanielsART.com.

JOLY & RIDDLE

Dave Joly & Mic Riddle

Illustrator, Flash, & Cinema 4D

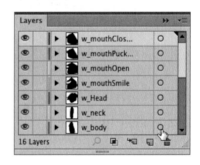

When Dave Joly and Mic Riddle col-
laborated on the "Trick or Treat" movie,
they produced a unique mix of 2D and
3D artwork, using everything from Flash
to Maxon's Cinema 4D, to After Effects,
to Apple's Final Cut Pro, and it all started
with Illustrator. To begin the 2D animation,
they drew all the parts in an Illustrator file that
they would use for a segment. Every part was
placed on its own layer. So, for example, the
man and woman seen here were created with
separate heads, bodies, and expressions—each
change in position on its own layer. They only
needed B&W in Illustrator; the color would
come from other programs. Once all the parts
were finished, they could choose either to create and name symbols in Illustrator for later
importing into a Flash library, or they could save
the file and import it to the Flash stage (which
is what they did for this scene). They chose to
have Flash convert all the layers as Flash layers,
which preserved Illustrator's layer names and
organization. After animating the husband and
wife talking, they were ready to export their 2D
Illustrator art as a QuickTime file with an alpha
channel (to create transparency around the animated characters), and from there take it into
Cinema 4D to become a "texture" for a 3D type
of "material" that controls how the 3D models
appear. Eventually, with the aid of other programs, such as After Effects and Final Cut Pro,
this 2D segment became incorporated into the
rest of the movie.

RIDDLE & JOLY

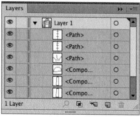

Mic Riddle & Dave Joly

Illustrator, Cinema 4D, & After Effects

Still working on their "Trick or Treat" movie, Mic Riddle and Dave Joly created the 3D scenes for the animation. Again, they often began inside Illustrator. Most 3D programs are able to import Illustrator paths and use them as the start for creating an extruded or lathed object, such as the doorway and clock shown here, both of which have dimension. It's these surfaces that, once lit in Cinema 4D or another 3D application, cast and receive shadows that convince us the objects are no longer flat illustrations. And just as they created a layer for each 2D part they intended to animate in Flash, they drew each "object" on its own layer that would be extruded in Cinema 4D, making extensive use of compound paths to represent both a solid dimensional surface and a hole for windows, or the cavity for a clock's pendulum. They added more animation and camera movements, color, texture, and pattern, then rendered their movie "scenes" to be imported into After Effects. They used After Effects both for features that were easier to produce there, and to save some time tweaking a scene by not jumping back and forth between programs. Finally, files were collected in Final Cut Pro, where they added sound and performed final edits, and saved as a .mov file (find a low-res version of the animation on **WOW! ONLINE**).

Finishing Touches

Adding Scenic Entourage Elements & Using Photoshop for Lighting Effects

MARIC

Illustrator, Painter, Go Media, & Photoshop

Overview: *Place a photo sky as the background; add entourage elements; create lighting effects in Photoshop.*

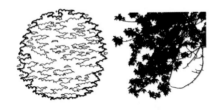

Sky background image created in Corel Painter

Go Media's bush and "foreground" tree vector entourage elements

To complete his architectural rendering created with Illustrator's perspective grid, Pete Maric inserted a photo background, added scenic "entourage" elements, and manually created lighting effects in Photoshop.

1 Replacing the sky background image and importing entourage elements. Maric decided to change the mood of the illustration by replacing the background sky image to reflect a dusk setting. In Illustrator, Maric created a new bottom layer and chose File> Place to choose a JPG of a sunset that he photographed and transformed with Corel Painter. Maric relies heavily on a library of entourage elements (cars, people, trees, bushes, etc.) to add interest to his illustrations. After importing a couple of his own trees, Maric opened Go Media's Architectural Elements Vector Pack and chose a bush and a foreground tree detail to copy and paste into his rendering. He sampled the grass color with the Eyedropper tool, then filled each bush with that color by holding Option/Alt and clicking. To populate the scene he duplicated each bush individually by holding Option/Alt while dragging it into place, using the bounding box to scale when needed.

The illustration with all entourage added

2 Creating lighting effects in Photoshop. In Photoshop, he rasterized the Illustrator file using File> Open, enabled the Constrain Proportions setting and set the Resolution to 300 pixels/inch. In order to help focus the image on the architecture, he darkened the corners by adding a blue solid rectangle layer, set the transparency to Multiply, created a layer mask, and applied a radial gradient to the center of the mask. Maric then manually created mood lighting effects by overlaying another series of gradient-filled layers on top of the image. He created the gradients by sampling color from his image using Photoshop's Eyedropper tool. He created the gradients on separate layers, then he painted on one layer, added layer masks as necessary to each of them, adjusted the layer opacity, and applied different blending modes.

2

The light effect layers created in Photoshop

3 Adding realistic reflections to the windows and simulating interior artificial lighting. To create a reflection in the windows, Maric used Photoshop's Pen tool to create an accurate selection inside the windows. He then opened a photo, selected and copied it to the clipboard, and pasted it into the window selection using Edit> Paste Special> Paste Into. To integrate the reflection photograph into the overall look of the illustration, he applied Gaussian Blur and Watercolor effects to it. To create an interior light glow effect, Maric added an additional 50px feather to the window selection using Select> Modify> Feather, created a new layer, filled it with a light yellow color, and reduced the layer opacity. For added interest and to mimic hotspots from interior lights, he created a new layer, used the Elliptical Marquee tool to select a small circular area within the windows, feathered the selection by 10px, and filled the selection with the same color used for the glow layer. To duplicate the highlight, he held Option/Alt and click-dragged it into place. He continued to duplicate the highlights for most of the front windows.

3

The window reflections photograph shown after being pasted inside the window selection

Window glow and highlights in Photoshop

Planning Ahead

Working Between Illustrator & Photoshop

Illustrator & Photoshop
Advanced Technique

Overview: *Plan ahead for export to Photoshop with layer organization; group or separate some objects on layers based on the Photoshop technique you will use; make a registration rectangle for precise placement.*

HUBIG

When Dan Hubig creates an illustration like "Soothing Nervous Patients," above, he relies upon both Illustrator and Photoshop to get the job done efficiently and quickly. Consequently, he constructs his files in Illustrator with Photoshop's strengths and weaknesses in mind. Because the two programs have very different features, even when those features share the same name (such as brushes), Hubig organizes his objects so their Photoshop layers will allow him complete flexibility and ease in creating the finishing touches. And by setting his layers to flatten sublayers on export, he reduces the RAM requirements of his large files and shortens the time it takes Illustrator to create the Photoshop file.

1

The Illustrator file before export to Photoshop

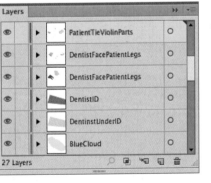

Keeping overlapping objects on separate layers, making it easier in Photoshop to add texture and effects to objects without making selections

1 Planning ahead. The main rule Hubig has when organizing his layers is that overlapping objects he will work on in Photoshop *do not* reside on the same layer. As long as they are on separate layers when exported to Photoshop, he'll be able to lock transparency (which acts like a mask limiting a tool to actual pixels), clip an Adjustment layer so it affects only that object, etc.—all without having to make tedious selections inside Photoshop. By constructing his layer organization this way, rather than grouping by subject (such as the dentist on one main layer, with its parts as sublayers), he can rasterize all the sublayers, so Photoshop doesn't import them as nested Groups when he uses Knockout Group to export the blends he likes to use (see the lesson "Ready to Export" for a full description of this method). The trade-off, however, is that if Hubig doesn't pay careful attention to naming the layers, once they're in Photoshop, his layer organization may not always be as "intuitive" as it would be if grouped according to subject matter.

In Photoshop, creating a Smart Object to apply a Smart Filter on two Illustrator objects placed on one layer, and reducing opacity for both at the same time

2 Preparing artwork for finishing in Photoshop. Aware of the Photoshop techniques he plans to use, Hubig is also able to save time by putting objects that will receive the same treatment in Photoshop on the same layer. If you look at the two floor shadows in the illustration, you can see they both have Gaussian Blurs and reduced opacity. By creating them on a single Illustrator layer, Hubig is able to apply the blur and change the layer opacity in Photoshop just once for both objects. On the other hand, by keeping the blue cloud on a separate layer, Hubig is able to make changes even though it overlaps other objects visually. He can adjust the cloud's opacity, and by locking the layer's transparency he can loosely apply a brush with a broad "Scattering" (set in the Brushes panel), knowing his paint won't spill onto other objects.

Locking just the transparency in a layer to limit the effect of a tool or command to just the pixels—essentially, "auto-masking" the object

3 Bringing new objects into Photoshop with a registration rectangle. Although Hubig typically eyeballs the placement of objects in Photoshop, you might have a need for precision when moving objects into Photoshop. Make sure your artboard and image sizes in Photoshop are the same. Then, to achieve precise registration, create an unstroked, unfilled rectangle on the top layer (to select easily) that is the same size as the artboard. Select both the object(s) and the registration rectangle, and copy and paste them as pixels in Photoshop. This positions your new art precisely where it belongs with respect to earlier artwork, and on its own layer. Finally, drag the artwork layer into position among the other layers, if necessary.

Creating a registration rectangle with no stroke, no fill, and selecting both it and an object to paste as pixels in Photoshop for precise alignment with existing artwork

DEL VECHIO

Gustavo Del Vechio

Illustrator & Photoshop

When Gustavo Del Vechio wanted an illustration to go along with his humanistic interpretation of an urban development project, he decided to make it appear as if the designer could make a real city rise up from his pencil-and-paper drawing. He contrasted the flat paper with the dimensional illustration, and the illustration with the full three-dimensionality of a photograph; then lit the whole to place the designer under a drafting lamp. He made the background from a simple rectangle filled with a white to black radial gradient. He filled another rectangle with white and used Effect> Stylize> Scribble on black-filled objects to create very flat-looking hatch marks representing the urban area. Del Vechio then linked the photos of each hand to a separate layer, adding Effect> Drop Shadow to one with a positive X value, and to the other with a negative X value, maintaining the illusion of radial light from above. Finally he added the completed illustration from his project for the urban development proposal. He had used 3D Studio Max for the initial structures, hand-traced the rendering, and later turned it into a Live Paint group to complete the colorful illustration (see his lesson in the *Rethinking Construction* chapter). Having placed his buildings in a designer's environment, his final illustration demonstrated what goes into creating a city, from the artist's initial concept to a three-dimensional reality.

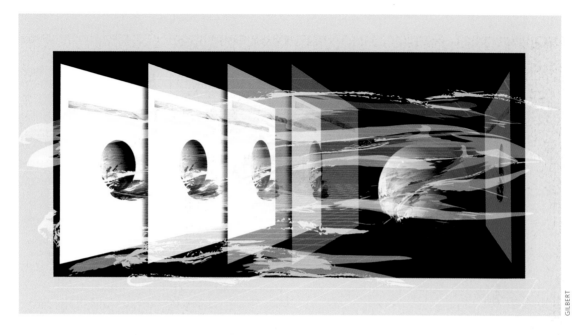

GILBERT

Katharine Gilbert

Illustrator & Photoshop

Katharine Gilbert moves freely between Illustrator and Photoshop, mixing vector, raster, and 3D to express her vision. For "Wind," Gilbert began in Illustrator with an abstract painting that she created with Art brushes (loaded from the Artistic> Artistic_Paintbrush and Artistic_Watercolor libraries). She then moved to Photoshop Extended where she applied the painting as a surface to a 3D sphere. After applying the texture image to her "world," she placed a rasterized version of it in a new Illustrator file to act as a guide for painting the "wind" layers. She used the same Art brushes as before, tweaking them slightly as needed. She turned off the image layers and exported only the vector artwork, which she saved with PDF compatibility. Back in Photoshop, Gilbert opened the .ai file as a Photoshop

PDF, then experimented with the sphere, her Illustrator art, and some Photoshop brushwork to add shadows and more depth to the sphere. She duplicated the elements, merging them into a 3D Postcard, rendered several copies at different angles, and added more image elements for added depth and contrast. She placed the sphere above, and then tied her universe together by placing her Illustrator painting of the wind over all.

The Executive Summary of Graphic Design News

Get 3 Free Issues:
www.design-tools.com/ilwow/

Design Tools Monthly brings you this selection of Illustrator tips from recent issues.

Batch-Convert Illustrator to PDF

Here's a trick for updating the file format of your old logos and other artwork to a more modern format such as PDF. Adobe Illustrator has a script that will batch-convert them for you! Just open them all in Illustrator (you can drag them all onto Illustrator's icon), and then choose File> Scripts> SaveDocAsPDF. All the open Illustrator documents will be saved using your current PDF settings.

New Document, Same Size

In many Adobe applications, such as Illustrator and Photoshop, you can instantly create a new document that's the same size as the last new document that you created: just press Option-Command-N (PC: Alt-Ctrl-N). This bypasses the New Document dialog box, using all its previous settings for size, orientation and color mode.

See True Object Sizes

By default, when Illustrator displays size measurements for a shape, it measures from the center line of its paths, without taking into consideration the width of any strokes applied to the paths. To see the true size of a shape, including the width of its strokes, you have to change Illustrator's Preferences. Choose Illustrator> Preferences> General and check the Use Preview Bounds checkbox.

Adjust Handles on All Anchor Points

By default, Illustrator displays the handles for only the currently active anchor point. If you want to see the handles for all selected anchor points, just change the preferences: choose Illustrator> Preferences, highlight the Selection & Anchor Display area and tick the checkbox named Show handles when multiple anchors are selected. After that, when you select more than one anchor point with either the Group Selection tool or the Direct Selection tool, all the handles will be available for adjusting.

Mark Center of Artboard

In Illustrator, you can mark the center of your Artboard by double-clicking on the Artboard tool. In the resulting Options window, check the Show Center Mark option in the Display section, and click OK. This creates cross hairs to mark the center of your Artboard. If you change the size of your Artboard, the cross hairs will automatically re-center themselves.

Easier Circles

In Illustrator, if you know where a circle should begin, you can press the Command/Ctrl key while using the Ellipse tool. This lets you begin the circle's arc exactly where you click, instead of at a virtual "corner" of an imaginary enclosing box. Use this tip when tracing a template that has rounded corners.

Round Corners Your Way

Instead of using the Rounded Rectangle tool, create a standard rectangle with the Rectangle tool and choose Effect> Stylize> Round Corners. You can then change the roundness at any time in the Appearance panel. As a bonus, you can use this effect on any shape.

Spiral Control

When using Illustrator's Spiral Tool, you can adjust the tightness drop-off and loops of the spiral by using the Option, Command, and Up and Down arrow keys. (PC: Alt & Ctrl)

The Key to Aligning Objects

You can easily align a set of objects to a guide in Illustrator. Using the Selection tool (V), select both the guide and all of the objects, then click on the guide again. The guide is now the "key object" with which everything will line up when you use the Align functions on either the Control panel or Align panel (Window> Align). You can do the same thing with any object—the key doesn't have to be a guide.

Change the Style, But Keep the Color

Graphic styles can save any appearance attribute (color, effects, transforms, etc.) to re-use on other objects, and the new additive graphic styles lets you apply these appearances without wiping out what the object looked like originally. Let's say you're drawing a set of tree ornaments with different Fill and Stroke colors and you want to apply a graphic style that has a scribble effect and a drop shadow, without changing the Fill and Stroke. Select all of the circles you've drawn for colored ornaments, then Option-click (PC: Alt-click) the style in the Graphic Styles panel (Window> Graphic Styles) to add it while retaining all of the original colors.

Use Live Color to Edit Blacks

If you get an Illustrator file that you need to print but you find there are five different types of black, don't fret — you can convert them all to a single black definition by using Live Color. Just press Command-A (PC: Ctrl-A) to select everything, and choose Edit> Edit Colors> Recolor Artwork. In the resulting dialog box, you can reassign the blacks.

Work Faster

In Illustrator, pressing the X key will switch between the current Stroke and Fill. Pressing the Forward Slash key (/) changes the targeted Fill or Stroke to None.

Choose a Complementary Color

In Illustrator, you can choose the complementary color of the current fill or stroke of a selected object by Command-Shift-clicking (Mac) or Ctrl-Shift-clicking (Win) in the color ramp at the bottom of the Color panel. You can also choose Complement from the side menu in the Color panel.

Better Dashes

When applying a dashed stroke, you can make the dashes distribute properly, with complete corners. The trick is to go to the Stroke panel (Window> Stroke), click the Dashed Line checkbox, and select the icon labeled Aligns Dashes to Corners and Path Ends, Adjusting Lengths to Fit. To keep this option turned on for future objects, go to the Appearance panel, and in its side menu turn off New Art Has Basic Appearance.

Better Buttons

Try using the 9-Slice Scaling feature to intelligently resize objects such as buttons and banners. For example, you may want to make a rounded-corner rectangle taller or wider, without affecting its text or the shape of its rounded corners. To do that, first make the object into a symbol by dragging it onto the Symbols panel. Then in the Symbol Options dialog, turn on Enable Guides for 9-Slice Scaling. Now when you resize the rectangle, its text and corners will not change.

Draw Inside and Paste Inside

If you draw a new object inside an existing object, the existing object will mask it. You can also Paste into an object or Place into an object — just click on the object and change the drawing mode at the bottom of the Toolbox to Draw Inside.

Taper Strokes

The Width tool lets you drag any place on a stroke to make it wider or narrower at that location on the path. You can even add multiple width points to make the stroke go from wide to narrow and back to wide again. Bonus tip: hold the Option/Alt key while dragging to create an asymmetrical stroke width (one that's thicker on one side than the other).

Simplify Strokes

It's easy to remove fancy attributes such as patterned brushes or art on a path, from a stroke. Just select the path, and in the Control panel look for the Brush Definition dropdown menu. Choose Basic from the top of that list. If you've applied a variable width stroke, also click on the Variable Width Profile dropdown menu and choose Uniform from the top of that list.

Another Use for Smart Guides

If you're having trouble selecting objects in a complex illustration, turn on Smart Guides (View> Smart Guides). The built-in Object Highlighting feature of Smart Guides will highlight objects as you mouse over them.

Easily Select and Edit Common Attributes

In Illustrator, you can easily select (and edit) all the objects in your file that have a specific effect applied. Just select the object and highlight the effect in the Appearance panel, and then choose Select> Same> Appearance Attribute and Illustrator will pick up all other objects with the same effect. You'll also see that the Appearance panel now lets you edit attributes that are common for all of the selected objects.

Easy Photoshop Textures

Want to add some texture to your object in Illustrator? Start by creating a texture in Photoshop in grayscale mode —white areas will become transparent, while black areas will become opaque. Place the image in Illustrator on top of the item to which you want to apply the texture. Select both the texture and the object and, in the Transparency panel, choose Make Opacity Mask. You'll be amazed.

Multi-column Text Frame

Illustrator, just like InDesign or QuarkXPress, can make a multi-column text frame. To do that, use the Type tool to create a text box, then choose Type> Area Type options. There you can enter the number of columns you want. You can even thread a story from text frame to frame box.

Rotate Individual Characters

Illustrator's Character panel, when in its expanded state, lets you rotate selected text — even one character. To expand the Character panel, choose Show Options from its side menu. To rotate selected text, type a number into the lower right field or choose an angle from its pop-up menu. The possibilities are limitless — or at least very odd.

Use Symbols for Graphs

Illustrator lets you use your own 'graph symbols' when making graphs. So, for example, you can use a column of CDs to indicate how many CDs were sold. Just draw your art (CD) and select it. Choose Object> Graph> Design, click the New Design button and then click the Rename button to give your design a name (CD). This saves your selected art as a repeatable element for your graphs. To use it in a graph, first create the graph by dragging out an area with the Column Graph Tool and entering or importing data. Then select the graph and choose Object> Graph> Column. In the resulting Graph Column dialog box, select the column design you just created and choose among the options of how it should be displayed.

The Executive Summary of Graphic Design News

Get 3 Free Issues:
www.design-tools.com/ilwow/

Design Tools Monthly's Jay Nelson shares his favorite Illustrator-related plug-ins and utilities!

Note: Many of the plug-ins are still in the process of being updated for CS6 and are currently not compatible.

Artlandia's **LivePresets** ($125) lets you create live pattern swatches and symbols that are editable on the fly with Illustrator's tools. Artlandia **SymmetryWorks 5** ($249) lets you easily create seamless patterns. You draw a simple shape and SymmetryWorks rotates, reflects, and spaces it to create a seamless pattern. As you edit the shape, the pattern updates in real time. (Mac/Win)   www.artlandia.com

Zevrix's **ArtOptimizer** ($120) reduces the size of linked images that were resized in Illustrator. If the effective resolution is higher than a target resolution you define, it backs up the image, opens the copy in Photoshop, changes its dimensions, and reimports it into Illustrator at 100% size. It can optionally also convert the image's color mode to CMYK, RGB or Grayscale, apply sharpening filters and flatten the image. (Mac)   www.zevrix.com

Hot Door's **CADTools** ($299) adds tools for computer-aided drafting to Illustrator, which already has filters for importing and exporting in DXF/DWG formats. It can add interactive dimensional text and arrows to any line or angle and measure and change angles, the areas of shapes, and radius of circles and curves. The Trim tool automatically trims excess from overlapping segments. The Fill and Chamfer tools let you automatically round or bevel a shape's corners. The Wall tool creates two-sided wall shapes, and the amazing Wall Healer tool cleans up the intersection of Wall shapes. (Mac/Win)   www.hotdoor.com

CValley's **FILTERiT** ($129), is a plug-in that provides a wide variety of options from simple distortion to 3D Transform on outlined objects. Its "killer feature" is that you work directly on your document page, seeing your results immediately as you change things, and that you can work on "live" type, while the objects and effects remain instantly editable—no more dialog boxes to open and close. (Mac/Win)   www.cvalley.com

GraphicXtras has many creative brushes and plug-ins, priced as low as $10 each.   www.graphicxtras.com

Jean-Louis Garrivet's **JLG•Dimension** ($25 euro) adds four new dimensioning tools. To use it, select a segment, angle, circle, or other path, and the dimensions of that selection are added to the outside edge of the selection. (Mac/Win)
http://perso.orange.fr/jlg.outils/Pages/ManuelCotationsUS.html

If you spend lots of time with paths and shapes, you can double your speed and enjoyment with this "ultimate upgrade" disguised as a plug-in: Astute Graphics'

VectorScribe is comprised of two sets: **VectorScribe Designer** ($60) and **VectorScribe Studio** ($110). Designer includes PathScribe, a path-editing plug-in with several tools that let you drag lines into curves, remove redundant points, control your Bézier handles, and more, along with the Dynamic Measure and Protractor tools, both aids to precise drawing. Studio includes all the tools in Designer plus Dynamic Shapes and Rounded Corners, "live" effects that let you edit basic geometric shapes without tediously adding and subtracting anchor points, and to interactively round any corner point by any amount. Read reviews and watch videos at their website. (Mac/Win)
www.astutegraphics.com

Avenza Software's **MAPublisher** ($1,399) lets you import CAD drawings and maps in geographic information systems (GIS) format, including shapes, boundaries, routes and elevations. MAPublisher also lets you automatically create legends and keys. It can import database tables, which can be linked to existing map layers, and can export to ArcView Shape files and SVG and dBASE formats. It even supports Google's KML file format for use with Google Maps. Their website shows examples of the beautiful, detailed maps made by customers. (Mac/Win)
www.avenza.com

Illustrator's Bevel feature can be too smooth; that's why Shinycore's **Path Styler Pro** is valuable. This plug-in for Photoshop or Illustrator ($99 each or $129 for both) creates sharp, clean bevels and accurate reflections with multiple lighting options. You can apply multiple bevels, and each bevel can have its own material, contour, texture, and procedural map such as wood, metal, plastic, glass, and others. Lights can be directional, omni, or tube. More than 100 presets are included. (Mac/Win)   www.shinycore.com

Astute Graphics' **Phantasm CS** (three versions, starting at £49) adds color controls similar to Photoshop's: brightness, contrast, hue, saturation, levels and curves—but you can use them on native Illustrator shapes and imported images. All controls are available as both a Filter and a Live Effect, so you can later edit or remove your changes. (Mac/Win)
www.astutegraphics.com

Code-Line's **SneakPeek Pro** ($20) lets you preview Illustrator, InDesign, EPS, and FreeHand documents in the Finder, without actually launching the application. (Mac)
www.code-line.com

CValley's **Xtream Path** ($139) lets you click anywhere on a path and drag it to into a new shape, instead of dragging anchor points around. A palette shows the numerical values of the position of anchor points and handles, as well as the length of segments. The palette also lets you copy and paste the position values from one anchor point onto another. You can symmetrically change a shape—pull on one side and the other side mirrors the change. A Smart Rounding effect changes sharp corners into rounded ones, even on editable type. A Multi-Line tool makes it easier to draw isometric shapes such as 3D boxes. You can even copy paths and insert them into other paths, bevel corners, round corners, and easily create arcs. (Mac/Win)

www.cvalley.com

Strata **Enfold 3D CX** ($695) is a sophisticated program for working with packaging graphics that span seams or folded edges. You can use linked Photoshop art, set die-cut lines and folding scores, and then preview your masterpiece—in full 3D—in Adobe Illustrator. You can then send the file to your own printer for a quick mockup, fire off a print-ready version for production, or export the art to Strata 3D CX Suite for further tweaking. Enfold 3D lets you fold existing art into 3D designs, rotate the Illustrator canvas to match the 3D view, and more. www.tinyurl.com/mxu6x3

The **Convert to Area Text** script (free) lets you select multiple text frames and convert them from the less versatile Point text to the more flexible Area text with a click.

www.ajarproductions.com

Astute Graphics' **DrawScribe** (£39) lets you intuitively create points and path segments without using the Pen tool and modifier keys. Path handles appear when needed for easier path editing, and points can easily be switched from corner to smooth without having to press additional keys. Path segments can be reshaped with DrawScribe by simply dragging on the path itself.

www.astutegraphics.com

Baby Universe's **EXDXF-Pro3** ($90) is a plug-in that lets you import CAD-standard DXF files and export Illustrator files to DXF as well.

www.baby-universe.co.jp

E-Spec's **JPEG Publisher** ($350), is a plug-in that automatically creates a JPEG whenever an Illustrator document is created or saved. You can choose to generate a JPEG from the entire file, from specific layers, or from layer combos.

www.e-spec.net

Shane Stanley's **PDF Pages to Artboards** is a free droplet for Mac OS X that sits on your desktop and, when you drag a PDF on top of it, creates an Illustrator file with one artboard created for each PDF page.

www.tinyurl.com/3s5ry99

The **All Group to Ungroup** script ungroups every object on every artboard in your Illustrator file.

www.tinyurl.com/4b2bh4r

Premedia Systems, Inc. specializes in automating workflows with custom plug-ins and scripts, personalized software, and training in all aspects of workflow, including production. Their commercial application, **PDF Comparator**, not only reveals differing content between two PDFs, but how each PDF will differ when rendered and printed. They also offer several free scripts for both Illustrator and InDesign. www.premediasystems.com

Collect for Output: two options

Adobe Illustrator—even version CS6—doesn't have a "collect for output" feature. (Its Collect for Output script only collects linked images, not fonts.) Here are two options to collect everything:

Worker72a's **Scoop** ($47) collects placed graphics and fonts and can also extract embedded raster images. (Mac)

www.worker72a.com

Code Line's **Art Files** ($50) is a utility that collects and packages placed graphics and fonts. Several Illustrator documents can be packaged at the same time, and any images or fonts that are shared among the documents are collected only once, saving disk space. (Mac) www.code-line.com

Rick Johnson: these and many more

www.rj-graffix.com

Concatenate ($20) lets you connect two or more paths into one continuous path. You tell it how close the endpoints should be to combine the paths, and whether to average the endpoints together. It's especially useful for cleaning up CAD drawings or connecting and filling borders in maps. (Mac/Win)

Cutting Tools ($5) adds new ways to cut paths: Hatchet cuts through all paths, not just the top path; Saber Saw cuts through all paths as you drag over them; Table Saw cuts a straight line through all paths; Vector Vac deletes all paths you drag it across. (Mac/Win)

Rick Johnson's **Select** (free) adds a "Select" item to Illustrator's Filter menu to select 15 additional things: guides, paths, open paths, closed paths, filled paths, unfilled paths, stroked paths, unstroked paths, dashed paths, undashed paths, compound paths, groups, live object groups, gradient meshes, envelopes, symbols, embedded raster art, and placed art. (Mac/Win)

Worker72a: focus on production

www.worker72a.com

Select Effects ($25) highlights any paths that use Transparency, Effects and Blend modes, which may cause problems when printing or flattening. (Mac)

Tag72a ($25) automatically creates and updates special text objects such as User Name, Document Name, File Path, Print Date/Time and Save Date/Time. (Mac)

More Plug-ins

PowerXChange sells many plug-ins for Illustrator, InDesign, Photoshop, Acrobat, QuarkXPress, and more:

www.thepowerxchange.com

Windows WOW! Glossary

and essential Adobe Illustrator shortcuts

Ctrl	Ctrl always refers to the Ctrl (Control) key
Alt	Alt always refers to the Alt key
Marquee	With any Selection tool, click-drag over object(s) to select
Toggle	Menu selection acts as a switch; choose once turns it on, choosing again turns it off
Contextual menu	Right-click to access contextual menus
Group	Ctrl-G to group objects together onto one layer
Copy, Cut, Paste, Undo	Ctrl-C, Ctrl-X, Ctrl-V, Ctrl-Z
Select All, Deselect	Ctrl-A, Ctrl-Shift-A
Paste Remembers Layers	With Paste Remembers Layers on (from the Layers panel menu), pasting from the clipboard places objects on the same layers that they were on originally; if you don't have the layers, Paste Remembers Layers will make the layers for you
Paste in Front	Use Ctrl-F to paste objects on the clipboard directly in front of selected objects, and in exact registration from where it was cut (if nothing is selected, it pastes in front of current layer with Paste Remembers Layers off)
Paste in Back	Use Ctrl-B to paste objects on the clipboard directly in back of selected objects, and in exact registration from where it was cut (if nothing is selected, it pastes in back of current layer with Paste Remembers Layers off)
Toggle rulers on/off	Ctrl-R
***fx* menu**	From the Appearance panel, click the *fx* icon to access effects
Select contiguous	Hold Shift while selecting to select contiguous layers, swatches, etc.
Select non-contiguous	Hold Ctrl while selecting to select non-contiguous layers, swatches, etc.
Toggle Smart Guides on/off	Ctrl-U
Turn objects into guides	Ctrl-5
Turn guides back into objects	Ctrl-Alt-5 (you must select the guide first; if guides are locked, you must unlock them first from the contextual menu or from the View>Guides submenu)
	Find related files or artwork in that chapter's folder on **WOW! ONLINE**
Illustrator Help	Access ***Illustrator Help*** from the Help menu

Mac WOW! Glossary

and essential Adobe Illustrator shortcuts

⌘ Option	The Command key (this key may have a ⌘ or a ⌃ on it) The Option key
Marquee	With any Selection tool, click-drag over object(s) to select
Toggle	Menu selection acts as a switch; choose once turns it on, choosing again turns it off
Contextual menu	Right-click to access contextual menus
Group	⌘-G to group objects together onto one layer
Copy, Cut, Paste, Undo	⌘-C, ⌘-X, ⌘-V, ⌘-Z
Select All, Deselect	⌘-A, ⌘-Shift-A
Paste Remembers Layers	With Paste Remembers Layers on (from the Layers panel menu), pasting from the clipboard places objects on the same layers that they were on originally; if you don't have the layers, Paste Remembers Layers will make the layers for you
Paste in Front	Use ⌘-F to paste objects on the clipboard directly in front of selected objects, and in exact registration from where it was cut (if nothing is selected, it pastes in front of current layer with Paste Remembers Layers off)
Paste in Back	Use ⌘-B to paste objects on the clipboard directly in back of selected objects, and in exact registration from where it was cut (if nothing is selected, it pastes in back of current layer with Paste Remembers Layers off)
Toggle rulers on/off	⌘-R
fx menu	From the Appearance panel, click the *fx* icon to access effects
Select contiguous	Hold Shift while selecting to select contiguous layers, swatches, etc.
Select non-contiguous	Hold ⌘ while selecting to select non-contiguous layers, swatches, etc.
Toggle Smart Guides on/off	⌘-U
Turn objects into guides	⌘-5
Turn guides back into objects	⌘-Option-5 (you must select the guide first; if guides are locked, you must unlock them first from the contextual menu or from the View>Guides submenu)
	Find related files or artwork in that chapter's folder on **WOW! ONLINE**
Illustrator Help	Access *Illustrator Help* from the Help menu

Artists

Anil Ahuja
Adobe Systems
I-1A, Sec-25A
Noida UP-201301
INDIA
+91-9810566779
ahuja@adobe.com

Kenneth Albert
www.kennethalbert@carbon-
made.com

Kevan Atteberry
P.O. Box 40188
Bellevue, WA 98015-4188
206-550-6353
kevan@oddisgood.com
oddisgood.com

Jean Aubé
785 Versailles #301
Montréal Québec
CANADA
H3C 1Z5
jeanaube01@videotron.ca

Janaína Cesar de Oliveira
Baldacci
São Paulo City, São Paulo
Brasil
(011) 37910918, (011) 73687068
janacesar@gmail.com
jana@janabaldacci.com
www.janabaldacci.com

Billie Bryan
717-363-8500
888-455-3384
billie@beethedesigner.com
www.beethedesigner.com

Pariah Burke
504-422-7499
me@iampariah.com
iampariah.com
@iamPariah

Cinthia A. Burnett
cinabur@yahoo.com

James Cassidy
860-223-8441
www.alliancewebdesign.com
@alliancewebdsgn

George Coghill
george@coghillcartooning.com
coghillcartooning.com
gcoghill

Charuca
www.charuca.eu

Sandee Cohen
33 Fifth Avenue, #10B
New York, NY 10003
212-677-7763
sandee@vectorbabe.com
www.vectorbabe.com

Sally Cox
408-628-2780
sally@kreatable.com
www.kreatable.com
@kreatable

Mike Cressy
www.mikecressy.com

Dacosta!
info@chocolatesoop.com
www.chocolatesoop.com
@chocolatesoop

Lee Daniels
+44 7909 583226
inbox@LeeDanielsART.com

Darren, *see* Winder

Gustavo Del Vechio
Brazil
gustavodelvechio@gmail.com
www.gustavodelvechio.com.br

Suzanne Drapeau
sdrapeau@sbcglobal.net

Dedree Drees
5307 Wayne Ave.
Baltimore, MD 21207
410-448-3317; 443-840-4423
dedreedrees@cavtel.net
ddreesart.wordpress.com

Elaine Drew
elaine-drew@comcast.net
www.elainedrew.com

Nicole Dzienis

EdWarner
www.edwarner.wordpress.com

Gary Ferster
10 Karen Drive
Tinton Falls, NJ 07753
732-922-8903
Fax: 732-922-8970
gferster@comcast.net
www.garyferster.com

Frazer
www.frazercreative.com

Monika Gause
Hamburg, Germany
post@vektorgarten.de
www.vektorgarten.de

Greg Geisler
512-619-3635
greg@raytracer.com
www.raytracer.com

Katharine Gilbert
550 Hazelwood Road
Aylett, VA 23009
804.994.2929
mail@truschgilbertdesign.com
www.inthewoodonline.com
@katgilbert

Von R. Glitschka
971-223-6143
von@glitschka.com
www.glitschka.com
@vonster

Mordy Golding
Design Responsibly LLC
320 Leroy Avenue
Cedarhurst, NY 11516
info@designresponsibly.com
www.designresponsibly.com
www.mordy.com

Steven H. Gordon
Cartagram, LLC
136 Mill Creek Crossing
Madison, AL 35758
256-772-0022
wow@cartagram.com
www.cartagram.com
@cartagram

Laurie Grace
laurie.grace@gmail.com
www.lauriegrace.com

Cheryl Graham
www.cherylgraham.net
@FreeTransform

Gusman, *see* Joly

Brad Hamann
Brad Hamann Illustration
& Design
brad@bradhamann
www.bradhamann.com

Dan Hubig
209 Mississippi St.
San Francisco, CA 94107
415-824-0838
dan@danhubig.com
www.danhubig.com

Lisa Jackmore
13603 Bluestone Court
Clifton, VA 20124-2465
703-830-0985
ljackmore@cox.net

Lance Jackson
Lax Syntax Design
www.noirture.com
www.lancejackson.net

Mahalia Johnson
mahaliaclarke85@yahoo.com

Rick Johnson
Graffix plug-ins
http://rj-graffix.com

Donal Jolley
10505 Wren Ridge Road
Johns Creek, GA 30022
770-751-0553
don@donaljolley.com
www.donaljolley.com
@donaljolley

Annie Gusman Joly
860-928-1042
annie@picturedance.com
www.anniejoly.com

Dave Joly
860-928-1042
dave@picturedance.com
www.picturedance.com

kaNO
www.kanokid.com

Killamari
www.killamari.com

Mike Kimball
PO Box 77492
San Francisco, CA 94107
mkimballsf@aim.com
www.MKSF-Gallery.com

Steve King
Senior Illustrator/Designer
U-Haul International, Inc.
steve_king@uhaul.com
www.uhaul.com/SuperGraph-
ics/
www.kingillustration.com

Stephen Klema
69 Walnut St.
Winsted, CT 06098
860-379-1579
stephen@stephenklema.com
sklema@txcc.comnet.edu
www.stephenklema.com
www.SnotArt.org

Raymond Larrett
715 Frederick Street
San Francisco, CA 94117
415-595-8240
rlarrett@puzzledsquirrel.com
puzzledsquirrel.com
@ PSquirreleBooks

Chris Leavens
chris@unloosen.com
www.chrisleavens.com

Adam Z Lein
40 Morrow Ave., Apt 3HS
Scarsdale, NY 10583
914-437-9115
adamz@adamlein.com
www.adamlein.com

Jean-Benoit Levy
Studio AND
2278 15th Street #4
San Francisco, CA 94114
415 252 05 06
jbl@and.ch
www.and.ch

Abe Lincoln Jr.
www.girlsbike.com

Amber Loukoumis

MAD
www.madtoydesign.com

Pete Maric
440-487-4205
contact@petemaric.com
www.petemaric.com

Jeffrey Martin
jmartin584@gmail.com

Danuta Markiewicz (Danka)
pazourek@gmail.com

Greg Maxson
116 W. Florida Ave
Urbana, IL 61801
217-898-6560
gregdraws@gmail.com
www.gregmaxson.com
@gregdraws

Aaron McGarry
aron@amcgarry.com
www.amcgarry.com

MCKIBILLO
josh@mckibillo.com
www. mckibillo.com
@mckibillo

Nobuko Miyamoto
3-8 Matuba-cho
Tokorozawa-shi
Saitama-ken Japan/359-0044
04-2998-6631
venus@gol.com
venus.oracchi.com/

Yukio Miyamoto
Matubacho 3-8
Tokorozawasi
Saitama Prefecture/359-0044
+81-42-998-6631
yukio-m@ppp.bekkoame.ne.jp
www.bekkoame.ne.jp/
~yukio-m/intro

Tamara Morrison
524 Torringford East Street
Torrington, CT 06790
860-806-2951
tamaramorrisongraphics@
gmail.com
www.tamaramorrisongraph-
ics.com

Gabriel Mourelle
www.gabrielmourelle.com.ar

Sebastian Murra Ramirez (mu!)
info@mu-illustration.com
www.mu-illustration.com
@muillustration

Stéphane Nahmani
sholby@sholby.net
www.sholby.net

Jared Nickerson
www.jthreeconcepts.com

Chris D. Nielsen
6662 Timaru Circle
Cypress, CA 90630
714-323-1602
carartwork@ca.rr.com
chris@pentoolart.com
www.pentoolart.com

Ann Paidrick
ann.paidrick@ebypaidrick.com
www.ebypaidrick.com

Podgy Panda
www.podgypanda.com

Ellen Papciak-Rose
info@ellenpapciakrose.com
www.ellenpapciakrose.com

Richard Perez
119 Haight St, Apt 28
San Francisco CA 94102
415-656-6576
info@skinnyships.com
www.skinnyships.com
@skinnyships

Stephanie Pernal

Mark 'Atomos' Pilon
www.markpilon.com

Ryan Putnam
ryan@rypearts.com
www.rypearts.com
@rypearts

Sabine Reinhart
Jakob Hoogen Straße 61
41844 Wegberg, Germany
sabine@sabinereinhart.de
www.sabinereinhart.de
@ SabineReinhart

Michael (Mic) Riddle
micrid3d@mac.com

Andrew Roberts
01223 571538
ar@andyrobertsdesign.com
www.andyrobertsillustration.
com
@arillustrate

Jolynne Roorda
www.folktheory.com

Andrew Rudmann
Long Island, NY
andrew@rudmanndesign.com
www.rudmanndesign.com

Rachel Sellers
256 282 9333
rachel@rsdirectionaldesign.
com

Shawnimals
www.shawnimals.co

Sharon Steuer
c/o Peachpit Press
1249 Eighth St.
Berkeley, CA 94710
www.ssteuer.com

Janet Stoppee
janet@m2media.com
light@m2media.com
www. m2media.com

Ilene Strizver
The Type Studio
Westport, CT
ilene@thetypestudio.com
www.thetypestudio.com
203-227-5929

Brenda Sutherland
345 Park Avenue
San Jose, CA 95124

Steve Talkowski
www.sketchbot.tv

Moses Tan
37 Kingloch Parade
Wantirna, Victoria
Australia 3152
03 97291120
mosestan@optusnet.com.au

Tokyo-go-go
www.tokyo-go-go.com

Jack Tom
1042 Broad Street
Bridgeport CT 06604
203-579-0889
art2go2006@yahoo.com
www.jacktom.com

Jean-Claude Tremblay
Proficiografik
135 Boul. Champlain
Candiac, Québec J5R 3T1
CANADA
514-629-0949
info@proficiografik.com
www.proficiografik.com

Junichi Tsuneoka
www.stubbornsideburn.com

David Turton
thegraphiclibrary.com

Warner, *see* EdWarner

Laurie Wigham
209 Mississippi Street
San Francisco, CA 94107
laurie@lauriewigham.com
lauriewigham.com

Darren Winder
Daw Design
darren@dawdesign.net
www.dawdesign.com

Jillian Winkel

Jamal Wynn
56 White Oak Avenue
Plainville, CT 06062
860-631-7767
MrJrWynn@gmail.com
facebook.com/JamalWynn

Brian Yap
briankyap@gmail.com

General Index

E

F

N

Nahmani, Stephane, 7
naming
    active artboard, 10
    color groups and pattern
        swatches, 149
    color groups in Recolor
        Artwork, 127
    each artboard in set, 40
    layers, 6
    layers in Photoshop, 239
    saving artboard stages for
        presentation, 78
    single color in Swatches
        panel, 120
    templates, 12
    text, 30
NaniBird project, 210
NaniPeeps, 210
navigation, Artboard panel
    layers, 11
New Art Has Basic Appearance,
    9, 157
New Brush icon, 103, 117
New Color Group icon, 131,
    135, 148
New Document, 36–37
New Document Profiles, 4
New Graphic Style button, 9
New Layer icon, 6
New Light icon, 158
new paragraph (Return/Enter), 26
New Pattern brush, 117
New Swatch icon, Swatches
    panel, 120
New Window, 10
Nielsen, Chris, 206–207, 219
No Shading option, 3D Surface
    Shading, 157
non-Adobe programs, moving
    artwork in Illustrator
    to, 223
non-contiguous layers, 17
non-contiguous shift points, 85
non-rotated rectangle, converting
    to artboard, 11
Numbers
    64-bit support, what's new in
        CS6, xv

O

Object Layer Options dialog,
    InDesign, 225
object management, workspace
    copy and paste techniques, 7–8
    graphic styles and Appearance
        panel, 9
    overview of, 5–6
    Select Behind, 7
    selection and target indicators
        in Layers panel, 7
    using Appearance panel, 8–9
    using isolation mode, 6
Object menu command, 189–191
objects
    building appearance for
        single, 18–19
    creating slices from, 231
    disappearing from artboard
        when entering
        PEM, 181
    making clipping masks
        from, 189
    modifying before or after
        blend, 187
    wrapping Area type around, 29
Offset Path, 125
one-point perspective view,
    163, 170
online resources, Help menu, xvi
online video game
    scenes, 164–165
opacity
    brightening artwork with, 135
    creating highlights using
        transparency, 202
    reducing, 184
    transparency referring to, 183
opacity masks
    constraining texture using, 217
    creating, 212–213
    interweaving objects using
        complex, 213
    overview of, 184–185
    precisely targeting and editing
        transparency, 185–186
    roping in paths using, 200–201
    with shadows for soft
        transitions, 212–213
Opacity settings
    adding transparency to
        individual mesh

points, 143
*The Adobe Illustrator CS5
    WOW! Book*
    cover, 215
    assigning to gradient mesh, 125
    basic appearance, 8, 18
    Blob Brush tool, 55
    California Magazine complex
        graphic, 214
    creating dragonfly image, 101
    creating glow, 205
    creating transparency with
        blending modes
        and, 203
    drawing complex elements, 173
    Drawing Inside mode
        example, 81
    drawing transparent
        brushstrokes, 102
    drawing with appearances, 9
    "Falling" complex graphic, 216
    Frosty Cones example, 51
    Golden Gate Bridge
        anniversary poster, 24
    object transparency, 186
    painting with Bristle Brushes,
        89–90, 110–111, 113
    Transparency panel
        controls, 184
    for type on terrain images, 45
    Vintage effect with, 74
Options dialog, modifying
    existing brush strokes, 90
Orientation, Blend options, 188
out port, Path type bracket, 27–29
Outer Glow effect, 45, 165
Outline mode
    isolation mode instead of, 6
    paths shown in, 86
outlines
    applying to stroke
        gradients, 124
    converting type to, 30–31
    creating background art and
        banners, 42–43
    example of, 49
    importing Illustrator paths into
        3D programs for, 226
    painterly illustration with
        Bristle Brushes/Draw
        Inside, 108–109
    Pit Bull poster example, 52
Overlap option, Art Brush, 88
Overlap option, Image Trace, 59
overrides, avoiding
    formatting, 29–30

P

P. See Pen tool (P)

Paidrick, Ann
    building gradient mesh objects, 125, 129
    creating pattern swatch combined with mesh, 144
    distortion of envelope mesh object, 145
    hand-drawn look of spirals using strokes, 99
    transparent mesh for realism, 142–143
    vector patterns, 199

paint bucket, using Shape Builder as, 57

Paintbrush tool
    Blob Brush tool vs., 55
    calligraphic attributes of, 54
    customizing Calligraphic brush, 103
    graphic illustrations of organic forms, 104–105
    painting fur and folds of bulldog with, 113
    setting preferences for all brushes, 89

painterly illustrations, 108–109, 110–111

painting, with Blob Brush tool, 55

palette of colors, Image Trace panel, 59

panels, arranging in workspace, 2–3
    finding, xvii

Papciak-Rose, Ellen, 184

Paperzebra, 211

Paragraph panel, 29

Paragraph Styles panel, 29–30

paste. See copy/paste

Paste dialog, creating Photoshop Smart Object, 224

Paste in Back, 7–8, 15, 61, 79

Paste in Front
    building from simplicity to complexity with, 15
    curving labels, 43
    forming shadows, 201
    ignoring drawing modes, 61
    masking with multiple objects, 213
    overview of, 7–8
    reshaping with Shape Builder, 79

Paste in Place, 7–8

Paste on All Artboards, 7–8, 34

Paste Remembers Layer, 7, 209

Path Eraser tool, 54, 188

Path type
    accessing Type Options dialog for, 33
    applying to circle, 28
    labeling curving features on maps, 44
    manually flipping to other side of path, 28
    overview of, 27
    using Appearance panel with type objects, 32
    working with threaded text, 28–29

Pathfinder
    building image with basic objects, 13
    combining paths with, 64–65
    creating frame for portrait, 111
    operating like compound shapes, 62
    overview of, 63
    PhotoRealistic complex graphics using, 206–207
    roping in paths with, 200–201
    simulating drapery folds, 144
    textured graphics using, 217

paths. See also compound paths
    altering/deleting with Live Paint Selection tool, 58
    applying Path type to closed and open, 27–28
    coloring line art, 66–67
    combining with Pathfinder, 64–65
    constructing shadows in 3D using, 167
    creating blends along, 187–188
    creating for envelopes, 153
    gradient, 138
    hiding/locking to protect from Eraser tool, 54
    making ends meet, 86–87
    modifying between existing width points, 84
    modifying with Blob Brush tool, 56
    moving artwork from Illustrator to

Photoshop, 224
    removing portion with Path Eraser tool, 55
    roping in, 200–201
    saving stroke profiles for other, 95
    Simplify command for, 60
    translating color into layers for filled, 218

Pattern Brush Options dialog, 114–115, 117

Pattern Brushes, 88–89, 114–115, 117

Pattern Editing Mode (PEM)
    complex layered patterns in, 196–198
    creating hand-drawn look for spiral patterns, 99
    entering, 180–181
    entering Recolor Artwork in, 148–149
    expanded pattern objects and, 180
    leaving, 182
    recoloring patterns in, 183
    what you cannot do in, 182

pattern fills, distorting using envelope, 153

pattern making
    complex layered patterns in PEM, 196–198
    complex vector patterns from photo, 199
    creating intricate patterns, 165
    creating pattern, 181–182
    creating variation on pattern, 182–183
    editing pattern swatches without PEM, 183
    entering PEM, 180–181
    layered patterns, 196–197
    leaving PEM, 182
    lesson in, 194–195
    mastering, 180–183
    NaniBird project, 210
    navigating Pattern Options panel, 194–195
    overview of, 180
    recoloring patterns in PEM, 183
    sample of unique patterns, 193

Pattern Options panel, 180–181, 194–195

S

sampling text, Eyedropper tool, 31
San Francisco Embarcadero waterfront, 217
Save A Copy, PEM isolation bar, 183
Save for Web, 226, 231
Save Grid as Preset, Perspective Grid, 177
saving
    artboards as PDFs, 35
    artboards as separate files, 35
    color groups and pattern swatches, 149
    with Create PDF Compatible File, 222
    current appearance, 9
    custom stroke profile, 85
    custom swatches as new color group, 131
    custom workspace, 3
    customized grid in Perspective Grid, 160
    layered Illustrator files as layered Acrobat files, 226
    map artwork as image and slices, 231
    New Document Profile to Library presets, 4
    program files as PDFs, 223
    stroke profiles and applying to other paths, 95
    swatch library, 131
    width profiles, 98
Scale Strokes & Effects, Scale tool, 60
Scale to Fit button, 3D effects, 158–159
Scale tool, 27, 60
scaling
    altering stroke weight and, 60
    applying 9-slice scaling to symbols, 91
    Area and Point type, 26
    auto-scaling art, 22–23
    gradients, 124
    mapping symbols onto 3D object with, 158
    text frames only, 27
scanned images, tracing template layers with, 12–13

Scatter Brushes
    gallery examples of, 118, 216
    working with, 88–90
Scissors tool
    creating Rubber Ducky, 97
    cutting ellipse for curved banner path, 42
    drawing arch, 21
    drawing tube, 201
scripts
    adding and editing colors with, 132–133
    Premedia Systems WOW! Artboard Resizer, 79
    Premedia Systems WOW! Colorizer, 78
sculpture, using Live Paint on, 75
Select All, 148–149
Select All Unused, Swatches panel, 120
Select Behind cursor, 7
selection indicators, Layers panel, 7
Selection tool, 13, 26
Sellers, Rachel, 12–13
shading
    adding to mapped surface, 159
    adding with Drawing Inside and Blob Brush, 81
    surface, applying to 3D objects, 157
shadows
    constructing in 3D, 167
    creating soft transitions using opacity masks with, 212–213
    gallery examples of, 101, 168, 203
    painting in layers with Bristle Brushes, 111
Shape Builder tool (Shift-M)
    building image with basic objects, 13
    building with multiple construction modes using, 80–81
    constructing objects with, 56–57
    gallery examples of, 77, 82
    rapid reshaping with, 78–79
Shape Modes, compound shapes, 63
shapes. See compound shapes
sharing artboards and libraries, 39

Shift-B. See Blob Brush tool (Shift-B)
Shift-D (toggling drawing modes), 61
Shift-M. See Shape Builder tool (Shift-M)
Shift-O. See Artboard tool (Shift-O)
Shift-W. See Width tool (Shift-W)
Shortcuts, xvi
Show Gradient Annotator, 124
Show/Hide Thumbnail, 9
Show Options, Transparency panel, 187
Show Transparency Grid, Document Setup, 183
Simplify command, 60
Simulate Colored Paper, Document Setup dialog, 40, 183
Single-line Composer, 31
size
    Color Guide panel, 122
    complex layered patterns in PEM, 196
    customizing Calligraphic brush, 103
    panel, 3
    printing artboards larger than your media, 35
Sky gradient, 175
slices, 231
Smart Filters, exporting layers to Photoshop, 239
Smart Guides
    coloring line art, 66–67
    creating and managing artboards manually, 10
    creating guides for arcs, 21
    Illustrator, Cadtools, and Photoshop art, 236
    organizing your workflow, 4
    rapid reshaping with Shape Builder, 78
    toggling for warps and envelopes, 153
Smart Objects, 63, 223–224, 239
smartphone case example, 142–143
Smooth Color, Blend options, 187
Smooth tool, 188
Smoothness control, Pencil tool, 13
Smoothness settings, Options, 81, 104–105

editing with Live Color, 126
gallery example with heavy use
    of, 116
mapping onto 3D objects,
    155, 158–159
placing artwork from
    Illustrator into Flash
    using, 227–228
replication/quick updates
    with, 39
saving artwork for maps as, 166
Scatter Brushes vs., 90
turning artwork on artboard
    into, 11
working with, 90–92
Symbols panel, 90–92

T

tabbed documents, 2
Tabs panel, 31
Taj Mahal building
    perspective, 169
Tan, Moses, 118, 218
target indicators, Layers panel, 7,
    19, 22–23
templates
    accessing, xvi
    in Cool Extras folder, 4
    drawing with Pencil tool, 211
    inserting art into, 210
    placing artwork as, 102
    placing sketch, 68, 94–95
    printing, 21
    scanning sketches as, 200
    tracing, 12–13
    using for artboards, 40–41
    using photo as, 52
terrain images, setting type on, 45
text. See also type and layout
    design
    attaching to perspective
        grid, 159–161
    formatting, 29–30
    moving between Illustrator and
        Photoshop, 224
    pasting into inDesign, 225
    wrapping Area type around
        objects, 29
Text tool, 43
texture, vector images, 217
threaded text, 28–29
three-point perspective view, 163
thumbnails, 9

Tiling tool, 21, 35
tints
    Color Reduction Options
        for, 128
    gallery example using, 75
    for layers showing different
        times of day, 163
    viewing colors as, 122
Tips, in book organization, xvii–
    xviii
titles
    arcing type for, 46–47
    creating depth for, 52
    creating with Type tool, 37
    Pit Bull poster, 52
Tom, Jack, 42–43
Tools panel, 79, 123–124
tracking, warp type, 43
Transform effect
    auto-scaling artwork, 22–23
    copying art between
        artboards, 11
    copying instances of artwork to
        another artboard, 34
    gallery example using, 50
    pasting Smart Objects from
        Illustrator into
        Photoshop for, 239
transitions
    color, color transitions
    masking with shadows for
        soft, 212–213
transparency
    applying to gradient mesh,
        125, 142–143
    brushstrokes for, 102–103
    creating highlights and glows
        using, 204–205
    creating highlights using, 202
    creating with opacity and
        blending modes, 135,
        184, 203
    dragonfly image showing, 101
    Flash retaining, 228
    gallery example using, 214
    locking to limit tool/command
        to just pixels, 252–253
    opacity masks and, 184–186
    overview of, 183
    SuperGraphics with gradients
        showing, 146
Transparency panel, 185–187
Trash icon, deleting colors, 120
Tremblay, Jean-Claude, 153
triangle, creating, 13
"Trick or Treat" movie, 248, 249

Turton, David, 70
two-point perspective view, 163,
    169, 172, 174–175
type and layout design
    advanced features of multiple
        artboards, 33–35
    converting type to
        outlines, 30–31
    formatting text, 29–30
    Glyphs panel, 33
    types of type, 26–28
    using Appearance panel with
        type, 32–33
    using Eyedropper with type, 31
    using type as clipping
        mask, 192
    working with legacy text, 33
    working with threaded
        text, 28–29
    wrapping Area type around
        objects, 29
type and layout design, gallery
    examples of complex
        type, 48–52
    labeling bold terrain image on
        map, 45
    labeling curving features on
        maps, 44
type and layout design, lesson
    arcing type with warps and
        envelopes, 46–47
    creating identity with multiple
        elements, 38–39
    graphic novel cover
        design, 36–37
    streamlining file output with
        artboards, 40–41
    type on curve and warping
        type, 42–43
Type characters, 32
Type objects, 32, 62
Type on a Path, 33, 43
Type Options dialog, 33
Type tool, 26, 32–33, 37, 49

U

"Using the Appearance Panel" section, 8
"Using Isolation Mode," 6
Undo, Pathfinder operations, 62
unified gradients, 136–137
Unite Pathfinder command, 64–65
updates, 33, 39
Untapped Cities illustrations, 106–107
User Defined library, 116, 131

V

vanishing points, perspective grid, 159–161, 171, 173–174
variation, pattern, 182
vector artwork
applying texture, 217
attaching to perspective grid, 159–161
book layout with, 37
converting from rasters with Image Trace, 58–59
from Illustrator into Flash, 227
from Illustrator to non-Adobe programs, 223
galleries converting from rasters with Image Trace, 72, 73, 74, 75
VectorScribe, 234
Vektorgarten site, 211
visibility
of attributes and thumbnails, 9
controlling how Illustrator file imports top-level layers, 226
of guides, 5
of layers in InDesign, 225
of layers in Photoshop, 214
of layers to organize complex objects, 15, 17, 50
of template layer, 102

W

Wacom tablet, 87–88
warps
applied to type, 30–31, 42–43, 46–47
applying and editing, 152–153
creating headline text, 69
envelope, 154
modifying gradient mesh shapes, 125
wash strokes, 103
web graphics, 226–227, 230–231
web slices, Photoshop, 224
Welcome Screen, xvi
Western Bullets WF, dingbat font, 52
white snap-to cursor, 54
Wide Fan Brush, 111
width points, Width tool, 84–85, 90, 94–95
width profiles, 84–86, 98
Width tool (Shift-W)
adjusting pattern brush fit, 114
gallery examples of, 96–99
modifying Art Brush with, 70, 88
stroke variance with, 84–85, 94–95
transforming brush strokes with, 93
Wigham, Laurie, 22–23, 233, 246
"Wind," 255
Winder, Darren, 139
word spacing, 31, 43
workspace
gallery example, 24
managing multiple artboards, 9–11
object management, 5–9
organizing custom, 2
organizing New Document Profiles, 4
organizing rulers, guides, Smart Guides and grids, 4–5
saving Pattern Options panel in custom, 180
workspace, lessons
auto-scaling art, 22–24
basic appearances, 18–19
guides for arcs, 20–21
navigating layers, 16–17
starting simple for creative composition, 14–15
tracing template, 12–13

WOW! Artwork Colorizer, 78–79
WOW! Books, epub versions, xv
WOW! ONLINE
accessing artwork from, xvi
downloading electronic version of book, xiv–xv
wrapping Area type, 29

X

X axis, 3D effects, 155–157

Y

Y axis, 3D effects, 155–157
Yap, Brian, 228, 235

Z

Z axis, 3D effects, 155–157
Zen of the Pen courses, xv
Zig Zag effect, 163
zoom, 11, 13, 206

The Adobe Illustrator CS6 WOW! Book Production Notes

Interior Book Design and Production

This book was produced primarily InDesign CS5.5 using Adobe's Minion Pro and Frutiger LT Std OpenType fonts. Barbara Sudick is the artist behind the original **Illustrator WOW!** design and typography, using Jill Davis's QuarkXPress layout of **The Photoshop WOW! Book** as a starting point. Cary Norsworthy and Mimi Heft (who also designed our book cover) contributed to new page-design specs. Victor Von Salza led the porting of our templates from QuarkXpress to InDesign CS, and modernized our style sheets. Cristen Gillespie keeps our copy-writing guidelines updated. Jean-Claude Tremblay is not only our technical editor, but his company Proficiografik produces (and troubleshoots) all the commercial and press-ready PDFs for the book. Computer Documentation Services (CDS) prints this book.

Additional Hardware and Software

Although most of the **WOW!** team uses Macintosh computers, we now have testers and writers who do Windows (or both Mac and Win). In addition to Adobe InDesign CS5, CS5.5, and CS6, we used Adobe Illlustrator CS6 (of course!), Adobe Photoshop CS5/CS6, and Ambrosia Software's Snapz Pro X for the screenshots. We used acrobat.com and Adobe Acrobat 9/10 for distribution of the book pages to each other, to testers, the editor, the indexer, Peachpit, and the proofreaders. Premedia Systems wrote a number of custom scripts to help us update and sync the many InDesign files. Many of us use Wacom tablets and Art Pens. Adam Z Lein created (and does emergency maintenence on) an online **WOW!** database so the team can track the daily details of the book production.

How to Contact the Author

If you would like to submit artwork that you've created using Illustrator's new features for consideration in future **Illustrator WOW!** books, please email a link to a web page containing samples of your work (no files please!) to Sharon at **www.ssteuer.com/contact**. For timely updates about all things digital, including future announcements about upcoming ePub forms of the **WOW!** books, find Sharon at **facebook.com/SharonSteuer** and **@SharonSteuer** (Twitter).

31901051592642